Praise for *Paranoid Publics*

"*Paranoid Publics* is an important and original contribution to our understanding of today's political movements. The book takes up a fascinating topic—the current political status of 'truth'—and shows how a psychoanalytic reading of its many manifestations help clarify its operations and its effects. A persuasive and subtle book."

—**Joan Wallach Scott**, Institute for Advanced Study

"By boldly foregoing the usual discrepancy between a subjective psychoanalytic category and collective life as such, and deftly traversing critical theory debates, mass culture practices, social media entrepreneurships, and algorithmic governance mechanisms alike, Chaudhary delivers an incisive dissection of the heterogeneous appeals to "truth" that bind knowing, belief, and political power play today. This book is a work of insight, imagination, and intellectual sophistication."

—**Rey Chow**, author of A *Face Drawn in Sand:*
Humanistic Inquiry and Foucault in the Present

"*Paranoid Publics* is a smart, original, and provocative take on some of the most pressing political questions of our time. Chaudhary examines the collective libidinal life of outrage, paranoia, scandal, and other negative emotions that have accompanied the ongoing assault on truth. He shows how psychoanalysis can help explain the libidinal eruptions of energy that have characterized the contemporary political horizon as truth and reason have waned."

—**Camille Robcis**, Columbia University

PARANOID PUBLICS

Paranoid Publics

PSYCHOPOLITICS OF TRUTH

Zahid R. Chaudhary

FORDHAM UNIVERSITY PRESS   NEW YORK 2026

Fordham University Press has no responsibility for the persistence or
accuracy of URLs for external or third-party Internet websites referred
to in this publication and does not guarantee that any content on such
websites is, or will remain, accurate or appropriate.

Fordham University Press also publishes its books in a variety
of electronic formats. Some content that appears in print may not
be available in electronic books.

Visit us online at www.fordhampress.com.

For EU safety / GPSR concerns: Mare Nostrum Group B.V.,
Mauritskade 21D, 1091 GC Amsterdam,
The Netherlands, gpsr@mare-nostrum.co.uk

Library of Congress Cataloging-in-Publication Data available
online at https://catalog.loc.gov.

Printed in the United States of America
28 27 26   5 4 3 2 1
First edition

For John Wood,
with love

Contents

Introduction: Psychopolitics of Truth   1

1 Exposure   31

2 Paranoia   54

3 Freedom   82

4 Hysteria   109

Coda   145

ACKNOWLEDGMENTS   149

NOTES   151

INDEX   175

There is no freedom without opinions that diverge from reality,
but such divergence endangers freedom.
—THEODOR W. ADORNO, "Opinion Delusion Society"

Nothing malfunctions more than human reality.
—JACQUES LACAN, *The Psychoses*

Introduction

Psychopolitics of Truth

You don't have to be paranoid to think we live in paranoid times (but you might be). Large segments of the public subscribe to the wild theories of QAnon, with many unaware that their beliefs are part of a fringe conspiracy theory gone mainstream. Paranoid discourse about border control and vigilance against immigrants can always be counted on to inflame the passions, with or without the aid of conspiracy theories. Protest movements against COVID vaccines and lockdowns are now organized as medical freedom organizations, fueled by suspicions about governmental and corporate control. Some people have taken to spending time and money obsessively shoring up their homes against societal collapse. Apart from these phenomena, paranoia also comes into play in a more general way in political polarization, in that one's political opponent is always presumed to be a menace to society. Insofar as paranoia is a form of defense, as Sigmund Freud has claimed, it is conditioned on agonism, rivalry, and the fight-or-flight response. Concerned as he was with individual cases of paranoia, Freud was less interested in whether paranoid beliefs could also make claims to truth. For Freud, working at the scale of the individual, the validity of a paranoid belief could be judged through recourse to the authority of shared and collective consensus about the truth. The veracity of individual paranoid belief was, in any case, less important clinically for Freud than the psychical reality which it illuminated. Can collective forms of paranoia similarly illuminate the social realities that give rise to them?

What happens when the truth claims of collective beliefs cannot be assessed by means of a *shared* standard of truth? These are the two fundamental questions *Paranoid Publics* will investigate.

There may be no better concept to characterize the disorienting present than "paranoia," a term whose etymology (*para* + *nous*) suggests being outside or beside one's mind. While in contemporary cultural politics paranoia is commonly associated with the resurgence of conspiracy theories, it applies across a much wider spectrum of social life. A feeling of dangerous exposure to forces outside of one's immediate control is central to paranoia, and this mood runs across widely different publics. From rising inequality to the steady withdrawal of states' protections of citizens, the devastating ravages of neoliberalism around the globe are, by now, well documented.[1] From this vantage, which includes scenes of catastrophic climate events, the feeling of exposure to danger seems a rational response to the social order. Paranoia is not the necessary outcome of such experiences, but it is both a symptom of vulnerability and a defense against it. Paranoia attracts by naming the unnamable, indicating the threat or the malevolence whose existence and unique powers it designates as "truth." Running across political divides, paranoia articulates with resentment and anger, the public feelings that dominate the contemporary moment.

An analysis of paranoia requires combining psychosocial considerations with political-economic ones. Alternative facts, delusions, and falsehoods are psychosocial realities as much as they are political-economic ones. The paranoid fantasy, for example, of a body under siege, shared by entrepreneurs as widely divergent as Alex Jones and Gwyneth Paltrow, and also by growing global movements against vaccines and medical expertise, bears a relation to political-economic realities, but is not reducible to these realities or fully explained by them. The fact that Jones and Paltrow sell the same health supplement to very different populations is a hieroglyph to be deciphered both for its political-economic insight into influencer economies and its illumination of shared psychosocial dispositions. Paranoid publics do not lend themselves to interest-based analyses, and the diagonal forms their politics take cannot be resolved by a tidy class analysis. In the chapters that follow, there will appear agents motivated by economic interest, and even some motivated by ideals, but their actions depend on psychopolitical operations. It is impossible to understand the political economy of new media ecosystems and the fabrications they incentivize without also taking account of the psychosocial conditions and unconscious processes that enable their operations. Such a sightline into contemporary cultural politics makes visible correspondences and contradictions that would otherwise go unnoticed. Instead of understanding unconscious processes as a reaction to or reflection of social and political realities, this book assumes that unconscious processes themselves constitute the political.

My subtitle, *Psychopolitics of Truth*, is intended as a provocation, since psychic realities and politics would in themselves seem to be inimical to truth. In psychic reality, truth is invariably refracted by desire or fear, and in politics, where facts are regularly instrumentalized, truth is often beside the point. Yet only by understanding the operations of psychosocial mechanisms such as fantasy, anxiety, paranoia, disavowal, projection, and the like can we hope to comprehend the politics of the stabilization or destabilization of truth. What interests me are the social, emotional, and even material satisfactions entailed in psychopolitical phenomena, specifically those that make an appeal to truth: whistleblowing, conspiracy theories, anti-vax movements, etc.[2] What, after all, does an appeal to truth accomplish, and what is it about truth that is so appealing? In legal contexts, truth holds out the possibility of rendering justice; in scientific contexts, truth claims universality and objectivity for itself; in politics, claiming to speak the truth shores up a minimal performance of honesty; and for businesses, truth claims can seek to create demands that an advertised commodity or service allegedly meets. Despite their differences, these heterogenous appeals all situate truth as a kind of authority that enables everything from justice and objectivity to votes and commodities. Truth is thus affiliated with power, and I will elaborate more on their relationship in the work of Michel Foucault later in this introduction. For now, I would like to consider the psychosocial nature of the constitution of truth.

References to "truth" abound in situations and contexts given to paranoia: the alt-tech social media platform launched by Donald Trump, from which he held forth about the "stolen election" and "witch hunts," is called Truth Social; Project Veritas is the name of an extreme right activist group that distributes misleading or fake videos of "undercover operations" meant to undermine progressive causes; playing the truth-teller is one of the central pleasures offered through participation in QAnon. "Truthing" is the word for "posting" in Truth Social's parlance; such rhetoric suggests that everything else is a lie. "Truthing" an alternative fact is both a form of and a call for political participation; the same dynamic applies to mainstream social media platforms, which were the first to perfect the art of online incitement. As with Project Veritas and various QAnon fora, on Truth Social (or Gab or Telegram or other alt-tech platforms) paranoia enters political practice as a conduit to certainty. If these references to "truth" seem Orwellian in their simple reversals—as Orwell writes in 1984, "war is peace, freedom is slavery, ignorance is strength"—it is because the social contexts from which they emerge have weaponized paranoia in the same way as the social worlds depicted in Orwell's fiction. Examples of these predictably extreme networked spaces with their Orwellian reversal of truth and falsehood do not capture, however, other contemporary itineraries of paranoia.

Take, for example, whistleblowers. They have been valorized in cultural politics, both lauded and hounded for their exposure of corporate or governmental malfeasance. Although juridical procedures can disqualify some kinds of evidence revealed in whistleblowers' breaches, the information they offer nevertheless also enters the public sphere where it operates somewhat differently than it would in a court. As I will discuss in Chapter One, "Exposure," whistleblowers such as Edward Snowden and Chelsea Manning tend to reveal facts that support an open secret. They confirm the existence of rot at the heart of authority. What good is an exposé when it reveals things that one has known all along? How does one understand truth-telling in a context in which the truth is already familiar and to some extent already known? What whistleblowers expose has less to do with veridiction—bringing to light some previously hidden truth—and more to do with verification—confirming a truth already known, whether claimed or suspected by others. While the kernel of truth may already be familiar, it can be salutary for cultural politics to have such truths verified and confirmed, keeping open the question of accountability in the public imagination.

Popularly heralded as preserving democracy, whistleblowing can also *generate* paranoia, by supplying irrefutable evidence for what had already been widely suspected. A malevolence that had been unnamable, now proven to be true, can make its appearance in the political imagination. Chelsea Manning's dissemination of scenes of American soldiers slaughtering innocents in Iraq (in a video that circulates under the title "collateral murder") not only raises questions about other atrocities that have been repressed by official narratives but also provides a visual idiom with which to imagine the repressed. To take another example, in 2016, a Whitney Museum solo exhibition of work by artist, filmmaker, and journalist Laura Poitras repeated the phrase "deep state" to critically examine the apparatuses of surveillance, social control, and military atrocities abroad. Poitras was the first journalist Edward Snowden had contacted when he blew the whistle on the National Security Agency (NSA). Her Whitney exhibition included an installation of a hallway with lighted slots in it at various heights, allowing the museum goer to bend down or stretch up to peer at a secret: copies of classified NSA or CIA documents concerning surveillance, memos about clandestine operations, a report from an interrogator at the infamous Abu Ghraib prison, and other similar documents. While the installation cleverly engaged practices of surveillance and state secrecy by inviting the viewer to inspect the administrative traces of these practices, it also positioned the viewer as both a peeping tom and a paranoiac.[3] The installation's wall text explained that the arrangement of the lit slots was like peering into the operations of the "deep state." The exhibition had earlier defined this term as unelected functionaries and agents of the state, including corporate entities—an assemblage of security and spy agencies, civil servants, business leaders, and technocrats. The term names a state infrastructure and a set of corporate alliances that endure through changing political administrations.[4] While Poitras deployed the term critically to indicate the durability of non-democratic tendencies within democracy, "deep state" nevertheless also invited paranoia. In the age of QAnon, the term has become ubiquitous for a politics diametrically opposed to Poitras's political commitments.

   That is not to say that whistleblowing is necessarily laden with paranoia, but that it always makes paranoia available, which, in its infinite quest for certainties, attaches easily to whistleblowing and its forms of veridiction. "Question Authority" is a dictum for progressive politics associated with youthful social movements. It is also a meme in QAnon communities and a sentiment familiar to anti-government libertarians such as Timothy McVeigh, who was responsible for the 1995 Oklahoma City bombing. There is an excessive element at the heart of paranoia, making it a feeling that "sticks" readily to existing structures and forms of knowing. In an Orwellian frame paranoid excess takes the form of inversion, and in other contexts it strings together trivial details or takes a verified fact and displaces its significance onto other facts.

Additionally, information provided by whistleblowers is subject to another psychosocial danger, disavowal. Here, as expressed in Octave Mannoni's classic formulation "I know well, but all the same . . . ," acknowledging the truth while refusing to take actions on its basis provides its own enjoyments. Knowledge of climate change is most often met with disavowal.[5] Disavowal bears a relationship to truth such that truth can be known and yet that knowledge makes no difference whatsoever. Truth is simultaneously adduced and canceled, voiced and yet neutralized. It is not merely an individual phenomenon but a collective one as well. At the collective—and therefore political—level, the operations of disavowal suggest that since the truth—even when known—does not matter, the relationship between truth and power is being reorganized.[6]

Disavowal and paranoia name different relationships to truth. In the former the truth is rendered politically ineffectual, and in the latter the truth is indisputable and yet requires constant retrieval and confirmation. In both disavowal and paranoia, the truth attaches to a form of enjoyment. Paranoia, for its part, offers up certainty as its own form of enjoyment, and often aligns itself with a moral higher ground, a superior vantage point from which the corruption of a cabal (for example) can be condemned. In Chapter Three, "Freedom," I analyze the moralizing impulses of paranoid politics, especially as these impulses intersect with neoliberal assumptions about the intertwinement of free markets with morality and truth.

I. On "Post-Truth"

Contemporary cultural politics are marked by the pleasures taken in breaking civil norms, proliferating anti-scientific sentiments, claiming racial supremacy, and spreading disinformation. These phenomena have been described as consequences of our "post-truth" era. The descriptor "post-truth" is associated with the deskilling of journalism, the multiplication of online information platforms, and the rise of extreme right-wing politics in the United States and Europe. Its most recent fruits are "Stop the Steal" claims about election fraud, the January 6th insurrection they inspired, and widespread belief among some people that the insurrection was instigated by leftist agents. By the time of his 2024 election campaign

Donald Trump was calling January 6th a "day of love." Yet if there is such a thing as a post-truth age, it was arguably inaugurated much earlier, perhaps with George W. Bush's false claims about Iraq's "weapons of mass destruction," the pretext for a catastrophic war that pundits from all sides of the political spectrum rallied around.[7] At the time, even liberal journalists like David Remnick and Ezra Klein supported the government's lies, warning against Saddam Hussein's totalitarianism while themselves demonstrating obedience to authority.[8] Peter Beinart even published a book in 2006 entitled *The Good Fight: Why Liberals—and Only Liberals—Can Win the War on Terror and Make America Great Again.* For such liberal apologists—"Bush's useful idiots" in Tony Judt's turn of phrase—the war on Iraq somehow conjured the heroism and moral clarity of World War II.[9] The psychopolitics of this catastrophic displacement deserves its own extended treatment. Crucially, even when it became clear that Iraq did not possess "weapons of mass destruction," many people continued to support the war.[10] This situation bore out Hannah Arendt's insight about the fundamentally adversarial relationship between truth and politics. Well before Foucault's more rigorous investigations into the constitution of truth (which I will discuss below), Arendt made a distinction between what she called "rational truth," which can be adduced through logical deduction or scientific experimentation, and "factual truth," which comprises basic descriptions such as what happened to whom, when, and where. As the domain of politics, factual truth is made vulnerable to injury, falsification, and erasure. This is so because political battles necessarily seek to marshal factual truth or to efface it altogether for the sake of instrumental ends. In another insight that continues to resonate with contemporary politics, Arendt notes that "factual truth is no more self-evident than opinion, and this may be among the reasons that opinion-holders find it relatively easy to discredit factual truth as just another opinion."[11]

What binds people to their opinions usually entails psychodynamic operations, an aspect of the social order Arendt was not interested in analyzing. Regarding the war on Iraq, it is not that the facts did not matter, but that factual truth did not interfere with people's unspoken racist beliefs in "Eastern despotism," which deserved elimination, or with their investment in the fantasy of just wars. For some, it even hardened their convictions. What happens to one's sense of reality when belief takes priority over fact and feeling priority over knowledge? Belief differs from opinion because it carries the force of *self*-certainty; it is a means of orienting oneself in the world, and thus conditions one's social and political comportments within it. Psychosocial dynamics can account for the priority of belief over truth and feeling over knowledge. The effectiveness of Bush era rhetoric relied on exploiting the conjuncture between psychosocial needs and political-economic exigency: a racist discourse about the clash of civilizations and the leveraging of collective fears in the wake of 9/11 helped to exploit the profitability of oil contracts.

More than two decades later, with the mainstreaming of QAnon-style politics in the United States and Europe, and the blurring of boundaries between fact and feeling, truth and delusion, the observation that global public spheres have become filled with noise and distortions is now commonplace. While understandably ubiquitous in recent academic and journalistic accounts, the phrase "assault on truth" threatens to become another meme in a collective life already given to outrage and paranoia.

Scholars have tended to locate the origins of public feelings, especially resentment and paranoia, in political-economic realities. The regnant analyses of contemporary "post-truth politics" put forth the following narrative: with the triumph of neoliberal policies around the world, an increasingly beleaguered group of majority populations feels adrift, forgotten, and "left behind." Disappointed by the promise of upward mobility, people feel cheated and hemmed in by the impoverished realities of their lives. When the state rolled back midcentury programs of social uplift and abdicated its age-old functions (protecting its citizens, ensuring equality before the law) to appease its shareholders, public infrastructures began to erode. These neoliberal techniques were practiced in South America and parts of Africa before being implemented in the United States and the United Kingdom, then were put in place in much of Europe and eventually throughout much of Asia. The state thus became the steward of the free-flowing circuits of capital that drove increasing income inequality around the globe. This inequality engendered the rise of populism, stoked by collective anger, and led to the endorsement of authoritarian tendencies and their attendant self-destructive politics.[12]

Meanwhile, the story goes, traditional media outlets, those erstwhile arbiters of truth, have been delegitimized by a neoliberal reordering of media industries, on the one hand, and by the rise of digital media, on the other. Every claim has become potentially plausible to someone. Online echo chambers proliferate, and people are networked even as they are atomized, increasingly social yet increasingly lonely.

The espousal of populist authoritarian tendencies that have arisen concurrently with this political-economic and technological transition is understood as a reaction to social ills, a reaction that misrecognizes the solutions for societal malaise. These solutions are interpreted by some commentators as forms of displacement. They include the demonization and desired elimination of minority populations; an embrace of non-democratic political possibilities; and a fervent attachment to (white, Christian) nationalism. In this transition—we are told—truth disappears only to return in displaced forms: collective paranoia and other negative affects are understood as representations of a genuine material and historical problem. The tension between real needs and desires and the limits that stand in the way of satisfying them is allegedly being worked out in the symbolic realm. Populist anger and conspiracies are the common forms of such substitutive satisfactions. As symptoms of social problems, they are each forms of social critique, and while they may have "misfired" they can nevertheless be read as a cry for help (no matter the content of the cry).[13]

These dominant accounts of "post-truth" politics describe an increasingly deformed or disappearing reality, yet they tacitly disclose their own embeddedness in a regime of truth which they take to be self-evident and necessary. Still, such accounts have much to recommend them: their willingness to take irrationality seriously instead of dismissing it, their broad economic view, and their historical contextualization of the conditions in which the current forms of truth demolition flourish. Yet at times such interpretations are suspiciously commonsensical as well, driven by unexamined assumptions about false consciousness that assume ideologies are largely the distorted effects of political-economic constraints and hence that assuaging economic anxiety can restore truth and public reason. To be sure, political-economic realities (income inequality, oligarchical alliances across corporate and state actors) can be adduced to explain a host of contemporary problems: political polarization, erosion of public reason, increased anger and paranoia, and the troubling incapacity to discern truth from falsehood. But such explanations are limited when they analyze the constitution of truth primarily as an effect of political-economic processes. In *The Guardian*, Samuel Moyn and Nicholas Guilhot conclude, "If we want to avoid the descent of politics into the factionalism of corrupt oligarchies, what we need is not the foiling of alleged plots or the debunking of conspiracy theories but a new political realism that takes a cold look at the economic and fiscal policies that have failed so many for so long."[14]

The trouble with Moyn and Guilhot's diagnosis is that support for anti-democratic policies and conspiratorial politics comes not only from those who have been failed or "left behind" but from middle classes and billionaires as well.[15] In addition, it has become increasingly clear that contemporary forms of "populism" not only entail a politics of resentment but also involve alliances between businesspeople, billionaires, and party politics. "Populism" has become a floating signifier, encapsulating politics as disparate as Bernie Sanders and Donald Trump (United States), Hugo Chávez (Venezuela), Narendra Modi (India), Silvio Berlusconi (Italy), Nigel Farage (United Kingdom), and Viktor Orbán (Hungary). As a term, "populism" has functioned similarly to "conspiracy," carrying a whiff of the disdainful and pitying about it. All anti-establishment movements or politicians—whatever their political leanings—risk the opprobrium associated with "populism." As Enzo Traverso writes, "When the neoliberal order, with its austerity policies and its social inequalities, is set up as a norm, all opposition automatically becomes 'populist.'"[16] As such the term explains less than it wishes to.

Tacitly, these liberal explanations for our "post-truth" era suggest that an authority with enough political will could rectify the underlying political-economic error, and then the psychic underpinnings of cultural politics would align once again with reason. Many such commentators leave untouched the operations of those psychosocial realities that had occasioned the analysis of populist anger and conspiracy in the first place. Such analyses are most productively read as warnings rather than explanations since the causality they offer is somewhat simple. What if conspiracy theories, falsehoods, and the overvaluation of opinion and feeling were not simply epiphenomenal? Not just some kind of vaporous distortion resulting from age-old economic contradictions that could be corrected with appropriate fiscal policies?

Conspiracy theories are not eradicated by debunking their claims. The QAnon injunction to "Trust the Plan," for example, does not yield to reason. Its authority-bound psychodynamics are not dissolved by an appeal to material interests. In Chapter Two, "Paranoia," I analyze the rise of QAnon and other paranoid publics, which I read as phenomena conditioned by both political-economic realities and psychosocial incentives. The play element in the participatory style of QAnon communities synchronizes with a neoliberal understanding of economic operations as a kind of game. This chapter develops an account of the constitution of truth in such ludic environments as the online fora where QAnon began.

II. Games of Truth

Truth, veridiction, and their relation to power are subjects that Michel Foucault spent much of his career investigating. His work offers less a grand theory of Truth than an analysis of truth as a matter of social, historical, and political representation. Foucault was a philosopher centrally concerned with the way truth was established: the procedures for apprehending it, its embeddedness in institutional and bodily practices, and its regulation of social relations. He was not proposing truth's demolition but a greater attention to its operations, although he is often misread and misunderstood.[17] For Foucault truth was far more than a problem of knowledge, information, or facts. The operations of truth extend to domains that at first appear oblique: statecraft and governance, secular and religious practices of self-cultivation and self-improvement, the forms of life that are enshrined under specific historical conditions. Foucault radically raises the stakes for any inquiry into the problem of truth, expanding it into the domains of politics, ethics, and history. He was interested in the contexts and conditions through which truth is adduced by specific procedures, protocols, or rituals—be they scientific experimentation, the confessional, or Delphic divination. He was then further concerned with how political, economic, religious, and ethical practices and forms of life came to be based on that adduced truth and how these varied practices and forms of life were construed by their practitioners as a necessary and inexorable consequence. Thus, Foucault distinguished two distinct aspects of the operations of truth: one concerns the context-specific ways of arriving at and apprehending truth, and the other entails the ways people are bound to the truth—that is, the self-evident, unthinking, or "obvious" ways in which individuals feel obligated to the truth and submit to its consequences. The first he calls "games of truth," and the second he refers to as "regimes of truth."

"Games of truth" are the domain of veridiction in which the distinction between truth and falsity is arrived at through rules, procedures, and demands internal to the game itself.[18] As such any game of truth produces verities that are autonomous with respect to those produced in other games: scientific truth and literary critical truth are mutually autonomous, for example. Yet the autonomy of truth produced in any game of truthing is not total because all games of truth occur in the context of what Foucault called a "regime of truth," which allocates and prioritizes the truths that have been variously produced.[19] Critically, it is the regime of truth that also determines what obligations one has to the truth.[20] These obligations may be spelled out or assumed, espoused willingly or unwillingly, be conscious or unconscious. Regardless, they bind a person to the truth, requiring that once a truth is made manifest, one must submit to it. Foucault explains it thus:

> To put things very simply, in an almost or completely infantile way, I shall say the following: in the most rigorously constructed arguments imaginable, even in the event of something being recognized as self-evident, there is always, and it is necessary to assume, a certain assertion that does not belong to the logical realm of observation or deduction [i.e. to the game of truth itself], in other words, an assertion that does not exactly belong to the realm of the true or false, that is rather a sort of commitment, a sort of profession. In all reasoning there is always this assertion that consists in saying: if it is true, then I will submit; it is true *therefore* I submit; it is true, therefore I am bound.[21]

Importantly, according to Foucault, this form of obligation, submission, acceptance—in short, the form of the self's binding to truth—has nothing to do with the truth itself (whether the truth concerns scientific deduction or a sense that one is a sinner) but with the form of power that links the self's life and practice to the truth.

This form of power, or regime of truth, is historically contingent, and it mobilizes truth in the service of producing subjects and of governing the social order. Both of these projects are grounded on the same generative logic, which Foucault expresses as the proposition "X is true, therefore I submit." To give some examples: since modern secular existence requires the separation of state and religion, therefore prayer in public schools should not be permitted; or, democracy requires political equality, therefore everyone must be enfranchised and encouraged to vote. Both secularism and democracy are associated with modernity's valuation of reason, and reason's regime of truth becomes consequential for each. Both entail cultivating a self whose values, field of action, and practices of subjectivation are oriented in relation to the truth. The point of interface between governing power and the self is the "therefore" that links the understanding that "X is true" with "I submit"—that is, as Foucault puts it, "you have to submit."[22] By articulating the oft-unspoken "therefore" that links the expression of truth with the self's submission to it, Foucault underscored the capacious and world-making effects of truth claims.

It is testament to the stability of any regime of truth that the "therefore" is accepted without question. Juridical truth must rely on the force of this acceptance if it is ever to deliver justice. When a regime of truth is well-established and supple, this "therefore" is assumed rather than stated. The force of a tacit "therefore" is all the more powerful for being invisible, especially in some games of truth like science. As Foucault points out, "this 'therefore' goes so much without saying that it is as if it is transparent and we do not notice its presence, [but] it nevertheless remains the case that standing back a bit, and when we take science as precisely a historical phenomenon, the 'it is true, therefore I submit' becomes much more enigmatic, much more obscure."[23] In contemporary cultural politics, scientific truth—whether about climate change or vaccines—is increasingly questioned, denied, or even more perniciously, disavowed. For Foucault, the mechanisms that are adduced in any game of truth and that make us submit to the truth—in effect, one of the operations of authority—are historically specific to a regime of truth. And yet, such mechanisms seem to fail regularly now. What are we to make of this? The binding force of an overarching and shared regime of truth has weakened, and people seem to have lost faith in the "therefore" that signals the stability (i.e., the internalized acceptance) of a regime of truth. When I refer to crises of authority—whether in government, educational institutions, or courts—I mean to indicate the weakening of a collective force that binds one to the truth.

Through his conceptual distinction between games of truth (which produce truth) and regimes of truth (which organize the way one submits to truth), Foucault intended to investigate one of the operations of power—namely, how power governs subjects by grounding itself on truth and how it produces different kinds of subjects with respect to truth (as deviant or normal, for example). Foucault hoped that understanding these operations of truth and power would enable and enhance critical practice. In "What is Critique?" (1978) he wrote that the "critical attitude" concerns "how not to be governed *like that*, by that, in the name of those principles, with such and such an objective in mind and by means of such procedures."[24] In other words, the basis of the critical attitude lay in grasping that nothing natural or necessary connected a particular truth with the ethical, political, and cultural comportments we might assume to follow from that truth. His was an attitude associated with emancipatory politics.

Yet increasingly, the questioning of formerly agreed upon truths, the refusal to be governed *like that*, and the loosening of the presumed synchrony between truth and conduct is practiced instead by white supremacists, TERFS (trans-exclusionary radical feminists), anti-vaxxers, Christian fundamentalists, conspiracy mongers, trolls, militia groups, politicized "warrior moms," and insurrectionists. Indeed, "Become Ungovernable" is now a catch phrase and a meme among progressives and the far-right alike. Foucault's theorization of the "critical attitude" emerges from his philosophical and epistemological method informed by Nietzschean genealogy and a critique of enlightenment reason, but insofar as Foucault indicated the critical attitude as a refusal to be governed a certain way, he explicitly situated this attitude at the heart of political contestation. Such contestation, however, does not in itself have a given or normative political orientation. Despite recent attempts to recuperate or imagine a normative force motivating Foucauldian critique,[25] Foucault's work does not lend itself to such normative or prescriptive analysis; this is a strength rather than weakness of his thinking. Indeed, in a lecture contemporaneous with "What is Critique?" he notes that "medical dissent," whether as opposition to vaccines or as espousal of alternate non-scientific forms of healing, is an example of a "counter-conduct" that, while refusing the prevailing regime of truth concerning medicine, nevertheless redirects and reinvents the body that was the object of medical scrutiny in the first place.[26]

Challenges to regimes of truth necessarily find within those very regimes their own priorities, even if these are points of refusal, delinking, or breakage. They are thus intimate with the regime of truth which they might oppose. Such challenges underwrite contemporary upheavals situated across a range of political, economic, and epistemological fault lines: the rise of ethno-nationalisms attended by an intensification of neoliberal forms of governance; scientific consensus on climate change in the face of political dissensus and inaction; the mainstreaming of conspiratorial forms of reason. Because all contestations of a regime of truth emerge from that regime does not mean that they are forever bound to it, since they can resolve into new regimes of truth. *Paranoid Publics* analyzes what happens to truth when it is no longer grounded in shared consensus or effectively regulated by a regime such that the manifestation of truth can be counted on to enforce what Foucault called the "therefore," or the necessary enactment of conduct in line with truth.

Truth and power indelibly imprint each other, as Foucault argued. While this might suggest that exposing power's excesses or violations ought to bear some force or authority, political power now appears preternaturally inured to such revelations. "The system is rigged" has become a truism for all kinds of political positions—at least within the United States—such that this *cri de coeur* declaiming the corruption of power is as likely to conceal that corruption as it is to expose it (it became one of Trump's most repeated complaints, in both of his election campaigns). The disorientation of contemporary life is accentuated by truths that that may seem plainly evident yet are rendered ineffectual because no power, whether normative, juridical, or otherwise, can enforce accountability to these truths. As Rudy Giuliani—not exactly known for veracity—once told a television audience, "truth isn't truth."[27] Was he speaking as a diagnostician or as a symptom? Can we tell the difference?

III. Psychopolitics

Following Foucault, I use the word "power" to refer to a dispersed net of institutions and discourses in which the presence of state power is simply one element. In the forty years since Foucault delivered his Collège de France lectures, neoliberalism has remade the world, and the modes of detection, knowledge-production, and evidence-gathering stabilized in the nineteenth century and reinvented in the twentieth century have been thrown into crisis. *Paranoid Publics* analyzes contestations over truth that are no longer bound by a regime of truth. These are games of truth such as whistleblowing, conspiracy theory, anti-vax activism, book banning, anti-trans politics, and the discursive emergence of mysterious illnesses. Investigating these phenomena has required modulating Foucault's own thinking about truth, which regards truth as propositional, manifested in a form of knowledge that might then become the basis of discursive formations and their forms of subjectivation. Yet truth interacts with psychical exigencies, and so a psychopolitical analysis of games of truth must necessarily consider the force of desire, compulsion, and demand at the heart of the search for truth, even when this search is authorized by reason itself, since reason and rationality are touched by psychical processes. As Theodor Adorno once noted, reason, like opinion, too has its subjective origins: "The moment called cathexis in psychology, thought's affective investment in the object, is not extrinsic to thought . . . but [is] rather the condition of its truth."[28] As alarm spreads about the alleged "irrationality" that has overtaken the world, one would do well to remember Theodor W. Adorno and Max Horkheimer's searing critique of Enlightenment reason in *Dialectic of Enlightenment* as itself the basis for domination and the guise in which myth returns in ever more destructive forms.

Foucault himself expressed his admiration for Frankfurt School critiques of reason even if he did not critically employ psychoanalysis as did the first generation of Frankfurt School thinkers.[29] *Paranoid Publics* combines psychoanalysis with Foucauldian genealogy, which replaces a search for origins with an account of interconnections across a range of social phenomena. Foucauldian genealogy shares with psychoanalysis an understanding of the social as a palimpsestic assemblage: in both, analysis aims to apprehend the patterns of subjectivation and social practice.[30] In addition, for both Foucauldian analysis and psychoanalysis, historical causality is a potentially interminable problem. Guided by these shared insights, *Paranoid Publics* offers provisional answers about why contemporary games of truth have become so destructive.

This book is inspired by the work of contemporary thinkers who have developed psychoanalysis as a form of social critique.[31] These scholars continue a heterogenous tradition of socially inflected psychoanalytic thinking that can be traced back to the 1930s and 1940s, when continental philosophers fused Marxist and Freudian thinking, from Frankfurt School critiques of modernity to early object relations theory. This tradition also includes later work, from Juliet Mitchell's path-breaking work on psychoanalysis and feminism, to Michel de Certeau's Lacanian-inspired analyses of history, to the Ljubljana school of theorists. As with any tradition of thought and its multiple trajectories, disagreements, debates, and conceptual tensions are as varied as the thinkers themselves, but what makes this genealogy of criticism so productive is its refurbishment of psychoanalysis as a discourse about politics, suggesting that the unconscious has a vital role to play in political and economic realities. Political-economic facts are not superseded by psychoanalytic insights but are co-extensive with them and disclose their additional dimensions. Emphasizing contradiction, rupture, discontinuity, and resignification over resolution, continuity, closure, or categorical thinking, this tradition of psychoanalysis is well suited for bypassing *both* strictly Marxist accounts that view contemporary cultural politics as the logical results of political-economic phenomenon as well as those wide-eyed analyses of "irrationalism"(which have proliferated exponentially since Trump's first election in 2016) that tend to conclude with appeals to normative idealism or liberal solutions, when it is liberalism itself that is in crisis.[32] Psychoanalysis assumes irrationality as a secret sharer of rational life, assumes that fantasy is a byway through which one arrives at truth. Whereas a liberal understanding of personhood assumes concurrence between desire and interest, psychoanalysis asserts a radical discrepancy between them. It takes as axiomatic that the unconscious does not conform to any normative expectation or injunction, given that rules, norms, laws, and prohibitions are foundational both for the generation of desires as well as for their repression and transgression. This insight about the unruly nature of the unconscious is ideologically neutral: it could be the grounds for emancipatory or authoritarian social change. As a result, not only does psychoanalysis not align neatly with a particular political outlook, but it makes it possible to discern identical psychodynamics across partisan divides and identify the unnamed satisfactions that forms of political discourse and practice offer.

My approach to contemporary games of truth and the challenges they pose to democracy assumes irrationality as a fundament of all experience, and it considers how phenomena as different as the anti-vax movement, QAnon, the 2017 "Unite the Right" rally in Charlottesville, the January 6th insurrection, and anti-trans rhetoric are all founded on variously paranoid forms of veridiction. What if "irrationalism" or widespread "disinhibition" entailed in the breaking of liberal norms is not a simple misfiring or displacement of social reality, but an expression of positive desire for authoritarian politics? Authoritarian politics promises a stable regime of truth, one in which a powerful authority (usually masculine and paternal) enforces the "therefore" to which one might submit.

These questions suggest the analytical richness of psychoanalysis for thinking about politics in general and about politics of truth in particular. In this book I will be less interested in the analysis of truth as conducted by psychoanalysis as a clinical practice, than in the usefulness of psychoanalysis for considering games of truth ungoverned by a regime. This does not entail using psychoanalysis as a diagnostic tool to explain away social symptoms, since this would instantiate psychoanalysis itself as regime of truth (a regime which, in any case, has been in crisis for some time). Instead, I deploy psychoanalysis to read social and political phenomena for moments where they overreach their own stated purposes, or promote actions and attachments that are diametrically opposed to their stated political aims and commitments, or create new norms in anticipation of a world to come. This approach to psychoanalysis emphasizes the shifting nature of truth rather than its fixation. It might, for example, consider the libidinal pulsions that attend the manifestation of truth with the understanding that these psychic pressures cannot be reduced to that truth's "meaning" but are its latent supplements. Psychoanalysis offers up concepts and vocabularies to designate a myriad of positions and comportments with respect to truth: adaptation to prohibitions or reality principles (in psychoanalysis, often themselves the products of social relations), fantasy structures necessary for lending coherence to experiences, absent causes affecting social functioning in contexts unrelated to them, etc. Psychoanalysis shows that the heterogeneity in people's relations to what they believe to be true speaks as much to the diversity of people as it does to the complexities of truth's intricate operations.

Games of truth that contest dominant regimes of truth have multiplied in the last twenty years, with new forms emerging quickly. In the United States these include MAGA "Stop the Steal" activism, digital echo chambers and so-called "algorithmic radicalization," the largely ineffectual liberal panic about Russian disinformation campaigns, the consequential emergence and integration of QAnon, and so on.[33] As constituted by contemporary networked information systems, the upheaval in the regime of truth that has governed our ethical and political values owes a great deal to telecommunication laws passed during Bill Clinton's administration, which included iron-clad protections for what grew to become "Big Tech."[34] In the Obama years, having become surrogate terms for an ideology of progress, the entrepreneurial values of "innovation" and "disruption" became the virtues of a truth-telling subjectivity, charged with delivering economic success for industry and nation simultaneously. In her account of surveillance capitalism, Shoshana Zuboff details multiple revolving doors between "Big Tech" companies and Barack Obama's administrations.[35]

While new media platforms are implicated in the de-prioritizing of truth, *Paranoid Publics* refuses a technological determinist account that would lay the blame for the crisis of truth on networked digital media. In the last decade, utopian rhetoric about how Silicon Valley innovations or disruptions might save the world has given way to disaffected accounts that single out the tech industry as the source of social ills. Essentially identical to the technological utopianism it opposes, technological determinism endows technology with magical and almost omnipotent powers. The analysis of media technology's role that interests me concerns the psychosocial satisfactions and challenges it offers. That it determines social phenomena to some extent is readily obvious, but technological determinism and its emergent dystopic imaginary has limited explanatory power when it imputes social malaise solely to technological development. Simply put, technology does not determine everything; it is an efflux of a collectively made social phenomena, for which it poses new social challenges and possibilities.[36]

IV. Paranoia

While disavowal, projection, anxiety, and enjoyment also appear as central to psychical engagements with truth or reality principles in the chapters that follow, I focus on paranoia as a critical sightline because it helps cut across many different contemporary culture wars, social divisions, and political climates. Paranoia names a feeling first and foremost, one that can deploy several psychical operations including projection, disavowal, foreclosure, displacement, and even fetishism. Felt as the undecidable edge between certainty and ignorance, experiences of paranoia give one back to oneself in sharp relief precisely by dispersing the self. One feels targeted, and this sense of being a target confirms the self by way of an external malevolent force, whether imagined or real.

Sigmund Freud understood paranoia as a form of defense against an unconscious wish or desire which—intolerable to consciousness—is projected onto the world and is refigured in the process. Paranoia offers protection from one's own desire, and with malevolence projected outward, it sets the stage for defensive maneuvers against the world.[37] Singling out paranoia as a primary experience in human development, Melanie Klein argued that because its experience of the world is fragmentary, the infant suffers a persecutory anxiety, which may be mastered (imperfectly) by a later depressive position, which accompanies a more holistic worldview.[38] Jacques Lacan considered all knowledge to have a paranoic dimension. In his account of the mirror stage, where one misrecognizes one's external image as oneself, the self is constituted through its foundational yet alienating dispersal, which lends a persecutory cast even to experiences of self-certainty.[39] The self's "dehiscence" that Lacan had located as a primal operation of the mirror stage (and which sets the stage for later identifications) might be experienced in the age of surveillance capitalism as a cell phone's notification that "you have a new memory," indicating an algorithmically identified photograph from your digital photo library, which you may or may not have been remembering. (Who, exactly, is doing this remembering?) Following Klein and Lacan, paranoia must be understood as ambient and capacious and as foundational in human experience. It is central to the experiences of being and knowing, and it entails the *necessary* projection of one's own needs or desires onto the world.[40] Two important implications follow from such an understanding of paranoia: First, even as a fundament of all knowledge and social phenomenon, paranoia needs to be historicized, given historically shifting forms of being and knowing. Second, when paranoia crystallizes into unshakeable political positions, these attitudes indicate historically specific systems of social organization, and paranoid publics are not therefore an aberration with respect to them, but emerge out of them. In *Paranoid Publics* I am interested in analyzing the forms of fantasy and autonomy that are generated by paranoid dispositions.

How is it that when paranoia becomes politics it takes on a destructive character? Paranoia has long been associated with fascist politics, most notably in Adorno and Horkheimer's *Dialectic of Enlightenment*, and more recently in Eric Santner's study of Daniel Paul Schreber,[41] whose *Memoirs of my Nervous Illness* was the basis of Freud's most sustained analysis of paranoia. Adorno and Horkheimer attribute the destructive nature of projection to epistemological habits of capitalist modernity, whose processes of mass production, standardization, and stereotypy promote a kind of perceptual automatism unable to apprehend the particularity of people or of objects.[42] They argue that this is the epistemological basis of antisemitism and other forms of racism—a projection resulting in a desire for dominating others that misrecognizes itself as self-defense, and thus "humanity's sharpened intellectual apparatus is turned once more against humanity."[43] Such destructive forms of paranoid projection block both self-knowledge and knowledge of the world. Crucially, what replaces knowledge is feeling—in particular, a feeling of mastery:

> This naked schema of power as such, equally overwhelming toward others and toward a self at odds with itself, seizes whatever comes its way and, wholly disregarding its peculiarity, incorporates it in its mythic web. The closed circle of perpetual sameness becomes a surrogate for omnipotence. It is as if the serpent which told the first humans, "Ye shall be as gods" had kept his promise in the paranoiac. He creates everything in his image.[44]

Adorno and Horkheimer's account of paranoia might be more fruitfully understood as a narrative about the miseducation of the senses. The world everywhere reflects to the paranoiac their own self, as perception contracts to admit less of the world, and this feeling of omnipotence is threatened by its own falsity. This unstable and destabilizing psychical solution to an originary disturbance (which, for Adorno and Horkheimer, is capitalist modernity itself) has the unfortunate effect of committing the subject ever more passionately to its schemas, since paranoia offers the lure of self-certainty. The initial malaise that had necessitated paranoid projection or repression is increasingly overwritten by new antagonisms, becoming unnameable on these new terms but nevertheless exerting pressures on them.

In Eric Santner's reading of Daniel Paul Schreber's memoir, paranoia emerges not merely as a concern to do with the singular and idiosyncratic psyche of Schreber himself, but from a social field that is experiencing crises of authority. Schreber was an important German judge who suffered from dementia praecox, a type of schizophrenia, that caused him to believe in an elaborate cosmology in which God planned to turn him into a woman and impregnate him with a pure race of new beings. Freud imputes Schreber's paranoia to unconscious homosexual desire and analyzes his paranoid fantasies as forms of projection. The itinerary of Schreber's projective fantasy goes like this: it is not that Schreber *loves* another man but that he *hates* this man because the man *persecutes* Schreber. Through a series of reversals and externalizations, paranoid projection protects Schreber from his own desire. Freud argues that in Schreber's case projection also takes the form of the assertion "I love no one," suggesting the psychological reality "I love only myself," giving rise to a sense of megalomania.[45] Thus, paranoid projection can be the grounds for self-aggrandizement.

Santner reads Schreber's pathological fantasies as figuring the cultural politics of the European *fin de siècle*. Schreber's malaise is that of society writ large, and in his symptoms one can detect the gathering of forces that Europe would unleash on itself catastrophically with the rise of fascism. Indeed, Schreber is something of an ur-figure in accounts of paranoia, and as a figure he is prismatic and ambiguous. Whereas he emerges ambivalently as a crypto-fascist in Santner's account, in Eve Sedgwick's account and more recently in David Eng and Shinhee Han's reading, Schreber represents the disfigurement of subjectivity given the corrosive effects of homophobia and racism in the social order.[46] One might wonder why it is that Schreber is so disfigured by the social order when others are not. Why or how does *he* become the representative of a collective social malaise? This question gets to the heart of why psychoanalysis is so productive as a conceptual framework and can operate across very different registers. To understand Schreber's individual experiences of psychical distress, one would deploy psychoanalytic categories as a clinician might. Everything from life history, family dynamics, parental relations, dreams and memories would need to be grappled with to understand why Schreber exhibited his symptoms. "The social" would appear in this material in variously mediated forms, each individualizing its effects: parental expectations, the shape of personal ideals, the assumptions regulating relations within the family, etc. But for the purposes of individual analysis, the aim is not to plumb the mysteries of the social order but that of the individual psyche.

Paranoid Publics takes the opposite approach, and its analysis is uninterested in individualizing paranoia, if "individualizing" means personalizing to a particular life history. I follow Adorno in his reading of the place of the individual psyche in psychoanalysis: "Freud made the discovery— quite genuinely, simply through working on his own material—that the more deeply one explores the phenomena of human individuation, the more unreservedly one grasps the individual as a self-contained and dynamic entity, the closer one draws to that in the individual which is really no longer individual."[47] The individual is "no longer" merely individual because the psyche is governed by needs, demands, and compulsions that are fundamentally social and historical in nature. Even if psychoanalytic categories are wrongly adduced by some practitioners (including Freud at times) as universal or transhistorical, the hermeneutics of psychoanalysis necessitate their transformation in light of the social compulsions that regulate any particular psyche. Such compulsions are always historically situated. My aim in this book is to understand how collective actions, shared fantasies, and emergent communities, and psychoanalytic categories are useful for apprehending psychical operations that are shared even among strangers. Though paranoia features prominently here, the examples I analyze also entail forms of repression, idealization, and somaticization. Psychoanalysis enables an understanding of how the psychic reality of specific groups gets generated, how shared fantasy can bind a group, and how such a psychic reality shapes the horizon of their actions in the world.

Some other recent analyses of Schreber's case have emphasized this social dimension of the forms of his fantasy. In Eng and Han's reading of Schreber, since paranoia entails a dispersal of the self into the external world, its psychodynamics have explanatory power in experiences of racial dissociation: a social field that announces itself as colorblind but tacitly endows Asian Americans with imagined capacities of the model minority makes it even more challenging to name the thing that troubles one's psyche. Hence, Eng and Han argue, experiences of racial dissociation among Asian Americans can ensue when one is unable to apprehend their own racial identity since one does not experience the boundedness of identity, either as a basis of solidarity or politics.[48] Taken together these diverse readings of Schreber indicate a central fault line that *Paranoid Publics* will trace, one between psychical realities and historical realities. For Eng and Han, there is indeed something to be paranoid about in the social order, but that very order makes it difficult to name this something. It becomes, then, the critical task of analysis to name the unnamable. For Santner, Schreber's paranoid fantasies are the result of a society's rituals of symbolic investiture having been emptied of their meaning and their function (which one might read as the fraying of a regime of truth). In their wake Schreber's fantasies seek to remake the world by destroying it. Both readings suggest that while psychical realities cannot be taken purely at face value or entirely on the displaced terms in which consciousness narrates the world to itself, it is the task of criticism and analysis to determine what relation psychical truth has to historical truth. No matter how unhinged a paranoid fantasy might appear to be, there is something in the social order that warrants the fantasy since the social order has generated it.[49]

V. In Real Life (IRL)

Of course, historically, people's distrust of authority and of regimes of truth can be warranted for fairly straightforward reasons. Given that the United States government permitted doctors to inject African Americans with syphilis for decades at the Tuskegee Institute in order to study the effects of the disease on the human body, that doctors routinely overestimate the pain thresholds of their Black patients, that Black patients tend to receive less attentive medical care in the United States, distrust of white doctors and the medical establishment among African Americans is widespread.[50] Even among African Americans, however, paranoid fantasy—however solidly rooted in reality—functions in ways more heterogenous than the historical reasons for the paranoia can explain. Patricia Turner's ethnographic account of Black people's paranoia in *I Heard it Through the Grapevine: Rumor in African-American Culture* gives a brilliant account of this. She demonstrates that even an organization as violent and extreme as the KKK, which has given ample grounds for mistrust and fear, still generates rumors of its machinations that far exceed the KKK's reach, capabilities, or actions. She analyzes rumors that a brand of fried chicken is purported to render Black men sterile, that Marlboro cigarettes are owned by the KKK and are specifically intended to cause cancer among the Black community, and that a brand of clothing popular among African Americans is a secret source of revenue for the KKK. With this kind of overreach, legitimate distrust becomes paranoia. Turner reads these paranoid rumors as folklore, which builds a community while simultaneously engaging in self-critique about consumerism or unhealthy habits. Additionally, the certainty offered by the rumor has a self-protective function. As Turner writes of her ethnographic informants, "They might not know when a racist comment would come their way, but they did know that they could protect themselves by avoiding this restaurant and encouraging others to do likewise."[51] Naming something more than the Ku Klux Klan, the acronym KKK makes concrete and definable threats that can sometimes be unpredictable or diffuse in

Black people's everyday lives. Turner's analysis suggests that even when paranoia is based in reality, it tends to produce effects in excess of that reality. To put this in psychoanalytic terms, psychical truth indicates less visible dimensions of historical truth; it is not independent of historical reality but provides a perspective on it.

In Chapter Four, "Hysteria," I analyze a similar dynamic among two populations who have legitimate grounds for their paranoia: children of asylum seekers in Sweden awaiting judicial decisions on their cases, and American spies and diplomats stationed abroad who are subject to various threats and countersurveillance. In the last decade or so, mystery illnesses have emerged in both populations ("Resignation Syndrome" in the children and "Havana Syndrome" in the diplomats), and all of the discourses (medical, journalistic, juridical, political) purporting to investigate and analyze the symptoms of these illnesses have reached an impasse. Mobilizing the much-maligned concept of hysteria, this chapter analyzes these bodily symptoms in relation to border politics, which involves mass hysteria concerning migration and border crossings. While *Paranoid Publics* largely concerns itself with developments in the United States, it does so with an eye to global political tendencies.

Liberal-left critiques of the "deformation" of reality explain the proliferation of paranoid politics as right-wing practice, citing the embrace of conspiracies like the "Great Replacement Theory" or QAnon among right-leaning people in the United States and Europe. But this assessment is often used to dismiss or render illegitimate others' political positions. There are several complexities to consider in this regard. Political polarization can sometimes hide heterogeneities within political collectivities. For example, QAnon has successfully recruited into its paranoid politics yoga moms and putatively liberal people who are concerned about saving children (a phenomenon known among researchers as "pastel QAnon"), and the QAnon Shaman (Jacob Chansley) espouses beliefs often associated with progressive politics: prison abolition, the end of borders, free healthcare, the end of homelessness, etc. That his political beliefs are somewhat confused would be an understatement.[52] Additionally, a libertarian anti-governmental tendency among segments of various paranoid publics brings together heterogenous groups of people united more by a concern about elite capture (technocratic, financial, governmental, and media) than about racial ideology. Followers of Robert F Kennedy Jr and activists for medical freedom are good examples of such publics, and not all such people fall neatly into line behind the same political party. Quinn Slobodian and William Callison have referred to such cross-ideological phenomenon as "diagonalism," which became more common during the peak COVID years, particularly among anti-lockdown protestors in Europe and the United States, and persists in the growing anti-vaccine movement.[53] Another example of surprising contradictions is the far-right group, Proud Boys, whose "pope" is Dante Nero, a liberal Black comedian and self-help guru, and whose leader is Enrique Tarrio, a Cuban-American. Some people of color proactively join white nationalist movements, and Trump won the 2024 election, in part, by appealing to more people of color. The power of psychopolitical appeals helps to explain these often surprising heterogeneities.

While identical psychical operations might well be shared across political divides, they do not always amount to the same political action. Take, for example, QAnon, whose adherents had a considerable presence at the January 6, 2021 insurrection in Washington D.C. At the time, QAnon largely comprised "extremely online" people connected to each other through networked message boards and social media platforms. Some Anons decided to transit from the virtual spaces of online fantasy—animated by sociality, play, and research—to the field of politics in real life ("IRL," in online parlance), even if participation now meant climbing through the broken windows of the Capitol building. Psychoanalytically, in this relationship between fantasy and reality, IRL political action served to make the fantasy "real," suturing the rift between psychical truth and historical truth, attempting to make them align. Undertaken in the abyss between fantasy and reality, such political actions have increasingly involved destruction. Examples of shootings at synagogues, mosques, and churches abound, and some people have taken to "saving the children" by kidnapping them. *Paranoid Publics* analyzes the forms of fantasy that energize destructive politics and the conditions under which such politics reveal themselves IRL. Indeed, the clear distinction between reality and fantasy that the acronym IRL expresses can be misleading, since online incitement in networked subcultures also happens "in real life." Although their actions are often sanctioned and even encouraged by right-wing politicians, these political actors will not be construed here as mere puppets of politicians and "dark money" investors, a common trope in conspiratorial thinking. It would be more accurate to consider destructive politicians or "dark money"[54] investors as themselves symptoms of a fraying social fabric, one in which capital trumps democracy. Hannah Arendt referred to the "alliance between the elite and the mob" as among the conditions for the rise of fascism. She indicated that this alliance is itself a psychopolitical phenomenon, noting that it "rested largely on this genuine delight with which [the elite] watched [the mob] destroy respectability."[55]

Paranoid Publics does not assume in advance that politics on the right have a monopoly on destructive political actions. Liberal Gwyneth Paltrow, for example, has hosted "experts" at her annual summit who deny the existence of HIV, who are active in the anti-vaccine movement (Dr. Kelly Brogan), and who have claimed that death does not exist (Laura Lynne Jackson). Such outlandish claims might be easily dismissed on the basis of scientific regimes of truth, but dismissal does nothing to further our understanding of these games of truth and of the calculus of danger that underwrites their forms of self-cultivation, in which vaccines can appear as a greater threat than HIV, a pandemic, or death. After running for the presidency in the 2024 election as a left-leaning libertarian, the most prominent anti-vaccine spokesperson, Robert F. Kennedy, Jr., was appointed by Trump as the Secretary of Health and Human Services. Presenting himself as a truth-teller and fortified with a sizeable following among women and wellness industry enthusiasts, Kennedy critiques malevolent elites (politicians and scientists) and their social control and offers a full-throated defense of free speech. These personalities aside, even putatively liberal institutions like universities demonstrated their willingness to violate their own values by punishing dissent and student protests on campus with shocking alacrity, even before the second Trump administration began its pressure campaign against universities.

The assassination attempt on Trump in the summer of 2024 kept paranoid publics on the entire political spectrum busy concocting conspiratorial explanations, politically opposed and yet participating in the same game of truth. The critical point here is not that "both sides" have their paranoid publics. Such "both sides" arguments are interested in apportioning culpability while maintaining the integrity of "each" side; they are no help in understanding the crosscurrents and pressures generated by shared dispositions. It is crucial to understand psychosocial phenomena without reference to predetermined political positions. Not to do so would mean to participate in the transferences offered up by political polarization rather than understand their psychodynamics. After all, what is political polarization if not a set of given subject positions at hand, opportunities to remake oneself by investing in these positions emotionally? Political polarization is most effective when its given polar definitions and categories feel irresistible because in themselves, they promise to be explanations of a polarized social reality. Such tautological reasoning is the surest indicator of the critic's enjoyment of a symptom overriding the analysis of it. My aim is to analyze forms of thought and being that were politically and culturally ascendent when I started writing this book, and that became well-established by the time the book went to press. This has entailed a greater focus on paranoid politics that are largely—but not wholly—aligned to the right. In addition, *Paranoid Publics* is interested in analyzing collective phenomena or reigning historical conditions to which everyone is subject: strategies of data capture, forms of border politics, neoliberal governance, the valorization of the family in cultural politics, entrepreneurial solicitations in the culture at large, and others.

Psychosocial analysis can illuminate the contradictory and fragmentary way that seemingly monolithic political solicitations—including authoritarian ones—appeal to a variety of people. I will also take it as axiomatic that liberal democracies under capitalism tend toward authoritarianism. This insight from Adorno and Horkheimer's New York and California exile in the 1940s remains relevant today. The authoritarian tendency in neoliberalism consisted of aligning economic necessity with objectivity, since markets were deemed to operate with the inexorability of natural law. In the ruins of neoliberalism—to use Wendy Brown's phrase[56]—the authoritarian strain in unchecked forms of capitalist modernity has become even more starkly apparent. But the fact that militia groups and QAnon adherents openly espouse anti-democratic rhetoric does not mean that authoritarianism is only to be found in these social segments.[57] The survival of fascist tendencies *within* democracy (and the liberal tradition) is potentially more dangerous than the survival of fascist tendencies against democracy, as Adorno warned his audience upon his return to Frankfurt.[58]

The chapters that follow seek to understand contemporary games of truth that are not stabilized by a regime of truth. What would it mean to take such politics and their enabling conditions seriously, not as wayward reactions to some pre-constituted reality, but as themselves constitutive of reality? My analyses are guided by an assumption that historical truth is never merely given or entirely settled since it results from changing procedures of veridiction and articulates with historically specific cultural and institutional demands. My wager in this book is that the erosion of what we once took for granted as truth signifies a realignment or reorganization of the ground on which truth legitimizes itself. It is not that truth is denigrated or demolished but that some rupture has occurred in the regime of truth that had, until recently, stabilized our collective notions. It would be a mistake to think of these games of truth as somehow radically new and forget their origins in existing—if frayed—regimes of truth, political-economic processes, and shared psychical mechanisms. Appeals to scientific truth and to democratic notions of equality and inclusion invoke an older and familiar regime of truth. Indeed, many (but not all) players in the games of truth this book analyzes look to the past to shape their fantasy of an authority to whom they might submit in the future.

1
Exposure

I. In Plain Sight

In 2017 Donald Trump held a press conference with his lawyer, Sheri Dillon. Basking in the glare of media lights, they presided over a long table whose entire surface was stacked with reams of documents in folders. These documents, Trump and Dillon attested, were just a small selection of the legal papers required to separate Trump from his businesses. Some viewers might have deemed this media spectacle to be evidence of Trump's truth-telling. The press conference suggested to its audience that there are no secrets, that all is visible, exposed in plain sight. But close-ups of the documents fueled speculation on social media that they were actually blank, and Trump's own account of passing the ownership of his businesses to his family contradicted the rationale for this spectacle, even as it fueled discourse around his conflicts of interest. Staged to allay concerns about corruption, while being an obvious instance of it, the "plain sight" of this scene provided an uncannily stark demonstration of concealment. Trump's news conference exemplified the field of truth's newfound games, in which the truth is out in the open—as the theatrics of the press conference suggested—but is also precisely the opposite of what is being stated. This is a different problem from "disinformation" or "misinformation," checkered terms that either recuperate Cold War paranoia about Russia or refer to the proliferation of targeted ads—sometimes posing as "news"—that spread non-truths to susceptible voters. In Trump's news conference the secret of corruption is transparent, yet its identification and recognition remains illegitimate within the terms of the spectacle's own logic. The cryptography of the social world is such that the secret is plain to see, and yet somehow not grasped, its truth not effectuated. Or perhaps more accurately, the open, ineffectual secret is of a piece with a social world whose civic norms, having been under duress, were losing even more of their governing force. After Trump's second election, in 2024, obvious oligarchal corruption became its own variety of political transparency.[1]

We no longer live in a world in which the relation among representation, knowledge, and political action feels as secure as it once did. Fredric Jameson had held out hope for a critical aesthetic practice of "cognitive mapping." Noting that it was an impossible task (as well as the ultimate aesthetic challenge), Jameson thought cognitive mapping would delineate a social field in which political action could be effectuated. Now cognitive mapping has been subverted by companies like Palantir and Meta for decisively instrumental and unaesthetic purposes. The former provides detailed mappings of the social world for both governmental repression and corporate coercion. One of its clients is the Central Intelligence Agency, whose venture capital arm, In-Q-Tel, contributed seed money when Palantir was founded in 2003. Palantir—named after the seeing stones in J.R.R. Tolkien's *The Lord of the Rings*—integrates vast amounts of data from disparate sources and makes them legible in the form of graphs, charts, heatmaps, timelines, and so on; it is understood by its government and corporate clients as a kind of digital panopticon. In 2025, Trump asked Palantir to compile data on all Americans through a series of contracts, including with Immigration and Customs Enforcement (ICE). Meta, for its part, deploys its dominance in the data economy—based on vast data sets about people across the world—for ceaseless self-expansion, despite the social costs of its old motto to "move fast and break things." Facebook's modus operandi has entailed facilitating ethnic cleansing in Myanmar and electoral subversion in the United Kingdom and United States.[2] To be sure, the maps of the social order that Meta and Palantir make available for their clients are not at all the kind of cognitive mapping Jameson had envisioned, but they nevertheless perversely affirm his assumption that political action requires first and foremost a representation—however approximate—of the totality of the social field.[3]

We are witnessing the operations of a new game of truth, one in which various forms of exposure (as revelation, as subjection to injury, as the grasping of knowledge) are entailed in the apprehension of truth. In the playing field, if you will, of contemporary games of truth, certain facts can be pressed as effectual or can themselves effectuate change while other truths, which once would have brought down entire political parties or demagogues, can come to naught. In psychoanalysis, truth paradoxically has the structure of a fiction, whether it refers to the generative misrecognitions as formulated by Lacanians, or the freedom to misperceive and reinvent one another as a condition for relating proposed by object relations theorists (Christopher Bollas, D.W. Winnicott, Melanie Klein). These psychoanalytic stances are reminders that our current notions of what counts as the truth (or "post-truth") might be misperceptions that aid our habitation in the world. Perhaps the ominous pronouncements that truth is dead are misguided.[4] They do not account for the ways that a transformation in the institutions that previously stabilized truth have now made it seem out of joint. If Foucault was correct that the exercise of power involves a game of truth—that is, that the exercise of power involves truth claims—then the radical mutations in the contemporary nature of authority (as an assemblage of juridical, corporate, and state power) have necessarily transformed the game of truth.

II. Exposure as Revelation

In his Collège de France lectures from the late 1970s, collected in *On the Government of the Living*, Foucault discusses how a key secret was encoded in the very architecture of the magnificent palace of the Roman emperor Septimus Severus. The public ceremonial hall, where the emperor "granted audience, delivered his judgments, and dispensed justice" had an ornate painted ceiling of a star-studded sky representing the position of the heavens at the exact moment of the emperor's birth, lending his judgments and decisions a sense of a foretold and objective necessity: the earthly power exercised by the sovereign was destined by the stars above, and the exercise of his sovereign power partakes of the same *logos* that rules the natural world.[5] Foucault explains that "what manifested itself as power here, down below, I was going to say at ground level, could and had to be deciphered in truth in the night sky."[6] The Gods know the truth, and the painted sky in the ceremonial hall discloses the operations of imperial power as an emanation of divine truth. On the ceiling of Septimus Severus's own room was another painting of a night sky, the corollary to this public display. In his room the painted night sky, like a horoscope, foretold the position of the stars at the hour of the emperor's death. It, too, represents the entwinement of truth and power (divine power in this case), but this secret truth about the end of Severus's life must be shielded from public view, left out of the public display of truth/power, in order for the emperor's judgments to be efficacious and grounded. Foucault's architectural mapping suggests that this setup is vulnerable to a possible exposure, since the hour of death is visible only to the emperor's intimates.

Placing Foucault's reflections in *The Government of the Living* in the context of his earlier work, we can see an intellectual trajectory that moves from a consideration of power-knowledge to biopolitics and governmental rationality, and on to the problem of truth and techniques of subjectivation. I would argue that *exposure* as a problematic brings into focus some of the sightlines Foucault sketches out across *episteme* and *bios*, truth and life, and, reaching back to his earlier work, knowledge and power. Or putting it another way, we can grasp not only the place of the secret (its valuation, necessity, and the kind of veridiction required to access it) in exposure, but through Foucault, we can also grasp another of its valences, exposure as modernity's commitment to fostering life by subjecting some forms of life to death. There is no better figure for the deep intimacy between truth, exposure, and mortal vulnerability than the image of Oedipus, who takes two pins from Jocasta's dress and blinds himself as prophetic truth catastrophically discloses itself to him and to the community. Divine and earthly justice finally converge, and Oedipus must cast himself away from the very community he had once saved. Such is, perhaps, the ur-image of authority brought under the yoke of accountability and justice, an image that serves well today as the ethical horizon for those who aspire to check tyrannical power—from whistleblowers to social justice activists. It is also a tragic image, one that combines grave harm to life itself as an instance of an inexorable and just fate. Truth still retains something of its piercing sting in our contemporary moment, as we will see, but the injury it deals is circumscribed by power's newfound games of truth, games that distribute the force of truth without much concern, incidentally, for justice.

Psychoanalysis teaches us that our relationship to truth has never been straightforward because our relationship to what we know is always fraught.

In Lacanian psychoanalysis the subject who is *supposed* to know (the truth) is a fantasized authority, Lacan's primary emphasis being on the supposition of such a subject, and secondarily on the knowledge imputed to this subject. Lacan, too, assumes a fundamental connection between authority and the possession of the truth.[7] This supposed subject of knowledge is a fantasy projected onto the analyst by the analysand, for whom this fantasy serves as a critical point of transference—the point at which all of the self's incoherence is imagined by the analysand to resolve in a flash of insight. Crucially, the analysand imagines this insight is withheld from them but is available to the subject supposed to know.[8] For the analysand, this relationship underscores their own radical ignorance, even as it consoles them that there is in fact a subject in this world who knows what is withheld from them. In other words, the subject supposed to know is the holder of a secret imagined by the analysand, a secret so critical, so radically unavailable (yet all the more effective for its unavailability), that it is no ordinary secret but The Secret itself—a secret that explains one's own truth. The promise of a revelation, one that reveals all, underwrites this fantasy. In this fantasy, truth can reassure the psyche, seeing as it is tucked away securely and might one day be vouchsafed.

This goes some way toward explaining the appeal of conspiracy theories, a conspiracy being a fantasy that someone is in charge and that this entity in charge can see how the disconnected signs that one experiences cohere. At stake in conspiracies is both a master explanation and the status of this explanation as a secret, one revealed in the telling but also preserved as the condition for the disclosure. Conspiracy narratives would lose their thrill without the persistence of the secret that is written into its exposure. As fantasy, the subject supposed to know operates by means of such epistemological and affective magnetism. Such a relationship to an imagined authority is often unconscious, and always infantile—and the more effective for being so. Yet the consolations of this fantasy are risky, since the supposition of a subject supposed to know can also generate its own affective turmoil.

Take, for instance, the contemporary fracturing of news sources. Conspiracies return us to the scene of user-generated content, troll bots, and monetized fake news, which have saturated the public sphere. Because digitally circulated narratives routinely compete with each other, they have given rise to multiple fantasies of a subject supposed to know. For some, this has entailed a wholesale rejection of mainstream corporate media, while for others, it has incited nostalgic longing for a bygone media landscape in which legacy news sources could once be trusted (British Broadcasting Corporation, *The New York Times*, etc.), and for others still, it has led to the insistence that only these corporate news sources can be trusted, however frayed those sources are by the depredations of neoliberal governance and by an old-fashioned nationalist allegiance that has always aimed to manufacture consent.[9] Amidst this fracturing, we can say we are experiencing something like an epistemological sublime—which, when not terrifying, results in general befuddlement, despair, or a desire to turn one's back on the noise altogether—ceding participation as well as knowledge about the collective world.

In this context the truth-teller emerges as a critical figure, and increasingly for liberal democracies, it is the whistleblower who occupies the place of the truth-teller. Whistleblowers promise a kind of authenticity that neither legacy media nor online echo chambers offer, since their knowledge usually comes from close involvement with the institutions and organizations they aim to expose. Whether it is Christopher Wylie, Chelsea Manning, Edward Snowden, or a member of Anonymous, the whistleblower is the unruly voice from within the inner sanctums of state, corporate, or religious power that has accrued the cultural and political authority of veridiction. This voice—when it is not anonymous—is individual, authoritative, principled, and willing to risk its own security for the sake of leaking the truth. Tarek El-Ariss has theorized what he calls "the leaking subject" as an increasingly common figure of the truth-teller whose disclosure is captivating not because it offers new information, but because of "the promise and anticipation it offers to further disrobe and humiliate those in power."[10] Given the befuddled sublimity of increasingly atomized and proliferating media on the one hand, and the "plain sight" signs of scandal becoming the norm on the other, the whistleblower promises the libidinal pleasures of a previous game of truth, in which the secret could be wrested from its sanctum and communicated in the forum, and on the basis of its exposure, some authority would enforce accountability. A corrupted Oedipus would thus be damned and exiled.

Yet often whistleblowers confirm what has been known all along: that governments lie, torture, and engage in all kinds of illegal activity. Slavoj Žižek argues that in the case of WikiLeaks, the true reveal is the shamelessness with which we have gotten on with our days despite having known the scandalous truth in the first place.[11] A similar argument could be made about some of the best-known whistle-blowing incidents: Chelsea Manning, Edward Snowden, the Panama Papers. Respectively, the exposés at issue here are the ruthlessness of American war machines (Manning); the surveillance state and its partnership with internet giants (Snowden); the legal as well as illegal management of wealth by the global 1% (Panama Papers). Individual whistleblowers expose themselves in the same act that seeks to expose their targets, whether these targets are the surveillance state, the military-industrial complex, or a corrupt global oligarchy, each of which are forms of sovereign or sovereign-adjacent power. These are examples of what rhetoricians have called *parrhesia*, a term that means speaking fully or saying everything. In Foucault's accounts of *parrhesia* it emerges as a kind of (free) speech that courts a certain personal danger; the parrhesiast tells the truth in spite of such risks. When the whistleblower is not anonymous then whistleblowing is a clear example of a kind of truth-telling that entails personal risk. Parrhesiatic speech acts oppose themselves to power, and the parrhesiast risks being at the receiving end of sovereign violence. The identification of the truth being spoken with the subject who exposes the truth is a critical feature of parrhesia, and this identification subjects the parrhesiast to a dangerous exposure.

The veridical procedures of whistleblowing have to do with the subversion of power, of rendering it vulnerable. Yet whistleblowers tend to be isolated; they tend to act individually. Their acts of civil disobedience, being highly individuated, are for that very reason limited. This is unlike, for example, the history of civil disobedience, in which the most effectual political struggles have involved the participation of whole populations or classes of people. While sovereign power has historically proved itself all too capable of inflicting violence on entire populations or classes of people, the individual whistleblower risks the wrath of this power being visited on him or her entirely. Therefore, whistleblowers will make all kinds of preparations to decrease their exposure to such vengeance well in advance by blowing the whistle only once they have left the country or securing some legal protection before disclosing the truth. I take the contemporary phenomenon of whistleblowing as an entry point for analyzing changing rationalities and cultural priorities concerning the manifestation of truth, part of a reordering of cultural and political landscapes. Whistleblowing's subversion of power partakes of a larger political impulse—namely exposure, which has become the currency of political praxis, and operates along the circuits and by-lanes of knowledge itself. My argument is that a logic of exposure subtends contemporary cultural politics and emerging forms of economic extraction. The politics of exposure are linked to forms of political power, of which state power is merely one (increasingly subordinated) form.

Most whistleblowers express a moral commitment to "informing the public" and seek to make available information that they feel ought to be public knowledge. However, this is a different register of veridiction than, for example, forms of evidence that might be viable in a court of law. The documents leaked by whistleblowers might indeed become critical for a future juridical process, which is often a priority for the whistleblower's moral charge. Such procedures of veridiction could not proceed without hard evidence. In 2018 the European Court of Human Rights ruled that the British intelligence and security organization, GCHQ (Government Communications Headquarters), violated the European Convention on Human Rights, specifically Article 8, which concerns privacy as a human right. This ruling would not have been possible without the documents Edward Snowden had made available to WikiLeaks and to news organizations. The ruling creates a legal basis for curtailing the government's scrutiny of its own citizens. So while we might say, with Žižek, that whistleblowing is surprising for how little it reveals (because we have known all along), we must not underestimate the importance of juridical truth—a formal truth, if you will, but no less important for that. Juridical procedures can sometimes yield results that work against the management of state and corporate powers. And yet, in the case of Chelsea Manning, the court would not consider the crimes of the state that her breach revealed, but only the crime that Manning herself committed.

Evidence of US military brutality, including the video Chelsea Manning leaked (popularly known in the press as "Collateral Murder"), has largely circulated as another unit in the increasingly derealized public sphere, with its "siloes," "echo chambers," and "halls of mirrors," phrases that turn up regularly to describe the public sphere now.[12] The media-theatre of news reportage and online social platforms is the strange court in which leaked documents circulate most widely, within these echo chambers that have blurred the lines between accusation and evidence, between reportage and conspiracy, and as observed so frequently now, between truth and falsehood. What do we make of the epistemological gap between the tedious leaked evidence—memos, bank records, emails, military video recordings—and the general conclusion that such evidence might be marshaled toward? In other words, how are we to understand the disjuncture between information and truth? Evidence is not the same as proof, and it is in the gap between the two that the most salient political and epistemic battles of our day are being fought, from climate change to a global reckoning with sexual assault to attacks on education. At stake in these battles is not a mere difference of interpretation of the same basic phenomena, but rather the weakening of collectively agreed-upon mechanisms for producing truth. Evidence is never merely given or stable, and proof stabilizes evidence as the manifestation of truth.

The alleged de-prioritizing of truth is not news (fake or otherwise), so I will not spend time bemoaning that truth seems no longer to matter, but I do register this lament itself as a symptom of our malaise. After all, there are enough truths that are plainly in sight, such as Donald Trump's history of sexual assault, his unmitigated racism, and his history of corruption. Even if his openly espoused racism and history of sexual assault were not quite considered assets in his 2016 presidential campaign, quite a few people were willing to turn a blind eye to both in order to support him. By the time Trump won the election in 2024 his voters were proudly sporting T-shirts with Trump's angry mug shot and the words "Convicted Felon." In his 1983 book *Critique of Cynical Reason*, Peter Sloterdijk discusses in depth how the rise of Nazism was made possible through practices of turning a blind eye, a practice of fetishistic disavowal: "I see that this is so, but nevertheless I will not-see it if necessary," or put another way, "I know X is false but I believe X and will act on it nevertheless." Hal Foster has suggested that one way to understand the place of truth in contemporary politics is to raise the notion of cynical reasoning "to a higher power . . . for cynical reason today doesn't care to know, or if it knows, it doesn't care."[13]

So perhaps it is not simply that truth-acts (such as whistleblowing) expose what we already know, but that the place of knowledge in an atmosphere of fetishistic disavowal lends such disavowal a libidinal frisson. In cynical reasoning, truth actually *matters* a great deal because acting *in spite of it* is what endows the action with its distinctive fetishistic pleasure. This is a different order of pleasure from what Wendy Brown describes as "disinhibition" of (Trumpian) libidinal politics.[14] While fetishistic disavowal requires truth for its libidinal satisfaction, it is not necessarily governed by a politics of resentment. For her part, Brown returns to Herbert Marcuse's notion of "repressive desublimation," a collective social atmosphere created under capitalism when pleasure is itself integrated into the operations of capital, thereby weakening the age-old opposition between conscience, or super-egoic prohibitions, and the pleasure principle. Words and acts that seem to be in tension with existing norms are fully indulged in the thrilling experience of a freedom that reactively shores up existing forms of repression:

> Free, stupid, manipulable, absorbed by if not addicted to trivial stimuli and gratifications, the subject of repressive desublimation in advanced capitalist society is not just libidinally unbound, released to enjoy more pleasure, but released from more general expectations of social conscience and social comprehension.[15]

From Trump rally participants attacking the press corps, to racist hate speech, to the pleasures of indulging in "anti-woke" tirades, to triumphant public expressions of misogyny, repressive desublimation as a form of disinhibited freedom is a *carte blanche* for the expression of aggression—in Brown's words, "this is humanity without a project other than revenge."[16] In the sense of turning a blind eye, disavowal is operative more generally across an array of violences, from sexual abuse and assault to pogroms against racial and religious minorities. For populations that find their autonomy and their voice through repressive desublimation, political and cultural hopes are underwritten by a politics of exposure: the fantasy that one can buck cultural and political norms and expose them as made-up, as vulnerable, and as unnecessary, all the while insisting on the most repressive forms of traditional values.

From this perspective, whistleblowing appears quaintly attached to an order of veridiction that assumes truth sets people free, that transparency is always a collective good, and that information ("informing the public") and knowledge are coterminous. In the face of such a widespread and collective phenomenon as fetishistic disavowal, including its variant of repressive desublimation, the truth that whistleblowers might reveal risks becoming mere fodder for the libidinal pleasure taken by acting in spite of any comprehension of the whistleblower's truth. In fetishistic disavowal, knowledge is overwritten by a libidinal pulsion; repressive desublimation gives free rein to the desire to tear things down as a way to restore some imagined "greatness"; in the supposition of a subject of knowledge, truth is imagined to be out of reach, and this supposition creates the conditions for dependency on the subject supposed to know. The logic of exposure is central to each of these phenomena. But whistleblowing differs from these entanglements of truth and power in one critical way: whistleblowers wind up communicating something in excess of their stated aims. Earlier I mentioned that whistleblowers make themselves vulnerable in the same gesture that exposes their targets. This double-exposure is part and parcel of the ethics of whistleblowing: stating the truth in one's own name, or exposing oneself to repercussions, is also an attempt to demonstrate that one is publicly accountable through the same action that demands accountability from the institution or agency that one has exposed. Foucault suggests that where sovereign power is concerned, operations in the domain of truth "are always in excess of what is useful and necessary to govern in an effective way," and that "the manifestation of truth is required by, entailed by, or linked to the exercise of government and the exercise of power in a way that always goes beyond the aim of government and the effective means for achieving it."[17] The truth escapes the control of the authority that would wield it, and it also escapes the control of the subject who speaks power's secret truths to power itself.

III. Exposure as Extraction

Whistleblowing is an overt act of exposure. Less overtly, the logic of exposure can limn the political mood concerning the place of truth in contexts far afield from whistleblowing itself. Let's take for a moment the phenomenon of leaks and leaking, which is often discursively framed as a crisis. We associate the terms *leaks* and *leaking* increasingly with digital circulation, and new media has made possible whole new forms of exposure. Wendy Chun and Sarah Friedland put it thus:

> From WikiLeaks to Facebook disasters, we are confronted everywhere with leaks. This leaking information is framed paradoxically as both securing and compromising our privacy, personal and national. Thanks to these leaks, we now understand the

extent to which we are under surveillance; because of these leaks, we are exposed. This leaking information and the problems/solutions it exposes/provides are often presented as oddly personalized and humanized. Snowden is a hero or a rogue agent; Anonymous are advocates or vigilantes; slanegirl [a woman who became a meme online] is a victim or a slut. But to what extent is leaking information an issue of personal human agency? [. . .] *New media are not simply about leaks: they are leak.*[18]

Chun and Friedland note that, for example, social media users often "leak," or expose, more than they realize to the tech companies who own the platforms and who can monetize their preferences. Although internet security purports to protect the end user, its real aim is to protect the tech company from data breaches. After all, the end user is increasingly solicited to expose more and more of their habits, preferences, lifestyle choices and the like to the tech giant. Based on Chun and Friedland's analysis, one might say that exposure is both a breach and *also* the very quotidian mechanism that motors online life. According to Tarek El-Ariss, this kind of exposure "generates a collapse in the subject itself and in the constellation structured around models of the public and private."[19] As the newest form of economic extraction, data capture is the scene of primitive accumulation in the heart of the most developed countries. Metadata concerning one's personal preferences, habits, moods, interests, and browsing histories has become capitalism's new frontier.[20] Products as wide-ranging as fridges connected to the internet, Google's search engine, Amazon's Alexa, and a Facebook profile are all channels for the extraction of personal data that can be monetized in a thousand different ways. Such exposure of users to data collection has become, from the point of view of tech companies, an objective economic necessity.

However, users are radically unaware of the uses to which such data might be put and of the other entities who may be granted access to it.[21] Facebook allows users to download all of the information related to their Facebook profile, but they cannot download the results of that information as it was processed by Facebook's various algorithms, not to mention its processing by third-party trackers. Various corporate entities monetize user data via proprietary algorithms, and multiple algorithms are used in conjunction with internet-tracking technologies. Whatever data about users these technologies collect is not available to users themselves. In fact, unless one has some technical know-how, it is becoming increasingly impossible to avoid trackers collecting granular levels of personal data that is then sold like any other commodity.[22] This data is far greater than the sum of its parts, and not reducible to the facts of the profile information one *can* download and access. The rapt users of digital products and services become more and more opaque to themselves, detached as they are from their existence as data, a digital index that paradoxically makes them increasingly usable to the powers that monetize it.[23]

Walter Benjamin spoke of the optical unconscious underwriting the manifest phenomenon of new visual technologies. The tech billionaires of today have made possible a cyber unconscious which, like the optical unconscious, is an effect of capital and no less real for being so. Users might know their data is being collected, but the circuits and processes in which that data morphs, or how it gets deployed, are as radically other to internet users as the processes of their own unconscious. Data becomes truth through algorithmic processing, and the multiplication of algorithms means that the same data set can be mobilized in an infinite number of ways. The cyber unconscious is networked, able to aggregate data as needed or focalize its precipitates for each individual user. The paradox of person-alization techniques—which tailor each user's experience online—is that personalization would not be possible at all without aggregated and net-worked data about demographics. The users of unregulated online plat-forms do not have many rights over their data, which enters cyberspace and becomes enmeshed in strange alchemies: the reserve of a precious resource (data) that is simultaneously the consumption and production of that resource. The resource is itself produced from the consumption/production of online users and only becomes legible as resource in its consumption by ad networks, spy agencies, and online trackers. Digital extraction synchronizes the ancient processes of production, consumption, and circulation into a single temporal instant that—as with the uncon-scious—knows no negation, and in which the past, the present, and the future are all subject to sudden valuation because nothing can be com-pletely deleted.

Creaturely life, as for the unconscious itself, is the ontological condition for the cyber unconscious, yet it remains detached from it in a crucial way: the cyber unconscious contains the data indices of life extracted through mechanisms of increased "engagement" (gathering clicks, focalizing attention, activating ludic loops) and then converted into a pure value-form. So-called engagement, or the point of extraction, can be leveraged via any physical or social need, from the alteration of the room's temperature in a networked home to the online purchase of a gift for a loved one. In this economy, the repressed returns as an ad for the perfectly pitched commodity, following the user across multiple websites. Or it takes the form of YouTube's perverse recommendations, powered by an algorithm attuned to showing what mass numbers of users cannot look away from, so that any of its near-infinite number of videos are linked to some of the most sexual or violent content on the platform through a set of algorithmic correspondences that unfailingly land in the same libidinally charged zone. A thread laid by a sinister Ariadne, this algorithm delivers users deeper into the labyrinth, to the place it assumes they secretly want to go, and which, in turn, habituates them to the new stimuli they find there. Such logics, which are not specific to YouTube, are self-perpetuating, creating new data sets based on their own nudging of users (which "prove" the truth of their original assumptions) while training new users to focalize their attention similarly. Such an aspiration of power is reminiscent of ancient gods for whom performative speech was indissociable from mere description. In the brave new world of digital economies, extraction and exposure are one and the same. Since data drives digital economies, the prized form of extraction—one that yields sustained streams of user data—is enhanced engagement, procured through a battery of techniques: ludic loops, algorithmic "personalization" and persuasion; integration of trackers across devices, household objects, and public spaces; click-bait and recommendations algorithms. Most techniques for enhancing engagement depend on the inescapability of fundamental subjective experiences, the bread and butter of Freud's theory of the unconscious: namely, desire and fear.

As the 2018 scandal surrounding Cambridge Analytica demonstrated, such base impulses can be exploited to manipulate the beliefs and behaviors of populations significant enough in number to swing elections.[24] Facebook itself has conducted mass social experiments on its platforms.[25] These targeting practices aside, *all* users of networked technology are exposed. The information one knowingly offers up morphs, via a set of channels both sophisticated and opaque, into a wholly different data set that seeks to anticipate one's desires, purchases, political persuasions, religious views, sexual orientation—the list could go on. Moreover, government spy agencies are often permitted back-channel access to troves of user data. Nor is there any possibility of opting out of surveillance capitalism altogether.

The defiant retort "I have nothing to hide" from otherwise thoughtful users displays their own commitment to fetishistic disavowal. Technology companies are highly skilled at psychological and behavioral modification, relying on libidinal pleasures to feed their algorithms while publicly assuming that the end user is a rational consumer who can choose not to consent to the fine print of the service's user agreement. The same platforms that keep working to perfect the addictiveness of their services insist that their users are rational agents whose desires and interests coincide—though such people (if they existed) would, of course, be deleterious to the extractive processes of big technology companies. In short, exposure is an economic, cultural, and political rationality unto itself; new media, insofar as they *"are leak,"*[26] crystallize one face of the politics of exposure, a politics based fundamentally on truth-producing mechanisms that are as important to the extraction of surplus value as they are to the strategies of governmental surveillance, political campaigns, and social agitation.

IV. Exposure as Biopolitics

Surveillance capitalism is so difficult to counter because the state authorities that might curtail Big Tech's excesses have themselves become the organs for spreading such forms of capitalist extraction. The digital revolution has reshaped media by atomizing both its content and its delivery to increasingly isolated users. A camouflaging of truth has attended this change, accompanied by a diminished sense of any shared social world and also by a dramatic increase in the scope of state and other kinds of authority. Powered by digital platforms, the gig economy, for example, extends the employer's authority by concealing it: Uber drivers or Deliveroo agents are not juridically designated as employees but as self-employed entrepreneurs—independent contractors whose health benefits, safety, and work environment are not the responsibility of the employer, even though gig workers expose themselves to greater risk than traditional employees.[27] The employer is not responsible for the workers' welfare, but his or her authority and discipline nevertheless regulate the workers' daily lives. That gig workers' designation as non-employees is starting to be challenged represents another turning point in the ongoing conflict between capital and labor, but the conflict touches on a secular theological doxa dear to neoliberal thinking: the market as the site of veridiction. This logic would argue that the significantly lowered price of the worker's labor represents a natural price. The depredations of labor under recent neoliberal governance abound: "zero-hour" contracts in the United Kingdom (in which employers need not guarantee even minimal hours of work), "marginal jobs" throughout Europe (in which contracts expire before the worker is eligible for benefits), "minijobs" or "midijobs" in Germany (a job with insufficient hours to qualify for unemployment claims once the job is terminated).[28] Foucault explains that under neoliberalism, "inasmuch as prices are determined in accordance with the natural mechanisms of the market they constitute a standard of truth which enables us to discern which governmental practices are correct and which are erroneous."[29] The market provides the truth on the basis of which governance occurs; the government becomes steward of the market and relies on the market's forms of veridiction. The truth-tellers of the market—economists—become central to the art of government, and, consulting the ideally autonomous and self-regulating market that emanates truth, they offer pronouncements that determine the kind of life the polity will lead.

Surveillance capitalism is aided by the neoliberal reordering of the world, a reordering that is also a moment of racial capitalist restructuring.[30] As Quinn Slobodian has argued, the high priests of neoliberalism—especially Friedrich Hayek, Milton Friedman, and Wilhelm Röpke—viewed decolonization as a profound threat to capitalist accumulation. Röpke was indeed an unreconstructed racist, arguing in favor of apartheid on the grounds that "the South African negro" was not only of a different race but of "a completely different type and level of civilization."[31] While Hayek and Friedman did not endorse this variant of racism, they too argued against the demands for racial equality when such a demand required the redistribution of property in the decolonizing world. Hayek even opposed sanctions against apartheid and would only favor Black majority rule if postcolonial state institutions were stripped of their power to regulate the economy. Milton Friedman defended white majority rule in Rhodesia. Global in its vision at the very outset, neoliberalism presumed that the economy itself was not political, sought to protect it from politicization, and rendered the global and local racial inequalities that the market generates into natural laws.

The neoliberal assumption that the economy is the site of veridiction must be challenged on all political fronts precisely because this assumption naturalizes capitalism's race and class arrangements. I am not referring just to the fact that digital technologies misrecognize racialized subjects or that algorithmic citizenship bakes in the social divisions it had sought to overcome.[32] A politics of exposure—exposure of life to risk—is now writ large, and it affects populations *differentially*. Exemplified by the governance of Margaret Thatcher and Ronald Reagan, neoliberal policies have rolled back the protections of the mid-century liberal state, multiplying the number of people left abandoned by the state. These vulnerable populations are the most radically exposed to material danger.

The veridical game of exposure links together the increased financialization of life itself with the increase in risk to that life. The *Oxford English Dictionary* tells us that "expose" is a relatively recent entry into the English language, adapted in the fourteenth century from French: a combination of the Latin *exponere* (to put out) and *pausare* (to rest, lay down). It is related to the French word, *poser*: to place or to pose. In English "to expose" means "to put out; to deprive of shelter"; "to unmask"; "to place in an unsheltered or unprotected location or to leave without shelter or defense; to lay open (to danger, ridicule, or censure); to abandon." In religious contexts "to expose" means to exhibit—for example, the Host or relics—for adoration. Taken together, these meanings are instructive: to abandon, to unmask or disclose, to deprive of shelter, but also to display for adoration. The power to abandon, to deprive something of shelter is intermixed with the capacity to disclose; this capacity remains, moreover, related to display, to putting out, to showing off. From the vantage point of exposure as a conceptual or theoretical frame, Foucault's intellectual trajectory appears in a new light. Foucault arrived at the thorny problem of truth and its relation to power after he had elaborated forms of state rationalities and their relationship to biopower; "exposure," crystallizes the affinities between truth, vulnerability, and power that preoccupied Foucault through his philosophical career. As the practice of biopower, biopolitics entails grasping the truth of a certain population for the purposes of regulating that population's life. Indeed, biopower is a concept that already suggests a theory of exposure.

As Foucault first establishes it, biopower is that regulative function by which a governing rationality seeks to encourage the flourishing of the population. It replaces the older form of sovereign power, which held sway over life and death. Biopower seeks to enrich and enable life by taking

48   EXPOSURE

charge of the conditions that regulate it, and to do so it necessarily practices
the power of normalization, producing the notion of a life that is worth
living, of life that deserves to live. By means of regulating life, biopolitics
thereby regulates death. How then does biopower, intending to regulate
and foster life, exercise the power to kill? Foucault explains that racism
plays a key role in squaring this circle:

> If the power of normalization wished to exercise the old sovereign
> right to kill, it must become racist. And if, conversely, a power of
> sovereignty or in other words, a power that has the right of life and
> death, wishes to work with the instruments, mechanisms, and
> technology of normalization, it too must become racist. When I
> say "killing," I obviously do not mean simply murder as such, but
> also every form of indirect murder: the fact of exposing someone
> to death, increasing the risk of death for some people, or, quite
> simply, political death expulsion, rejection, and so on.[33]

Foucault refers to racism as "the precondition for exercising the right
to kill"—that is, it makes killing acceptable by situating some people as a
threat. By eliminating these people or by exposing them to danger, biopower putatively encourages the flourishing of the "right" forms of life.[34]
Hence biopower can practice the old sovereign right to kill in the name
of protecting life itself. It is hard to read Foucault's words today without
thinking of populations around the world who have recently been abandoned by the law, and exposed to all kinds of danger: the Rohingyas of
Myanmar, Syrian refugees, children of Mexican immigrants in detention
camps, Black men and women subject to police brutality, Palestinians
under occupation, Yemeni lives endangered not only by bullets and bombs
but by the destruction of the infrastructure that supports biological life
itself. The list could go on.

V. Exposure as Mood

Attending the increased immiseration for these populations, made vulnerable because abandoned, there has been the haunting of the middle
and upper classes by the real or imagined threat of falling from their
comfortable perch. In other words, alongside the material forms of exposure for poor and racially different populations, there has emerged a *feeling*

of exposure for those who are far less vulnerable. This feeling is a kind of ambient anxiety experienced by some of the most privileged people in society. Within Western nations income inequality is at an all-time high. Some economists may tout a low unemployment rate, but what good is that when a single job increasingly does not provide enough to live on? These days, the metrics of economic health tend to index, more than anything, the economic health of the already wealthy. Television shows depicting the crisis of the American middle class all circle the same ground: an upstanding nondescript white middle-class parent must turn to crime in order to make ends meet (*Weeds, Breaking Bad, Ozark*, etc.). These shows depict the wounds of moral injury sustained by national subjects attempting to live up to the nation's idea of the good life. They evidence the strange double fantasy generated by neoliberalism: the entrepreneurial self can overcome and can win, and at the same time, that very entrepreneurship is required because survival itself is at stake.[35] Extreme vulnerability attends fantasies of dominating and taming the course of one's life. In these narratives the injuries dealt by the social order have to be managed by individual cunning, and yet these are not triumphant old-fashioned narratives of people overcoming adversity. Even as the middle-class mom or dad begins to enjoy becoming a drug lord, the moral compromises entailed in the journey combined with the increased exposure to brute violence display these anti-heroes as having revealed their inner potential for corruption, venality, and murder. The feeling of economic exposure that leads the protagonists of these shows to make ends meet by means of criminal activity takes on the form of another kind of exposure: the danger that one might be found out as a criminal, and threat of *this* kind of exposure comes to lend the narrative its distinctive thrill. The narrative shuttles from threats to life (*bios*) to the threat of being found out (*episteme*): exposure as a biopolitical threat and exposure as a disclosive truth are intermixed. This is the case in fiction and in reality, in the United States and elsewhere. It is also the case for people living in situations of extreme precarity. For refugees, for example, exposure to threats to life becomes, when crossing borders, an exposure to governmental scrutiny: everything from life history, education level, vehemence of religious conviction, personal dress, manners, and comportment figure into the political calculation of decisions about asylum, detention, or deportation.

Yet the global bourgeoisie consider themselves to be living in a state of heightened exposure. To care for oneself means to scrutinize oneself for the slightest sensitivity—somewhere between the menace of gluten sensitivity and a terrorist attack lie the lineaments of bourgeois whiteness. These might well be adaptations to a pervasive atmosphere in which everyone *feels* insecure, even as more and more people are rendered objectively insecure. An atmosphere can be considered the very medium through which one orients oneself to the world. This is close to what Martin Heidegger referred to as mood (*Stimmung*), the affective ground from which one experiences being and comports toward objects in the world. In Heidegger's sense, a mood is an attunement to the world, and it can be collectively produced, stumbled into, made an object of scrutiny, or assumed as the basis from which one's attention, actions, and utterances flow. In an essay concerning the relationship of *Stimmung* to literary texts, Jonathan Flatley has described it as "a historical form that orients us in a specific world [and] is felt on an intimate and individual level even as it is not 'psychological,' and is a key player in the psychic life of power."[36] As a kind of generalized mood, exposure certainly describes the self-cultivation and extreme sensitivity of first-world subjects whose lives feel to them like a series of vulnerabilities they have to manage. Dangers abound to one's bodily sovereignty, well-being, household, class position, and career. Psychopolitically, such a mood has become the corollary to the ever-present wish for some segments of the middle and upper classes that an abstract cipher of value, whether meme stock, NFT, or crypto currency could magically deliver abundance to oneself as it has for some. Exposure becomes a mood when political economic processes remake life itself into a kind of lottery. Until one wins, however, exposure must be managed, and the feeling of risk runs across radically different kinds of populations.

Take, for example, two very dissimilar entrepreneurs who cater to divergent kinds of consumers: Alex Jones and Gwyneth Paltrow. Jones is the infamous professional conspiracy monger, who has faced three defamation lawsuits for publicly claiming on Infowars that the Sandy Hook school shooting[37] was a hoax. Paltrow is the wholesome face of the wellness and lifestyle company Goop. It would seem they have more in common than one might think. One of the "health supplements" that Jones sells, Brain Force Ultra, contains the same ingredient (Ashwagandha) that Goop also sells under the product name, "Why Am I So Effing Tired?" How to understand this seemingly incidental overlap between the consumers of Goop and the consumers of Infowars? If anything, the consumers that Goop appeals to and whose interests it promotes are among the most cosseted and secure populations. These are mostly wealthy women, largely liberal, with time and money enough to practice everyday vigilance against perceived environmental threats, and to cultivate an ethics of self-enrichment and wholesomeness. There is an anxious component to this ethics, however, subtended as it is by a persistent sense of the body's vulnerability and the ever-present possibility that some persecutory force (whether toxin or bad habit) will violate the body and an individual's practice of self-care. In contrast, the consumers of Infowars are largely male Trump supporters, self-described "patriots," and insurrection enthusiasts. By Jones's own 2016 metrics, his audience is 72% male, and 63% of his total audience has an annual income of less than $100k.[38] Yet an anxious attention to the body's vulnerability is present here, too. While Brain Force Ultra can hardly undo the damages wrought by deepening income inequality, it provides libertarian succor for anxieties about imagined government control of the body. Like most products Jones sells, Brain Force Ultra offers freedom instead of social control; similarly, Goop's product supports "balance in an overtaxed system," protecting the body against excessive environmental demands. Both companies offer their consumers psychic release conditioned on a notion of the body as a fortress under threat. The gendered and political differences across these consumers are sutured by a fantasy whose fundamentals they share—a paranoid vigilance that is simultaneously relieved and cultivated by consuming the products. Yet while it is surely generated by these products, for susceptible buyers, paranoia must also precede the encounter with the commodities on offer. Since a sense of danger attends paranoia, the resulting desire for self-protection is felt not as desire but as need. Such experiences of desire *as* need make paranoid people ideal consumers. Infowars and Goop share the same economic logics, and appeal to identical solutions for mitigating the threats posed by an imagined hostile environment. What Nick Srnicek has called "platform capitalism"—the conjuncture of digital technological development and rentier capitalism—does not simply divide and polarize the *demos*, but also unifies it in ways that may not always be readily apparent.[39]

While our contemporary insistence on exposure has a history and a genealogy worth excavating, it is also worth considering more closely how such a priority underwrites the contemporary game of truth's linkages to power. A politics of exposure results in the abandonment of lives and their exposure to risk, in part because under neoliberal rationality more and more of life is monetized and given over to risk. Surveillance capitalism and platform capitalism both assume exposure for their extractive processes. They also link up the most minute details of a user's life to the dispersed and nebulous—but no less coercive—power of technology companies, as well as subjecting those details to governmental scrutiny. These aspects of capitalism synchronize with already existing neoliberal techniques of subjectivation, in which subjects are not directly oppressed but the conditions of their choice are subtly managed. Hence the enthusiasm for so-called nudge economics, a political-economic theory advanced by Richard Thaler and Cass Sunstein that aims at subtly guiding and manipulating the choices given to the populace so that people can make "better" decisions. These would be decisions in line with people's putative economic interests, supposedly already anticipated by the experts and policymakers engaged in nudging everyone. Hence, as well, elaborate rationalizations by right-wing politicians for the kind of manipulative work engaged in surreptitiously by Cambridge Analytica (which has become more common and less scandalous since the Cambridge Analytica scandal of 2018). Within contemporary games of truth and power, truth is both the mark of vulnerability and the ultimate prize. In a climate where information and disinformation are hard to tell apart, exposure as an epistemological priority becomes all the more critical. Yet exposure differs from mere truth-telling because in its political, cultural, and economic operations, disclosure of the truth and banishment from the circle of life operate in tandem with each other.[40] Such a regime of exposure—in which disclosive truth constitutes a form of life—has implications for subject-formation, collective moods, and economic extraction, and this chapter has outlined some of these implications. When our contemporary games of veridiction consistently offer up exposure as the means for achieving justice, and for saving democracy from authoritarianism, we ought to consider as well the dangers to truth that attend exposure, the reduced notion of justice that can underwrite these hopes, and the deep intimacy between the truth disclosed and the body injured.

The global disruptions caused by COVID made exposure a central concern for everyone: millions of deaths worldwide, the lockdown and quarantine of cities around the world, the shuttering of whole economies, skyrocketing unemployment claims, and measures of social distancing recommended and unevenly enforced. The destruction wrought by COVID revealed the societal fissures often disavowed by governments and corporations. The most vulnerable tended to be those in low-paying professions suddenly deemed "essential" (grocery store clerks, hospital workers, transit workers, construction industries, etc.). Although the pandemic starkly demonstrated mutual dependence among people, exposure as a collective mood also took the form of a volatile anxiety seeking discharge: calls for large-scale sacrifice of the elderly and the weak for the sake of economic health were heard alongside the largest anti-police uprisings in US history.

COVID offered an opportunity for profiteering by finance capital and the pharmaceutical industry, and, as virus tracking, virtual workspaces, and more of social life became available for data mining, platform capitalism became more deeply entrenched. QAnon and its psychosocial promises of exposure gained traction during this time, moving from a fringe online community to become the guiding spirit of mainstream GOP politics. As Chapter Two will show, QAnon claims the certainty but also the challenge of conspiracy, whose Latin root we would do well to recall in the age of COVID and the cracks in democracy it accentuates; *conspīrāre* means "to breathe together."

2
Paranoia

I. Insurrection Content

The January 6 insurrection was a carnival, a logical endpoint for the libidinal and spectatorial politics that installed Trumpism as a political symptom of American politics. Witness the self-professed QAnon Shaman, shirtless, with painted face, feral horned headgear, carrying a long spear, who took to howling in the Senate chamber after breaking into the Capitol building along with the rest of the mob: a surreal display of an insurrectionary primitivism that claims to root out corruption and restore the law by breaking it. Participant of a scene intended to "stop the steal," the Shaman and influencer (real name: Jacob Chansley) concretizes the storming of the Capitol as an elaborate spectacle intended for the eyes of ubiquitous digital cameras. Indeed, the world was watching. Posing for pictures, making "content," and playing dress-up was, however, combined for some rioters with deadly intent: killing a person with a fire extinguisher, concussing police officers with flag poles, attacking security personnel with chemical sprays. And the spontaneous collective effervescence of the crowd was coupled with a premeditated effort by some participants to monetize digital livestreams of themselves at the Capitol. The theatrics of January 6 shocked in part because scenes of play-acting, phoniness, and collective fun appeared dissonant with an event that demonstrated all too spectacularly the damage to democracy that has been ongoing in less visible ways over the past three decades. The imagined injury—a stolen election—was even more galvanizing for being unreal. It was also a cipher for multiple other psychic investments: being wronged, seeking justice, acting in the interests of an aggrieved self, and feeling dispossessed in one's own country. The Shaman emerged from a mixed crowd of Trump supporters—small business owners, middle managers, white supremacists, ex-military personnel. Multiple politicians also tacitly or explicitly lent support to the crowd and the narrative of election fraud that mobilized it.

A study of the demographics of those arrested or charged in the Capitol attack found that 95 percent were white, 85 percent were male, and most came from regions that have seen an increase in nonwhite populations.[1] Those actually dispossessed could not afford a trip to Washington, D.C., if they had wanted to join at all. Since almost all those charged or arrested were professionals, narratives of economic immiseration, of being "left behind," are not sufficient explanations for their "radicalization." What motivated them were forms of misrecognitions and conjuring—of injury, grievance, and malevolent enemies—that constitute their paranoid ideation. The January 6 crowd represented an amalgamation of paranoid publics comprising QAnon, antivaxxers, and various militia groups, among others. The Shaman is an eco-warrior who only eats organic foods, and while extremist right-wing militia groups like Proud Boys and Oath Keepers also joined the melee, so did yoga instructors and suburban moms angry about lockdown measures and vaccine mandates. Everyone's grievances converged around the fantasy of a stolen election. When an imagined injury, or an injury to one's fantasies of nationhood or collective belonging, is the effectual element in one's political participation, we are clearly in the presence of powerful psychodynamics. At the same time, this conjuncture of paranoia and political mobilization suggest that the psychodynamics of this event are indissociable from their economic and political aspects. It is the transit from paranoid ideation to political action that interests me in this chapter.[2]

The oft-repeated QAnon dictum, "Enjoy the Show," is key both to Trumpism as well as to the media ecology in which QAnon germinated. Instead of assuming false consciousness on the part of paranoid publics, or dismissing them as merely delusional, I consider QAnon's paranoid game of truth as a symptom illuminating the social formations that produce it. QAnon is one product of Trumpism and a valuable lens on this political strain. That strain is likely to outlive Donald Trump and has already sur-passed QAnon itself.[3] As a "big tent conspiracy," QAnon assimilated other conspiracies into its multiverse. This means QAnon itself is an amalgam of different paranoid publics; its set of beliefs is mobile and flexible, and therefore capable of recruiting believers from a variety of ideological persuasions. It has grown organically out of the mediascape where it ger-minated, and its growth is instructive for understanding the powers of new media. QAnon shares features with other paranoid politics such as anti-mask, anti-lockdown, and anti-vaccine movements, as well as evangelical Christianity and millenarian movements. Its membership overlaps with extremist movements such as the Proud Boys and Boogaloo Bois, but also with consumers and practitioners in the wellness industry. For all these reasons, I will repeatedly return to QAnon as my example. To understand how right-wing extremism, the devaluation of truth, and the polity's increasing exposure to various forms of risk form our contemporary con-juncture, we must delineate the terms of these mass psychological phe-nomena along with the forms of subjectivation, self-cultivation, and world-building they make possible.

Although initially a lurid fringe phenomenon, QAnon grew exponen-tially during the COVID lockdowns and eventually seeded mainstream paranoiac ideation about sexual "groomers," the deep state, social control, and bodily exposure to pharmaceutical malfeasance. All of these notions pre-dated QAnon, but the QAnon movement reenergized them and brought them together into a constellation that purports to describe an intricately networked and formidable malignant power which is respon-sible for all societal malaise. As these notions have become mainstream, many people expressing them are unaware that they have been transmitted by QAnon influencers and content producers. Central to QAnon's games of truth is a technique it shares with other forms of paranoid thinking: questioning established truths—sometimes for entirely valid reasons—but filling in the resulting doubt with a fixed certainty about alternative explanations whose basis is neither fact nor firm evidence, but whose libidinal charge is one of insinuation, grievance, and aggression. The fact that QAnon could emerge out of specific psychopolitical and social conditions and then become so easily assimilated to the social order—so much so that its fundamental paranoiac commitments no longer traffic under the banner of QAnon—indicates that its game of truth relies on psychodynamics and political-economic processes that are shared across the socius. The online spaces where QAnon emerged initially determined the rules and demands of its historically specific game of truth, and in this chapter, I trace these ludic solicitations to the political-economic conditions that pre-dated them.

This chapter will concern itself with the psychopolitical conditions that have given rise to emergent paranoid publics. These publics espouse paranoid politics as wayward forms of counter-knowledges involving scrutiny of the self and also of the world. These knowledges relieve psychical tension because a newfound paranoid explanation explains everything, yet they also give rise to psychical unease because this same explanation indicates an ongoing danger. The conspiratorial explanation represents a fear that is simultaneously a desire; it is a wish-fulfillment that doubles as a warning. As Robyn Marasco puts it, "conspiracy theory is a love affair with power that poses as its critique."[4] However irrational its own forms of reasoning, it assumes that the powers and authorities it is exposing operate rationally and are not merely powerful but *all*-powerful—that is to say, are ideal and pure forms of power.

One of the guiding principles of my exploration is Sigmund Freud's insight drawn from his analysis of Daniel Paul Schreber, whose *Memoirs of My Nervous Illness* (1903) would become an ur-text for later psychoanalytic accounts of paranoia as well as of psychosis, proto-fascism, and delusional ideation. Reading Schreber, Freud argues that paranoia represents an effort to hold together a world that seems to be disintegrating.[5] Noting that ideation around "world catastrophe" attends many cases of paranoia, Freud writes:

> [W]e shall not find it difficult to explain these catastrophes. . . .
> The end of the world is the projection of this internal catastrophe;
> his subjective world has come to an end since his withdrawal of
> his love from it. . . . He builds it up by the work of his delusions.
> *The delusional formation* [Wahnbildung], *which we take to be the*
> *pathological product, is in reality an attempt at recovery* [Hei-
> lungsversuch], *a process of reconstruction.*[6]

Paranoid delusions are a *Heilungsversuch,* or a "healing attempt," that entails a reworking and refashioning both of the self and the world. Paranoid delusions are "healing" because they position oneself as a bounded person— coherent and significant to others and to oneself—and the assumption of a malignant force that targets oneself might cause anxiety, but it also alleviates a greater repressed anxiety. Delusional formations (*Wahnbildung*), insofar as they are a type of *Bildung,* or self-formation, entail not only projecting idealized fantasy images onto the world but also transforming and cultivating oneself by means of such projection. In its obsessive scrutiny of external signs and patterns, paranoia might appear to be directed outwards, but it is at the same time a form of self-recuperation and self-cultivation. A paranoid belief can feel like one has just discovered a whole new aspect of the world and one's own truth in the same instant, and so the delusion provides coherence to both the world and to oneself. For paranoid publics like QAnon with its participatory and networked formation, anti-vaccine activism with its moral charge to protect values of self-ownership and self-sovereignty, and for preppers who aim to organize life in relation to a future catastrophe, the delusion is indeed a healing attempt because the paranoid belief, being an overly coherent explanation, returns one to oneself as a person now endowed with knowledge, significance, and purpose. Participation in paranoid publics takes forms similar to ordinary solicitations in the social order for self-cultivation and self-making. As such the paranoid, too, are subject to historically particular limits and practices of self-formation and moral solicitation. Paranoid formations are therefore not a break from reality as such but arise from an accentuation and intensification of its features.

Contemporary conspiracy thinking is unique to its historical conditions even as it also invokes (often literally) older narratives of conspiratorial fantasy.[7] Critiques expressing alarm that distortions and untruth have entered the sphere of politics, supposedly inaugurating a new "post-truth age," are not helpful for understanding what is at stake in paranoid politics. Even when not delivered in a nostalgic or elegiac tone, these accounts remain tone-deaf not only to the historical existence of other eras of truth-demolition but also to the fundamentally adversarial relationship between truth and politics. Theodor Adorno observed that mass delusions arise from opinions that have sedimented into a semblance of truth.[8] "Opinions" in general are widely deemed to be value-neutral, everyone is naturally entitled to them and sometimes even solicited to form them as a basis for individuality. Some opinions are delusional and pathogenic at the outset—Adorno mentions American pamphlets of "an insane periphery of society, [. . .] whose body of ideas also includes ritual murders and *The Protocols of the Elders of Zion.*"⁹ These supposedly aberrant and extreme delusions—all resting on a concatenation of opinion—must nevertheless *not* be seen as distinct from "normal" opinion, Adorno insists, because in their mass psychological and philosophical underpinnings they share the same conceptual ground as opinion in general. The distinction between delusion and accepted opinion, in practice, is determined by power. People operate with all manner of normative delusions, some of them "healing attempts" akin to Schreber's. For example, the so-called war on terror distributed democracy abroad, and the cost of democracy is such destruction; truth will always come out; the principle "when they go low, we go high" (Michelle Obama) as a means for electoral victory. To be sure, these widely divergent instances are not paranoic because they do not consequently lead to distrust—which Freud indicated as the "primary symptom"¹⁰ of paranoia—but they are idealized fantasies and healing attempts. Each of these beliefs, no matter how false or misguided, has normative implications—that is, even as each belief assumes a world that corresponds to it, it also legitimizes that world as the one that *should* exist. There are no easy correctives to the problem of mass delusions, then, if one understands this phenomena only as one involving some bad or incorrect knowledge whose rectification is all that is required. The psychosocial payoff that delusions provide is as crucial for understanding them. Also, collective delusions have to be understood as continuous with the conditions of history, psychology, and political economy that have given rise to them, not as aberrations.

II. LARPolitics

QAnon's central doctrines seem designed for the clickbait era: politicians, the film industry, Jews, and "elites" form a cabal that thrives on ritual sexual abuse and murder of children, whose blood these elites drink to renew their vitality; Trump plans to put an end to all this by arresting or executing the cabal; the day this happens is called "the Storm." As QAnon began to grow and received significant press coverage,¹¹ Q opined on media critiques of QAnon, questioning why resources were being spent on discrediting something that mainstream media claimed was a conspiracy theory: "ALL FOR A LARP?" The acronym stands for "live action role play," a game in which players assume an identity and perform scenarios in real life (think *Dungeons and Dragons*). The term *LARP* performs important interpretive work, suggesting a host of relationships between performance and community formation, play and reality, and between public, private, and anonymous selves. A LARP assumes not only a make-believe subject position but also a make-believe world in which that newly assumed identity resides: its environment, its web of relationships and their orders of hierarchies, and the possibilities of action in the alternate universe. LARPing fuels the attention economies of platforms like Reddit, the chans, and alt-tech platforms, not only at the level of content (users pretending to be fictional people) but also as economic exigency.

In internet parlance, LARP has accrued an additional meaning: it refers to someone whose online persona paints them as privy to an exciting secret or an interesting life though in reality they may be Mr. Generic who lives next door. This valence of LARP, which refers to individuals rather than to a collective practice, is sometimes used in a derogatory fashion, as a kind of exposure of an online persona as fake. However, such an exposure does not diminish the entertainment value or other kind of fascination with that very fake persona. In other words, when someone is deemed to be a LARP, the game is not over. Lobbing accusations of LARPing is a part of 4chan's culture of aggressive content and extreme irony. For users of 4chan—where QAnon initially took hold as a collective phenomenon—a LARP is someone pretending to have inside governmental or political information. Before Q there were other well-known LARPs posting on 4chan, with names such as "CIA Anon," "High Level Insider," and "Highway Patrolman." Their pronouncements on 4chan were delivered as aggressive truth-telling, and the necessity of both aggression and truth-telling presupposed a hostile world of opaque signs, duped citizenry, and oblivious politics. The persona of the truth-teller would become a central libidinal attachment for QAnon participants.

Mimicry and role-playing are LARP's fundamental techniques. The original LARPers—communities of sword-carrying real-life role-players—dress up in costumes they often make themselves and together act out a narrative whose key points are decided in advance, but whose central themes are fodder for improvisation and elaborate play-acting. This close imbrication of theater and spectacle with gamification—connoting play, in all of its senses—endures in the multiple meanings and practices of LARPing taking place not just on fringe platforms like 4chan but regularly on mainstream platforms. The selfie, the thirst trap, the vlog confessional, the well-observed nature scene, the photograph of the airline wing in air, the viral tweet: all are fodder for LARPing. Paranoid publics emerge out of such familiar everyday LARP practices of digital life: Twitter and Instagram users, YouTube personalities, and of course influencers regularly engage in a game of pretend, meeting the demands of increasing user engagement and donning the required persona for followers. The fact of knowing that online life is often filtered, enhanced, and contrived for the spectacle changes nothing in the fundamental operations of LARP. The self is dispersed between the real one and the online image, which is further split between the anonymous and the non-anonymous persona, and variegated across the moods and protocols of different online platforms. Such dispersal of subjectivity is taken as given and is key to paranoid subjectivation because even as one participates in make-believe the knowledge that one's environment is the product of others' make-believing is never successfully repressed. Thus LARPing itself is a phenomenon far larger than 4chan or QAnon.

Influencers are more likely to be aware of their own participation in a world of playacting than the average user of Instagram, because they are fully aware of their roles as content providers. Regardless, the fun in LARPing combines a break from one's ordinary self—through the assumption of another identity—with the release of one's true self. Its power resides in the existence of the true in the guise of the false. Arguably, this is the case for all fictions and fictionality, but in a LARP, this power is focalized around self-making and world-making. The real world is a cipher for a hidden world that exists alongside it, and one's actions in that hidden world—now magically visible everywhere—consolidate the true (previously hidden) self and reaffirm the terms of the game. One can participate in a LARP without having any awareness that one is participating in a LARP, and even if one has such an awareness, the power of LARPing is not much diminished for the cultivation of personal and collective worlds of make-believe. Influencers, for all their awareness of the staginess of the life they represent online, nevertheless must not call out this online existence as a LARP, not because it would break the spell but precisely because it is assumed that online life is contrived, yet such contrivances continue to exert influence nevertheless. Indeed, when LARPing becomes a generalized phenomenon, no opprobrium attaches to the figure of the influencer; this figure's mysterious powers of influence have become an aspiration. LARPing is a quotidian solicitation and practice for users of new media, hardly restricted to the fringe regions of the Internet. The horned and winged LARPers of yore had a clear demarcation between the space of play and the space of reality; digital platforms blur this distinction. Such a convergence of the unreal with the real is critical for the formation of paranoid publics.

"Delusion" derives from the Latin root, *ludere*, meaning "to play." The ludic grounds of paranoid ideation include new forms of economic necessity as well as psycho-historical processes entailing the constitution of enemies. The problem of collective paranoia persists stubbornly in the inequities of an administered world that promises the good life. My wager is that we are witnessing the gamification of paranoia. From this perspective, the paranoid publics of previous eras might also appear in a new light, as collective formations activated by what Roger Caillois called the "play instincts." These instincts are now solicited from users of contemporary digital platforms, which are not mere tools that preexisting paranoid publics deploy; rather these new media solidify paranoid publics. They may not originate paranoia, but they do feed it, sometimes lending credence to delusionary ideation because the algorithms favor more extreme content that resonates with previously engaged content. Deployed as a theoretical formulation, what I am calling "LARPolitics" can provide critical sightlines into formations of paranoid publics and the conditions of emergence they share with other related cultural and political phenomenon. Such an understanding of LARP as a conceptual category helps us to see the conjoint operations of economic necessity, affective commitments, and subjectivation. In psychoanalyst D.W. Winnicott's account of play, make-believe blends the real with the fantastical to train the self to be able to tell them apart—this game mediates distinctions between fantasy and the real. Now, in a LARP, this distinction is lost.

The sense of community offered up through play is one mechanism that blurs the real and unreal. QAnon is first and foremost a community, however diffusely and heterogeneously constituted. [12] The user interface on 4chan, where QAnon began, is deliberately low-tech and user-unfriendly, reinforcing a sense among users that they are a part of the 4chan community, with unique skills to navigate the platform. People outside of this community are "normies." Q encouraged community formation by indicating in parentheses that certain words, such as "timberwolf" and "warlocks," were "inside terms," codes for particular people or particular alliances. 4chan threads are up-ranked based on user engagement, which in /pol/ (politics) and /b/ (random) boards index how incendiary or offensive the remark or meme is found by other users. This may or may not, however, be someone taking actual offense at a post, since a mood of supreme irony rules all terms of engagement, and anyone taking a meme or post at face value can be, and often is, publicly shamed by other users. A spirit of LARP already underwrites participation in the chans, whether or not one is a part of QAnon. A given member of QAnon might hold fast to some or none of the core doctrines. The game, such as it is, entails sharing content that either creates an overall mood of outrage or moral panic or offers new interpretations of Q's cryptic posts. Insofar as the Anons participate in a LARP, paranoia marks the affective script of the game or the mood in which this game is to be played. Put simply, the game solicits paranoia from its participants, whether as performance or as "true belief."[13] It thus detaches belief—in the sense of commitment—from political action, thereby increasing the reasons for taking action. Even if one might believe, such belief is not necessary to the operations of the game, which makes available psychosocial satisfactions and enjoyments in which belief may or may not play a part.

In a LARP, the participant is both actor and audience, aiming to fascinate themselves, other participants, and anyone on the outside looking in. In QAnon land, the outrage and offense expressed by "normies" is a part of the show. Thus, even the nonparticipants in the LARP are included in it, and the scope for play expands far beyond the boundaries of the playground or the stage, if you will.[14] For this politics, the ordinary world has the character of being itself temporary, and the people in it all players in spite of themselves. Since the whole world has now become a play space, the LARPers of QAnon insist they are not a LARP. Q's mocking statement, "All for a LARP?" suggests that the powers ranged against QAnon understand its central doctrines as the truth rather than make-believe, and this rhetorical flourish situates those powers as players. "All for a LARP?" became a refrain in QAnon forums. As an utterance, it is a feat of paranoid projection and an invitation into the rabbit hole: QAnon knows the truth, and this knowledge is imputed to those who seek to criticize or de-platform QAnon precisely because they do not want the truth to come out. Thus "All for a LARP?" reaffirms the truth QAnon already knows and suggests that none of this is a game. The world is reduced to a belief already suspected, but at the same time this utterance also belies the anxiety it is intended to repress, that all is in fact make-believe. The Anons are often fascinated with their newfound role as truth-tellers and search for opportunities to develop it further, all the while being ready to discard or transform it as the requirements of the performance shift. QAnon does not require belief in the sense of an enduring conviction whose propositions can be taken at face-value; instead, belief is a provisional matter, like the temporary world of the game, held in relation to the demands of the game and discarded or revised as these demands shift. The adventure of the game and corollary to this, the cultivation of the self, are the primary drivers of participation.

As a form of play, LARPing aids in integrating oneself to a larger whole, with all the libidinal comforts and tensions that come with such integration. The gaps in logic, the phantasmatic nature of friends and enemies, and the associative links across different claims, personages, and events, all indicate a deferred plenitude that is the endgame for QAnon participants. The piecemeal nature of the information available on the internet is enticing for would-be Anons because it extends the experience of half-conscious accrual of a conspiratorial plot. The repetition of stock tropes (e.g., Hilary Clinton as devil incarnate, the COVID vaccine as microchip serum), the expressions of nationalist sentiment, and the insistence that the world is in a sorry state because of the cabal's activities all take place in the half-light of conscious conviction similar to the state of consciousness Freud discovered in his experiences in hypnotizing patients. To be clear, I am not suggesting the Anons are like hypnotized zombies, but that their relationship to reality can be understood through psychoanalytic thinking about the ambiguous place of reality in hypnosis. Subjects under hypnosis are prone to a strange regression in which the emotions they are experiencing under hypnosis are both fully present and yet understood as phony: "Some knowledge that in spite of everything hypnosis is only a game, a deceptive renewal of these old impressions, may, however remain behind and take care that there is a resistance against any too serious consequences of the suspension of the will in hypnosis."[15] Adorno reads this moment in Freud's analysis as an account of how the phoniness at the heart of fascism becomes integrated into the social world.[16] QAnon demonstrates that such phoniness results from the operations of the game but this is so because the game is not "only a game."

By means of its rhetorics of extreme unseriousness, irony, and pastiche, overlaid on a current of aggressive ideation, QAnon forums reproduce aspects of what Theodor Adorno analyzed as psychological features of fascist propaganda: the glib jokiness that "is not so much an obstacle as a stimulant in itself."[17] Also, the deindividuating experience of being in a group facilitates destructive forms of disinhibition, but with the addition that for LARPolitics such disinhibition also meets the requirements of the game.[18] The online culture of "lulz," with its conscious attempts at offending sensibilities combined with the cultivation of extreme irony and the drive to outperform other posts in sheer engagement through a greater show of aggression or prurience all appeal to conscious and unconscious wishes and affective needs of the users. Such demonstrations of the violations of norms—often for the sake of the performance—serve to bind the audience as a paranoid community, with access to otherwise opaque truths and now linked to one another by the libidinal glue of shared aggression, made permissible because the game requires it.

As instances of such destructive forms of disinhibition, consider some other details from the January 6 insurrection. One member of the January 6 melee had brought home-made napalm in his truck for the fight. Another texted his friends a picture of himself in blackface with the note "I'm gonna walk around DC FKG with people by yelling 'Allahu ak Bar' randomly."[19] Such is the political unconscious of the American gothic: crafts made by tinkering in the garage, the nostalgia for blackface and playing dress-up, the enjoyment of adolescent sadism. Two miles away from the Capitol building, on the steps of the National City Christian Church, one (white, male) Trump supporter lay on his side while a second (white, male) pretended to press his knee on his friend's neck, mocking the killing of George Floyd under the Black Lives Matter sign that the church had hung on its entrance. Their mockery was itself a repetition of a viral Tik Tok video that had circulated in the summer of 2020, made by Iowa high schoolers to make fun of George Floyd's murder even as protests for racial justice were being held around the country. Two New Jersey men—an officer in a prison and a FedEx employee—had indulged in the same reenactment that summer to provoke BLM protestors, yelling to the marchers: "Black lives matter to no one."[20] On the mall outside the Capitol building, others erected a scaffold with a noose, suggesting a prehistory of the LARP in the American tradition of lynching, complete with its carnivalesque forms of enjoyment.

The storming of the Capitol was a LARP similar to the white supremacist march on Charlottesville in August 2017 that had marked the spiritual inauguration of Trump's regime. The specter of the noose haunted, as well, the scene of the hapless St. Louis couple anxious to defend their property against imagined threats from Black Lives Matter protestors, taking the opportunity to act out the fantasy that attends gun purchases. The noose also hangs over incidents too numerous to count of an enraged white person threatening a person of color. Karen, that perennially anxious and angry figure of contemporary racial capitalist modernity, has elective affinities with the Anons because for her, ordinary encounters with (non-white) people set off paranoia and its attendant feeling of aggrievement. For her, such aggrievement becomes an occasion for *performing* supremacy. LARPing gives rise to the expression of latent desires and wishes.

These LARPs involving napalm, blackface, parody performances, and "Allahu ak Bar" are of a piece with the hanging noose—all components of a fever dream in which violence against racial minorities at home is a project contiguous with America's forever wars abroad, including its expansive "war on terror." Cold War paranoia, which authorized American imperial wars beginning with World War II, morphed into hysterical anxiety about the so-called New World Order in the 1990s, and eventually returned after 9/11 to the classic paranoid form it had in the Cold War: an anxiety that persecutes the entity it claims to be persecuted by. The widely popular television show *Homeland* crystallizes the intermingling of racism and misogyny central to the zeitgeist: a white female CIA agent in the grip of hysterical anxiety is proved correct time and again about the threats Muslims pose to the nation. Her paranoia—however far-fetched it seems to others—is warranted every single time, and she carries in female form the vulnerability of the nation. She has an uncanny knack for getting the kill list just right. *Homeland* appealed to many otherwise liberal audiences because it cast a woman in the lead role of the oracular—albeit hysteri-cal—CIA agent. Islamic signs and gestures are usually attended in the show by foreboding music, and with the ineluctability of the paranoic *idée fixe* that drives the narrative, the heroine discovers a scheming, conspiring Muslim at the heart of every mysterious threat. Classic antisemitic tropes are thus refurbished (and made palatable) in this "liberal" War on Terror drama, since they are transposed onto Muslims. Thus, antisemitism is the latent script for the show's overt Islamophobia, and the heroine repeatedly demonstrates that bigotry is the surest path to truth, security, and self-defense. A perverse demonstration of the catchphrase "believe women," the show subverted feminism in the service of both misogyny and paranoid politics. The Cold War and the forever wars coincided with voter suppression, the rise of incarceration rates, and the persistence of police impunity, all of which eroded civil rights gains. These associative links were apprehended by the January 6 rioters in their zeal to oppose Black Lives Matter, Jews, Muslims, and communism. In their political theology, these profanities all require elimination. Hence the mocking reenactments of the murder of George Floyd. The LARP involving racialized murder is a part of the same game that attacks democratic symbols. At stake in these performances is the "making real" of forms of aggression cultivated over time, often online. A wished-for performance, including one of losing self-mastery, took the opportunity for embodied action on January 6. As Jim Watkins, the owner of websites that hosted QAnon, said at the scene of the Capitol's storming: this began as a LARP and "it became real. It's American history now."[21]

Such are the adventures of paranoid healing attempts, that this entire endeavor is a feat of collective projection and all the more riveting and fun for being so. The enemies imagined by QAnon are racial and sexual minorities on the one hand and an elite cabal of operators on the other. Each of these imagined enemies is a result of projection, and the connections between them become clear in the passionate invectives against "woke ideology" that intensified after QAnon went mainstream. Having been assimilated into GOP rationality, one of the policy results of such paranoid projection was the targeting of Diversity, Equity, and Inclusion (DEI) initiatives. Malevolent powers, in addition to their hold on key institutions, allegedly give preferential treatment to all kinds of minorities, and so therefore both the cabal and these minorities need to be opposed. Intimations of the cabal's racial betrayal already circulated as memes in QAnon fora before January 6. LARPing entails projection in the sense that all play involves projection: the world is reinvented through make-believe while simultaneously "found" anew, as if it existed there all along.[22] Projection is a psychic defense against the limits imposed on one's life-world by reality. It names a neutral operation by means of which people rid themselves—often unconsciously—of a desire, thought, or feeling, by displacing it onto an external entity, where it appears changed from its original form. An internal excitation is experienced as an external perception; this can become pathological, curative, or remain simply neutral depending on the context in which it occurs. Projection can be at work in paranoiac experiences, but it is not reducible to paranoia, which itself makes use of projection as one among other psychological mechanisms. By means of paranoid projection, a person masters an original unease, and paranoid desire aids in orienting oneself in the world, however temporarily. Freud suggests that paranoid projection entails shifts within ego formation, often giving rise to a sense of megalomania, ego aggrandizement, paired with epistemic certainty.[23]

As I suggested earlier, beyond these psychodynamics, LARPing also entails political-economic processes that feed the expansion of paranoid publics. Contemporary paranoid ideation during the rise of QAnon was tied to dominant forms of neoliberal governance, not only in the existence of literal revenue streams but also in the often deleterious ludic dynamics of economic calculation. The influencer represents the gamification of performance, the imbrication of economic logics with the realm of make believe—a figure of "LARPonomics," if you will.[24] It was Friedrich Hayek, the arch-priest of neoliberal thought, who described economic operations as a game—"namely, a game partly of skill and partly of chance."[25] This "game of catallaxy" encourages improvisation, is itself "undesigned," yet it proliferates information, advances progress, and encourages liberty. Naturally Hayek's vision of this game is a utopian one, deriving as he does the word "catallaxy" from the Greek word *katallattein*, "which meant, significantly, not only 'to exchange' but also 'to admit into the community' and 'to change from enemy into friend.'"[26] Grounded on agonism (competition), the game nevertheless delivers a reconciliation or adequation of diverse needs. Crucially, the game rewards not effort but strength, skill, or discernment: "It would be nonsensical to demand that the results for the different players be just."[27] Hayek refers to calls for the redistribution of wealth as "unjust" because these calls invoke an authority other than the inexorable laws of the market. By figuring market imperatives as the impersonal and objective demands of a game, Hayek explicitly sequesters these imperatives—emanating from the oracular diktats of the market— from the sphere of ethics. In a game, just as "truth" is the result of the game's various rules, and "belief" is a lever for improvisation and subject to reinvention, "justice" can only be understood as an end that conforms to the operations of the game. In the attention economy, "gaming" the algorithm to increase engagement is a mark not of the cheat but of the skilled player. Gamification cedes ethics in the service either of rule-bound action or of improvisation, depending on the kind of game at hand. In either case gamification—like politics—is fundamentally inimical to factual truth.[28]

The algorithmic up-ranking of posts, the clamor for user attention, the desire to be viral all feed into circuits of monetization that make participation in the LARP a central necessity not only for the influencers within paranoid publics, but also for tech companies that profit from the platforms and the advertisers the platforms serve. LARPing is therefore a cultural, political, and economic logic. Vying for user attention, QTubers perform alongside influencers, Qvangelists, entrepreneurs, online-only warriors, vigilantes, interpreters (known in QAnon parlance as "bakers"). Participation options abound and are always flexible. Increasingly, as QAnon has entered the world of the wellness industry ("pastel QAnon"), it resembles lifestyle marketing, as with digital content created by self-professed "tradwives." There is always merchandise and swag to consume and multiple books for sale describing the Great Awakening or the Coming Storm. QAnon has also seen success at the ballot box, in Georgia (Marjorie Taylor Greene), Colorado (Lauren Boebert), and Oregon (Jo Rae Perkins, who did not win the election but won the Republican primary). Some of Trump's appointees after the 2024 election are former QAnon promoters. Its growth into multiple positions of institutional and cultural influence is a mark of successful improvisation, with its attendant willingness to bend the rules. Roger Caillois had described games of make-believe as being fundamentally free of strict rules—as he put it, "*mimicry* is incessant invention."[29] The flexibility of the QAnon multiverse—its accommodation of all past conspiracy theories and openness to new ones, its adaptation to various political and economic spaces—is nevertheless underwritten by norms that entail an adherence to a political game that tacks right.

III. Anxiety

What accounts for the destructiveness at the heart of the politics of paranoia? How does play become oriented toward a twofold destruction, of the
world and of oneself? While answers to these questions are already implied
in the account given above of the dangers of make-believe, I would like to
draw out the implications of the LARP's psychodynamics more explicitly.
Ressentiment, which imagines that others steal the rightful satisfaction of
one's own desires, requires a form of expression, some thrilling speech or
action that would gratify it. So it targets the perceived enemy who must
be eliminated, even if that destruction is injurious to oneself. Ressentiment
names one of many dynamics for channeling the collective anxiety at the
basis of projective fantasies. Freud understood anxiety as a vital component
of survival mechanisms because it prepares one for situations of danger,
priming the organism for its fight/flight reactions in response to an anticipated external danger. When danger is present in the external environment, anxiety is a natural and even necessary response. Neurotic anxiety,
on the other hand, is triggered not externally but internally; it suggests a
libidinal disturbance causing sensations that feel like danger but the effect
of which is far in excess of any reasonable external danger.[30]

According to Freud, anxiety in general is always a ready "substitute for
all 'repressed' affects."[31] Emotions other than anxiety (shame/embarrass-
ment, anger/rage), once repressed, can reemerge as anxiety: "anxiety is
therefore the universally current coinage for which *any* affective impulse
is or can be exchanged if the ideational content attached to it is subject to
repression."[32] Phobias are projective attempts at taking flight from an anxiety
whose source is internal, by locating the source in the external environment;
obsessional neuroses mitigate anxieties through the creation of elaborate
rituals (handwashing, for example). Both, like repression, are flight responses
and both are inadequate to dispelling the internal danger of unbound
libidinal impulses that seeks discharge in the form of anxiety.

Franz Neumann was among the first thinkers to consider the political,
mass psychological implications of anxiety. Neumann argues that the
oft-used word "scapegoat" is inaccurate for describing the subject-position
of this enemy though, because scapegoats are "substitutes whom one only
needs to send into the wilderness."[33] The libidinal cathexis involving
the-enemy-within brooks no substitutes however, and indeed spells the

end of figuration and the hardening of conviction, what Neumann refers to as "false concreteness." According to Neumann, true historical anxiety—which, in his examples from midcentury Europe, is the result of inequality, hunger, or war—transmutes into neurotic anxiety, which is then assuaged by renouncing the ego through a false concreteness secured through identification with an authoritarian leader. Since the enemy is fundamentally evil, singular, and therefore un-substitutable and exempt from the play of signification, one's conviction about the enemy's guilty and rotten nature cannot be shaken. Projection entails a conjuring of such truths to which one must hold fast because their certainty is the grounds not only of the self but also of the group. The noose erected in front of the US Capitol stood as a warning to Black people, Muslims, Jews, immigrants, "globalists," and the "cabal" of elites. These enemies, for all the differences among them, are treated as a single bloc, against which the mob constituted itself as united in order to "Stop the Steal."

What are the psychodynamics underwriting this phenomenon of the mob acting in concert against common enemies? Freud's account in *Group Psychology and the Analysis of the Ego* turns on his account of authority and its surrogates: totemic forms, collective ideals, and the figure of the leader provide focal points for an otherwise dispersed collectivity. These forms of authority appeal to the individual's narcissism insofar as identification with these forms promises the fulfillment of narcissistic fantasies (aiming at becoming an ego-ideal, being in the know and therefore superior) and binds the individuals to one another. People in a group identify with each other because each identifies with the same authority figure; the emotional tie with the leader (for example) becomes the basis of their (narcissistic) tie to others who share in the bond with the same leader. [34] Authority does not operate in group psychology as a form of coercion or brute power but rather as a promissory note or a lure. For the Anons, Trump is always on the cusp of gutting the government of the "deep state" and hanging the cabal publicly. The failed prophecy is always about to come true, if only you "Trust the Plan." Adorno follows Freud even as he revises him in his own analysis of the group psychology of fascism: "The leader image gratifies the follower's twofold wish to submit to authority and to be authority himself. . . . The people who obey the dictators also sense that the latter are superfluous. They reconcile this contradiction through the assumption that they are themselves the ruthless oppressor." [35] This assumption of ruthless capacities is the beginning of the LARP. The ego aggrandizement entailed in these psychodynamics relies on the transfer of authority from the leader (an external reality) to the self's internal capacities and powers. Thus begins the adventures of paranoia in the realm of self-cultivation. Trump is simultaneously just like his followers and also figured as an ideal. It is not that leaders are adept at techniques of mass psychological manipulation in any conscious way such that one has to impute brilliance and calculation to leaders who are indeed often incompetent and even ridiculous. Rather, it is the repeated voicing of an uninhibited latent wish of the group that proves so effective for mass mobilization. This explains why the fascist and quasi-fascist leaders' arguments operate not by means of rationality but rather by means of association, as in paranoid formulations. Wearing one's unconscious on one's sleeve becomes a strength for the leader—what Adorno refers to as making "rational use of his irrationality"—and language takes on psychopolitical significance over and above the meaning of words.[36] That is, it provides cathexes even as it signifies.

Leaders and demagogues function, therefore, as phantasmic forms. In libidinal politics, the putative powers of the leader do not require military control, intellectual prowess, and certainly not a life already lived according to the group's shared ideals. It would therefore be fruitless to search for explanations for libidinal politics in the personalities of particular historical leaders. The logical conclusion to be drawn from Freud and Adorno's accounts is that the leader or demagogue's necessity to a group is short-lived at best, and specific leaders are superfluous with respect to the libidinal politics that they might have helped to focalize. Neumann suggests that if Freud is correct that for masses of people identification with a leader is a means of identification with one another as well, it means identification is a mechanism for mastering anxiety. The leader is idealized as being capable of addressing one's distress, and corollary to this is the positing of certain others as the source of distress, and the management or elimination of these enemies, in turn, renews one's faith in the leader.[37] The enemy is crucial for installing the promise of a reprieve from collective anxiety.

Nationalism, even in its ordinary and non-exceptional forms, shares in such group psychodynamics. According to Benedict Anderson's classic account of nationalism, it takes over from religion as a form of collective imagining, a secular belief in transcendence. The political theology of nationalism is "a secular transformation of fatality into continuity, contingency into meaning."[38] Such collective imaginings—not specific to nationalism—are forms of psychic suturing that allow accidental and contingent facts to become significant for collective life. For nationalism this might mean that certain features of the landscape, ancient ruins, or flora and fauna become symbols of the collective. A similar overvaluation of the contingent detail is involved in QAnon's participatory group dynamics. Not only do Anons often refer to themselves as (true) patriots, but there are also a variety of Q flags and banners, some of which were carried by insurrectionists on January 6. The overt patriotism and flag-waving of QAnons adherents aside, as important for the group formations of QAnon are the "Q Proofs," a form of truth-telling through elaborate diagrams and flowcharts that decipher Q's "drops." The classic image of the person who has done their own research used to be a corkboard with pieces of evidence and information linked with one another by string. This practice has endured in digital form in elaborate proofs, from images connecting the time stamps of Q's posts to real-life events or numbers that are made to correspond to them, to the "Q clock," an elaborate diagram through which one can confirm whether Q predicted a future event in a prior drop. The world appears less fatalistic, and accidental details become highly meaningful. Where nationalism is concerned, Anderson puts it well in his pithy statement, "it is the magic of nationalism to turn chance into destiny."[39] It creates continuity between the dead and the unborn, inserting both into national history. It also integrates one's immediate experience with collective history, as does participation in paranoid politics. Both paranoid politics and ordinary nationalism require the projection of a fantasized world overlaid on the one experienced daily.

The continuity that nationalism forges between the self and the group allows one to transmute one's own powerlessness and contingent existence into a supreme force understood as collective will and destiny. Whether in the form of nationalism, racist hatred, delusional paranoia, or conspiratorial explanation, projection marks a narrative reversal for the subject caught in its thrall, who can then guarantee itself the upper hand. Projection seeks to rid the self of negative feelings by imagining them as existing in other people or institutions; it converts anxiety into aggrievement. Such a position longs to remake the world in the image of the illusions it has already deemed to be truth. Even a cursory consideration of the recent political discourse in light of collective projection brings to mind the denigration of truth as "fake news," the longing to consolidate executive state power by invocations of a shadowy "deep state," railing against "cancel culture" while ensuring that some viewpoints or voices do not find a home in the public sphere, trying to "Stop the Steal" by attempting to steal the election, proclaiming a conspiracy at work in order to conspire, and so on. Projection is a psychological mechanism that operates in an obscure zone between epistemology and phenomenology; when indulged in the grip of paranoia, it replaces knowledge with knowingness. In the internet age, its privileged genres are the headline and the meme. Destructive forms of mass projection are an elaborate LARP, investing the world with forms of the group's psychic needs and wishes, but such a solution spells disaster because it ensures that the image of the world reflected back to the paranoid subject is a repetition of itself, caught now in pathological forms of symbol formation that assure certitude but fail to relieve anxiety. New data is easily assimilated into the schema as a repetition of the self-same because for the paranoid all evidence confirms what is already known and all that is contingent becomes necessary. These are games of truth that have turned veridiction itself into a form of enjoyment.[40] Byzantine "Q Proofs" and their surrogate forms in other paranoid publics multiply. In such games truth is not the same as knowledge. Where knowledge might bring closure, the paranoiac search for truth renounces closure and seeks surplus enjoyment in the limitless possibilities of truth's exposure. Since its certainty is based not on knowledge but on knowingness, the pleasures of repetition become indissociable, as well, from the satisfactions of veridiction.

The confluence of capitalism with collective being prepares the political and affective ground for highly destructive politics, according to Adorno, since capitalism demands that people submit to its economic necessities, resulting in a gradual repudiation of the very subjective autonomy that liberal democratic ideals promise.[41] Critical to such an experience is that repudiation itself *feels* like subjective autonomy, especially for the middle classes who have long provided support for atavistic and counterrevolutionary politics. Hence the dubious itineraries of "freedom"—reconceived in our contemporary political climate as the right to "free speech" even when such speech is a ruse for the suppression of social critique and social change or sometimes an outright call for violence.[42] Daily adaptation or identification with the status quo—even when it poses as its demolition—prepares the ground for the acceptance of authoritarianism. This was strikingly evident immediately after the 2024 election, in the anticipatory obedience of institutions, universities, politicians, and corporate policies to the new administration's desires, even before it had expressed them through official pronouncements. As in a LARP, people are incentivized "to preserve themselves only if they renounce their self."[43] Adorno was analyzing the dissatisfactions and disappointments of capitalist reality, whose betrayal of democracy's promises means that "people remain indifferent to democracy, if they do not in fact secretly detest it."[44] The psychodynamics of the group offer intoxicating possibilities of projection, introjection, and the surrender of freedom; such intoxication spills over party lines, ideologies, and class positions.

IV. Double Realities

I have tracked how paranoid publics emerge from the conjuncture of political-economic processes that encourage gamification and performance with group psychological processes as common as nationalism. My aim has been twofold: to demonstrate that seemingly aberrant social phenomena depend on familiar political-economic and cultural solicitations, and to follow the psychosocial itineraries of QAnon with its lurid claims across new media platforms to its boots-on-the-ground manifestation at the Capitol on January 6. Paranoid ideation turns into political action because these political-economic and group psychological processes encourage such ideation to do so. But paranoia has a special affinity for these outlets because it fundamentally assumes that the world as it appears conceals the malevolence that determines it, and so the feeling of paranoia is always an uneasy experience of living across different realities simultaneously. Paranoid projection, far from being merely illusory, winds up altering reality by treating it as a battlefield. Reality, then, is insufficient for dispelling projection. This indistinction between reality and fantasy is precisely the kind of experience encouraged in LARPing and in group formations. It is no wonder that paranoia integrates so easily into the political-economic and psychodynamic processes of LARPing. And the anxiety that paranoia evokes—about the malignant force that targets one—can be managed by a range of actions: further participation in supporting the paranoid belief through additional proofs, singling out enemies and aiding in suppressing them, identifying with a group in whose midst one's beliefs feel like truth, and taking political action on the basis of one's paranoid belief.

Fundamental to paranoid politics is the division of people, institutions, events, and policies into those that are good and those that are evil. Insofar as paranoia is a form of defense, it assures oneself of one's own innocence in the face of evil. Such a division of the world into poles, although experienced as certainty, nevertheless leads one to reassess one's judgments again and again—hence the persistence of "false flags," "crisis actors," traitors, and secret signals in QAnon lore. The truth is indisputable, yet the world manifests signs whose ambiguity must be interpreted, and thus the truth already known is constantly in the process of expansion as signs are interpreted in conformity to it. This suggests that the polarized world the paranoic has projected requires a great of psychical effort to maintain. Melanie Klein understood projection to be a defense against anxiety, but of a different sort from Freud's reflections on anxiety. Crucially, for Klein, infantile anxiety stems from the intrusion of the death drive, understood not as a vague biologistic notion but as a mode of social relation, which is "felt as fear of annihilation (death) and takes the form of persecution" (4).[45] Such a fear becomes externalized—projected, for babies, onto the mother's breast (the object at hand). Should the breast be withheld when it is needed—an inevitable course of events—it is experienced as a bad object; when it gratifies physical need, it is introjected as a good object and idealized, as capable of delivering limitless gratification. Such is the experience of what Klein calls the "paranoid-schizoid" position. Key to understanding Klein's account of projection is to understand that both extreme idealization of the good object and demonization of the bad object are forms of repression. Idealization represses the unease created by the bad object, and demonization of the bad object represses the persecutory anxiety that this object had unleashed. Thus, both idealization and demonization are forms of adaptation to changing realities, and such splitting of the world into idealized poles entails a split within the ego itself.

Yet the bad object that had rid the ego of its original anxiety can also be introjected back into the ego, in a process Klein called "projective identification." As a result, the hatred of one's own parts can be directed (for example) at the mother, now seen as the arch-persecutor: "this iden-tification of an object with the hated parts of the self contributes to the intensity of the hatred directed against other people."[46] Such extreme forms of splitting weaken the ego itself, increasingly bereft of a sense of self which it now experiences as disintegrating, "falling to bits," and dispersed and dissociated. Such dispersal of the self and de-individuation that attends projective identification is an experience that can be overcome if the good object is successfully introjected, but even so, it remains an ever-present potential in interpersonal relations. Ego integration is an ongoing project, but the stark appearance of the polarized world—divided between those who are good and those who are evil—aids in psychic splitting.

Such splitting, an attempt at channeling the disturbances of the death drive, makes possible the expressions of sadistic and masochistic release, as in the outrages committed on January 6, despite risks to oneself. The deliberate flouting of norms and the ratcheting up of offense as a collective project for QAnon has imbued this paranoid formation with an anxiety always at the ready for fight/flight. This has persisted well past QAnon's de-platforming and mainstreaming. To follow QAnon channels on Telegram means to enter a Manichean world in which an immediate fight/flight response is necessary. QAnon shares this aggressive quality with militia groups such as the Oath Keepers, Proud Boys, and Boogaloo Bois, who have installed aggression more explicitly as their raison d'être. Often attended and fueled by these other groups, anti-Lockdown protests and anti-vaxxing demonstrations also exhibit this aggression.

Such aggression, however, functions psychically to secure one's own innocence and goodness, and nothing makes the expression of aggression feel more righteous than the feeling of persecution, whether imagined or real. It is a short step for the paranoic self to tip the certainty of its own innocence into supremacy. The spectacular scenes of January 6 and repeated scenes of distrustful white people having a meltdown in interactions with nonwhite people in daily life bear witness to this psychopolitical process. As I hope has become increasingly clear in my analysis, such psychopolitics are not beholden to Trump or only shared among his supporters. Indeed, even for Trump supporters, he exists as a phantasmatic figure.

The psychoanalyst Wilfred Bion went as far as to posit a leaderless theory of group formations, locating group psychology not in the centrality of a shared locus of authority but in the (Kleinian) dispersive and self-disintegrating mechanisms of the psyche. Leaders and figures of authority that might seem to draw to themselves collective projections are, Bion argues, merely symptoms of a preexisting psychotic social formation. Bion's critical insight into group psychology—key to understanding contemporary paranoid publics—is that the requirement of a leader is "to be devoid of contact with any reality other than the reality of the basic-assumption-group demands."[47] In other words, the leader is a placeholder for the emotions of the group; leaders are like phantasmatic forms, invented and reinvented over the history of the group. For QAnon, insofar as LARPing is a game, the hierarchies within its formations are necessarily contrived and subject to reinvention. In groups, emotional release and spontaneous action correspond to anxieties similar to primal object relations. Bion states categorically that it is this *earlier* form of object relations, in the paranoid-schizoid mechanisms of infantile anxiety, that the "the ultimate sources of all group behaviour" reside.[48] Bion's reflections on group psychology are particularly helpful for understanding contemporary paranoid politics, whose invocations of messiahs, leaders, or demagogues are less vociferous than their insistence that the unreal is real, and also whose fundamental forms of understanding are nimble enough to incorporate contingency (as in QAnon).

The Boogaloo Bois do not have a leader and are a decentralized group, unlike the Proud Boys, with whom they share an apocalyptic sense that the US government needs to be overthrown, a new civil war fought, and new forms of freedom therefore made possible. Although Anons looked to Q for "crumbs" that would help them play the game of paranoid truth-seeking, Q was only one node in the game that has taken on a life of its own and continues to evolve in spite of his extended silence. Although adherents of QAnon exalt Donald Trump, their arcane interpretations of everything from Trump's misspellings to Melania Trump's wardrobe treat them as phantasmic part-objects that conform to collective projection. Not being beholden to a specific leader is a strength rather than a weakness to a politics of the LARP. Such politics are equally available to extreme groups as well as mainstream politicians, industrialists, funders of "dark money," and political parties who encourage extremists and feel energized by them.

Considering the conjoint problems of paranoid publics, truth-demolition, and political polarization through group object relations illuminates several key points. The alarm over the neoliberal corrosion of communication systems and information ecologies—a staple of discussions of post-truth—conceals a longing for an order of authority (or regime of truth) that was itself an invention of group psychological dynamics. That is, in spite of critiques that indicated the deeply compromised and ideological nature of established and authoritative media, these media nevertheless retained their hold on people. For Europe and the United States, the catastrophes of the twentieth century—fascism, the atom bomb, the Vietnam War, etc.—invented not only their own forms of abolishing factual truth but also produced new enemies, internal and external. This was also the case, however, for recently decolonized countries whose own intellectuals presciently warned of the pitfalls of nationalism. The Cold War division of the globe into blocs—a profoundly paranoid-schizoid formation—even more effectively channeled collective aggression while also building the conditions for ongoing coercion in the forms of capitalist exploitation. So while the contemporary crises of democratic rule are not exceptional, they differ from twentieth-century crises in that the forms of idealization-as-repression are undergoing a change. After the fall of competing Cold War utopias, the pretext for new wars in Afghanistan and Iraq claimed "freedom" and "democracy" as the reasons for aggression. Domestically, the roll-back phase of neoliberalism extolled the virtues of "choice" and "freedom" as it stripped workers of basic protections. This idealizing of freedom as well as democracy served to undermine both, domestically as well as globally. Still, such idealization appealed to utopian aims, however cynically. QAnon and the militias that have surfaced in recent years seem attached to their own notions of utopias, notions based on these received ideas about choice and freedom. Their endgame is the Storm or some similar vision of catastrophe that is not to be welcomed passively but rather to be precipitated actively, as quickly as possible.[49] The overriding affect of their politics is the thrill of vengeance paired with the practice of a scandalous freedom that evades accountability, destroys existing law, and overturns the existing order—such are the pleasures of *jouissance* as proffered by QAnon. The imminent "Storm" is also going to be a show, a world-historical entertainment.

Such LARP fantasies are collectively cultivated through performative iterations of memes and expressions of outrage. The performative LARP of online projection prefigures the politics of the LARP to be embodied on the ground: white supremacists carrying tiki torches in Charlottesville, the Storm arriving in an attack on the Capitol, the GOP closing party ranks to ensure impunity for Trump's actions. As Freud explained long ago, the death drive operates in a deceptive manner, often appearing in forms that can feel freeing. For example, the fantasy of heroic action represses the mortal dangers to such actors by idealizing them. "Question Authority" shows up regularly as an exhortation on QAnon paraphernalia, and Lauren Boebert, a QAnon congresswoman tweeted, "Never let anyone tell you that you shouldn't speak up for what you believe in. The 'powers that be' fear our voice more than anything. That's exactly why we need to be more vocal than ever." These exhortations are not subversions of the freedom-seeking impulses at the heart of well-worn American platitudes but expressions of the fascist apocalypticism that has always underlain their banal repetition.[50] In the QAnon multiverse, the world-to-come is only possible after the fearsome yet desirable cataclysm, one that can be hastened with increased calls to punish the evildoers. In this worldview, dystopian visions light the path toward national salvation.

But even social movements that aim for a more genuinely egalitarian world express their protests by holding up a dystopian mirror to contemporary forms of inequality: "We are the 99%"; "Black Lives Matter." For the Occupy Movement, for BLM, and for climate activists, the storm is already here and has been brewing for decades. An expression of racial injustice, "I Can't Breathe" also speaks—emblematically—to the world's current uninhabitability for many. World catastrophe, then, is a critique of the existing order for one politics and the solution to worldly ills in another. Whether it is an orientation toward a dystopian cataclysm or a mirror held up to one already occurring, it is dystopia that lends politics its charge.

In Freud's analysis of Schreber, he notes that such megalomaniacal ideation tends to become haunted by images of world catastrophe, of everything being burned to the ground, of the world falling away to make room for a new order, and so on. Such visions of the ruined world are an acknowledgment of an unconscious withdrawal of libido: "The projection of this internal catastrophe; his subjective world has come to an end since his withdrawal of love from it." News images of climate disasters and footage of lockdown-induced emptiness in world cities wracked by COVID not only demonstrated that classic filmic tropes of dystopian fantasy are now available in the form of reality—the objective world appearing in the garb of the LARP—they have also intimated how the Storm might look for an imagination given to delusional paranoia. A QAnon meme showed the face of Donald Trump pasted on the head of a US soldier in full body armor, leading his prisoner Joe Biden across a blighted landscape. The figure of the US soldier remains heroic in the mythology of QAnon and the militia groups whose membership draws significantly from former members of the US armed forces. As the jingoistic imperative of post-9/11 America that was often weaponized against critiques of American imperial wars, "Support Our Troops" has in some memes come to mean supporting the overthrow of the US government, in the most literal-minded way of bringing the war home. The pardoning of January 6 insurrectionists by Trump underscores powerfully their sense of their own innocence and recommits them to paranoid aggression. The Anons are least delusional when they refer to themselves as the Storm. For all their putatively fringe existence, they share in the same forms of idealized subjectivation that neoliberalism makes available: the entrepreneur, the influencer, the Instagram and YouTube star, and the hustler who has mastered the art of "pivoting" (in neoliberal parlance, an injury displayed as virtue or skill). These forms of subjectivation—not specific to extremist groups—are how the politics of the LARP transit from the virtual to the real.

3
Freedom

I. Truth-Freedom

In Sarasota County, Florida, a clinic named We the People Health & Wellness Center offers its clients ivermectin for treating COVID infections. Its name suggests that within the confines of its campus there exists a true democracy of treatment options and consumer choice. Billing itself as a "Freedom based wellness center" on its website,[1] the center offers treatments that promise more than cures. The center assumes that freedom is a problem concerning truth, since it offers clients the gratifications that come from knowing a truth that is opposed to normative and institution-alized medicine, and empowers them to act on this knowledge. For ivermectin enthusiasts and anti-vaccine activists, the truth is sometimes presented as a personalized and individualized notion that corresponds to a notion of individual freedom, which is conceived as a personal choice or a personal right—often expressed as "my truth." Yet the same activists and communities also express rhetorics of collective emancipation and anticipate building a social order in which their truth-telling would no longer be required, because "my truth" would now be understood by everyone, codified in institutional practices, and in new laws, protections, and rights.

Tanya Parus, a Florida-based activist, has been vocal in insisting that doctors be able to prescribe ivermectin for COVID. Parus is a member of

Moms for America, which began as a group promoting "medical freedom" but has widened its mission into three objectives: "Empower Moms, Promote Liberty, Raise Patriots to heal America from the inside out."[2] It is not incidental that Moms for America has added "parental rights" to its greater mission (more on this below). When asked by a journalist why she spends so much time and energy militating for the use of ivermectin, a widely discredited cure, Parus responded, "It's about freedom. It's not ivermectin. [The point is that] the doctors should be able to prescribe whatever they feel the patient could benefit from."[3] A medical prescription expresses, in other words, a *feeling* (whether hunch or certainty), and freedom means not having any legal barriers to rendering this feeling into a medical assessment. Behind this feeling, that an alternate treatment is the right one, is another that Parus shares with the imagined doctor: a feeling of paranoia, a sense that established protocols of scientific inquiry are an elaborate plot for social control or maximal profits. Alliances between corporate and state entities surface in paranoid fantasy as the workings of a cabal. Feelings of paranoia and exposure underwrite the claims of a growing medical freedom (or health freedom) movement, which aligns with anti-vaxx interests though its remit is broader than vaccines, and extends to placing limitations on scientific research.[4] As a social movement it is an assemblage of anti-vaxx and anti-lockdown supporters, alternative medicine advocates, and wellness industry enthusiasts. This movement, though heterogenous, has come to be represented by conspiratorial health skeptic and Health and Human Services Secretary, Robert F. Kennedy, Jr., and his MAHA (Make America Healthy Again) movement, with its growing ranks of "MAHA Moms." Since most people who promote ivermectin or other alternative cures for COVID allude to some personal experience or anecdote concerning its success as a treatment for the virus (in stark contradiction to the scientific consensus), they vehemently oppose suggestions that medical science with its controlled studies might have guidance to offer them. This overvaluation of personal experience aids in producing a belief that they are medical freedom fighters ranged against a powerful and organized medical establishment.[5] Personal experience, deemed to be beyond contestation, also elevates them as privileged subjects whose speech then takes on the force of self-evident truth.

In May 2023, Florida's governor Ron DeSantis signed four medical freedom laws. These laws block businesses and government offices from requiring vaccines, masks, testing, or proof of post-infection recovery from COVID to access services. They also create protections for those prescribing alternate treatments and expand exemptions for those opting out of public health services. Erstwhile pro-choice slogans like "my body, my choice" are increasingly taken up by anti-vaccine movements but recast in a libertarian frame suffused with paranoia, as injunctions to escape "the biomedical security state." After he signed these laws, DeSantis proclaimed in a speech at CPAC, "In Florida, we reject the biomedical security state which erodes liberty, harms livelihoods, and divides our society. We've stood for freedom across the board, and the result has been, Florida has defeated Faucism. Freedom has prevailed in the Sunshine State."[6] Clearly aligning CDC mandates with fascism, DeSantis positions himself as a freedom fighter.

In the rhetorics of right-wing groups in the United States, "freedom" has become an agreed-upon value among otherwise heterogeneous conspiracists, lobbyists, online trolls, and activists. While their emphases may shift, with some voices espousing anti-statism and others emphasizing personal license, by and large, it is the banner of freedom that mobilizes right-leaning people. How does freedom become entailed in the politics of truth? By means of what political and psychodynamic mechanisms does freedom manifest in opposition to science and expertise? Because there is no authority that can broker knowledge or stabilize truth, everyone has their own partisan "right to know"—a phrase frequently twinned with "freedom to choose" in the YouTube videos, pamphlets, and other paraphernalia of these movements. Freedom emerges, strangely, as both a pre-requisite and a product of this right to know. In Chapter One, I discussed how Michel Foucault's reflections on truth and power demonstrate that the exercise of power entails a game of truth. In the games of truth engaged by medical freedom and parental rights activists, what forms of power do they wish to release? What does freedom mean when it is aligned with these forms of power?

Given that appeals to freedom underwrite a host of right-leaning paranoid projects, from banning books to passing anti-trans legislation to mandating religion in public education, freedom has veered far from its understanding as emancipation or liberation from systems of social domination. Instead, freedom is invoked by many political actors in the service of strengthening existing forms of domination. This suggests that freedom, like truth, has been subject to a nihilistic hollowing out of significance, and its meanings have become fungible and untethered from their foundations.[7] As social and economic policy, neoliberalism diminished understandings of freedom as liberation or emancipation from an unjust social order, encouraging instead an imaginary of freedom grounded in markets and capital, on the one hand, and in religion, family, and traditional morality, on the other.[8] I assume, here as in previous chapters, that neoliberalism is a fundamental governing condition under which heterogenous right-wing social movements have emerged, from New Right to alt-right to far-libertarian. Thus, neoliberalism's reworking of the meanings of freedom affects myriad political positions, some opposed to each other. As Wendy Brown has argued, "while orders of governing reason [such as neoliberalism] build and recede slowly; their effects generate their own logics and trajectories, subject and social formations."[9] Extending Brown's claim, I submit that "orders of governing reason" also entail psychosocial effects, and that such orders adhere and persist over time because of their effects on "subject and social formations." This means, then, that a symptomology of the psychic dimensions of these social formations is critical for understanding them.

Founded during the pandemic in response to school closures, COVID restrictions, and mask mandates, Moms for Liberty initially asserted a freedom meant to exempt individuals from collective responsibility. "Do not comply!"—a rallying cry for anti-lockdown protestors—became a governing principle for Moms for Liberty. Over time Moms for Liberty changed its political mission by making rights and responsibilities—rather than noncompliance—the center of its platform, under the moniker "parental rights." Yet their fight for parental rights entails, in fact, the suppression of others: public school teachers, medical care providers, librarians, trans people. Moms for Liberty receives critical support from the Council for National Policy, a network of organizations from the Reagan era that has connected big money with Christian conservatism to influence political agendas on the right.[10] Imagining themselves as the ultimate authority with respect to their children, parental rights advocates (of which Moms for Liberty is only the most visible and influential group) assume authoritative stances with respect to public education, medical treatments for trans youth, the content of library shelves, and so on. Their politics thus operate in a double-movement. Acting as the arbiters of morality, education, and traditional values, parental rights activists call for an

iron-clad authority that would secure their visions for the social order. The
defiant and rebellious cry of "do not comply!" has resolved into a wish for
submission to a form of state authority that would ensure and protect
parental rights, thereby making parents the ultimate authorities regarding
children. The children are thus sequestered, in this political imagination,
from the social altogether.

There is a revolving door between movements for medical freedom and
movements for parental rights because these movements both concern
themselves with the family as the fundamental unit of social reproduction.
They are also often lead by women who primarily identify themselves as
"Moms." From protesting on the streets and lobbying politicians, Moms
for Liberty shifted its operations to fighting "woke indoctrination" in
schools, by successfully taking over school boards and demonizing teachers
for teaching what they (wrongly) call "Critical Race Theory" or accusing
teachers of adhering to "gender ideology" and "grooming" schoolchildren
to becoming queer or trans. As such this group has wielded the discourse
of rights and responsibility against democracy and against the state. Their
merchandise prominently features apparel with the slogan "Fight Like a
Mom." Sovereign citizen movements, for their part, make freedom from
existing law the very basis of their self-definition. Preppers, whose ideological allegiances range across the political spectrum and who cannot be
said in any simple way to be on the "far-right," want to ensure not mere
creaturely survival but the capacity for sustaining a zone of personal
freedom and self-ownership after the end times have laid waste to everything else. If such a future exemption from collective catastrophe is to be
secured, one must make the most of the time that remains and accumulate
the best skills and resources now. That the uses of *freedom* are cynical for
at least some of these political actors does not render them meaningless.

Freedom for these groups comprises self-ownership, personal license,
and exemption from state regulation and social responsibility. Under the
sign of freedom, some of these groups seek to violate public health ordinances, prevent women's control of their own reproductive health, ban
books from public libraries, keep children from learning histories of race
and of sexuality, overturn gay marriage, introduce religion into public
education. Wendy Brown rightly dubs this resurgent strain of freedom
"antidemocratic authoritarian liberalism." She writes:

If classical liberalism's identification of freedom as a private, individual good quietly ignored social powers of inequality, marginalization, and abjection that bear on its use, *antidemocratic authoritarian liberalism* is the political form converting liberty into a rabid defense of those powers. Divested from popular sovereignty in particular and democracy and democratization in general, and animated by the unprecedented social disintegration of neoliberalism, freedom within this form is more than anti-statist. It is antidemocratic, anti-political, antisocial, and sometimes anti-life.[11]

Indeed, as Brown notes, the history of notions of freedom is an exclusionary one, arguably reaching as far back as the Greek polis, in which men were the subjects of freedom, but not slaves and women. The latter were, instead, people over whom freedom could be practiced as a kind of entitlement or power. Over time freedom became riveted to the rights and practices of domination. The historical as well as philosophical entwinement of freedom with domination has been a central concern for recent thinkers. Tyler Stovall, in *White Freedom: The Racial History of an Idea*, has analyzed how Enlightenment notions of freedom in America and France are discourses that fundamentally assume a white subject.[12] Aziz Rana and Jefferson Cowie have also parsed how hegemonic notions of freedom rely on producing unfreedom for others, whether through dispossession, slavery, or the withdrawal of civil rights or political power.[13] Brown contributes to these critiques by tracking how, in the wake of neoliberalism, reactionary notions of freedom emphasize personal, civil, and economic liberty not merely to produce a free democratic sphere for some at the expense of others. Rather, they weaponize these liberties, turning them against democracy itself. Realizing democratic ideals would require interventions in the spontaneous (and supposedly "natural") order secured through unregulated markets and traditional morality—a spontaneous order that neoliberal rationality aims to protect at all costs—so its forms of governance detach equality from the practices of freedom. Thus, freedom is transformed into a "right of aggression against social mores, social protections, and social justice; it becomes an entitlement to refuse democratic principles and accountability; and it becomes compatible with political autocracy or authoritarianism."[14] Alberto Toscano dubs this "fascist freedom." An outgrowth of liberalism itself, fascist freedom aims to deliver "the promises of liberalism though illiberal means," complete with anti-statist rhetoric often delivered by state agents themselves.[15] Whether fascist freedom or anti-democratic authoritarian liberalism, contemporary rhetorics of freedom that position themselves against social justice and social equality offer up the space of politics as an arena for psychosocial satisfactions. The key pleasure they offer is a practice of freedom without accountability, responsibility, or any sense of dependence on the well-being of others. In short, such freedom is a promise of impunity as the glimmering hope of a fascistic utopia.

Insofar as liberalism understood rights to be instantiations of freedom, rights remake the subject politically, economically, socially, and psychically. If authoritarian forms of freedom presume a subject entitled to refuse accountability (as in Brown's formulation), what are the psychodynamics of this form of subjectivation? Arguably, as they are grounded on Lockean assumptions about self-ownership, liberal notions of freedom have long entailed producing unfreedom since they do not include equality or interdependence in their political calculus. Already then, the history of liberal notions of freedom is a history of producing subjects of entitlement—that is, subjects sanctified by their claims to moral right even as they are endowed with powers of personal autonomy. In turn, the liberal state positions itself as the guardian of freedom, which is rendered into a secularized totem, in whose name the state can discharge violence and coercion. Having grown out of this history, the contemporary authoritarian form of "freedom" is best thought of as such a totem, one that has come to be overloaded with signification, especially when its totemic expression takes the form of a logo or a meme. As with any totem, it promises self-evident truth through social obligation to the totem itself, and it organizes the social field with the authority of a newfound reality principle that governs one's comportments and relations in the world.[16] Erich Fromm once referred to such authority as "anonymous authority." Not locatable in a person or an institution, anonymous authority is a reigning common sense that governs normative practices and ideals. As Fromm puts it, such authority "does not demand anything except the self-evident."[17] The authoritative grounds of truth are to be found in notions of what is "natural" or "inherent" (as in self-ownership being a natural right, etc.) The presumptive self-evident truth of natural rights—the "obvious" nature of which

Foucault would consider an indication of a game of truth—is thus the kernel of authority in liberal understandings of freedom. Conceived this way, in the game of truth that invokes it, freedom takes on the semblance of totemic authority. Simultaneously law and fetish, it recruits political actants into the service of its doxa—which, in neoliberal times, resolve into the twin sacrosanct freedoms of the market and family (with religion and traditional morality serving a key supports for the latter). Thus freedom obscures elements of social relations (including interdependence and varied organizations of the family form) that fall outside the realm of what appears to be self-evident and obvious projects of freedom. As a totem, freedom combines authority with the force of truth, and it provides the foundation for community as well as enmity toward those outside the fold it has established. Those under its ken are positioned as the elect.

In medical freedom and parental rights movements, the elect enjoy the satisfactions of stating truths opposed to prevailing scientific or educational norms. According to the political imagination of these movements, existing educational and governmental institutions and scientific norms are the results of a broken social pact, and this brokenness requires that all manner of imagined ideal pasts be reinstated. For parental rights advocates, society's broken pacts are figured in the family that has been unmoored from traditional morality; for medical freedom activists, it is the body itself that is beset with dangers from a corrupt political-economic system that profits from hiding the truth and keeping the body ailing and vulnerable. The body as body politic must be made healthy again on the basis of truths increasingly hidden by malevolent interests. Existing social arrangements must be treated with paranoid skepticism, since the fundamental political fight is about truths that society obscures. For these social movements the political aim is to enable the emergence of an authority that could enforce these hidden truths. In the meantime, because freedom can be enjoyed by speaking such truth—online, in courts, at medical board hearings—it is as much a matter of will as veridiction. That is, freedom as a value sanctions political action. For medical freedom advocates a minimum political action is to spread alternate truths in order to "inform the public"; for parental rights advocates this means fighting for the heteronormative family unit as the truest form of family and one that is autonomous with respect to the state. Truth-telling makes the will to power feel like freedom, and hence freedom can be opposed to science, to public education, and to expertise.

In the discourse of medical freedom, paranoia underwrites the triad of freedom, truth, and psychical gratification. If paranoia is a form of defense as Freud understood it, then like any defense it assumes rivalry and antagonism, which in the case of social movements resolves into political antagonism. As previous chapters have illustrated, the feeling of exposure and danger is a mood that cuts across many different publics, and paranoia is a common element for such a mood. For medical freedom and parental rights activists this leads to concrete political practice: reorienting the agendas of school and hospital boards, protesting in the streets, militating against teachers' unions, organizing conventions, doing your own research, and other such practices are part and parcel of freedom practiced as an ethics of paranoia. So not only does paranoid fantasy become political practice, but the resistances and oppositions one encounters in the social field affirm the basis of the original paranoid beliefs, which now, retrospectively, appear self-evident and true. Political action in real life (IRL) aligns psychical reality with historical truth (see Introduction). Because one has disrupted drag queen story hour, for example, and faced some resistance in doing so, this event must be a part of a concerted effort to turn kids queer; because a hospital has cleared one's anti-vaxx posters from its façade, the hospital must be a node in a larger scheme to keep one sick.

With truth as the guiding principle, and with freedom operating as a kind of totem, paranoia itself becomes an ethics, in Foucault's precise sense of a set of practices and beliefs that aid in subjectivation. The ethics of paranoia make available social, emotional, and material gratifications that are legitimized all the more when practiced under the banner of freedom. The freedom imagined by medical freedom activists, Moms for Liberty, and other such groups entails obligation, necessity, and responsibility, a freedom unlike the utter disinhibition practiced by anonymous users of 4chan, Telegram, Gab, and other such platforms, explored in the Chapter Two. Whether expressed in the form of disinhibition or desublimation (anonymous online ranting against women, smashing the windows of the Capitol in DC) or in the form of superegoic sublimation (stockpiling resources for future personal use, researching medical exemptions), newfound practices of freedom offer up a range of psychosocial enjoyments.

Additionally, the *collective* nature of political action (whether an insurrection or a school board gradually populated with like-minded people) confirms the validity of individually held beliefs. For medical freedom fighters, freedom is practiced through a variety of political actions. While the ideal action helps to enact laws that would curtail governmental regulation of medical treatments, in the absence of such laws there are additional political strategies:

- Attend and disrupt the board meetings of public hospitals, since these boards are imputed to have ulterior motives.
- Seek election to such boards to change hospital policy and make way for truth in policy.
- Protest in front of vaccine providers.
- Legally challenge the basis of medical-licensing protocols.
- Work to expand the recognized exemptions (religious or medical) for vaccines or other treatments.
- Become a digital warrior and spread the truth about established medical treatments.

These actions are not an unchecked will to power. Rather, these actions assert their authority by working alongside the social demands of politics, while being ready to subvert these social demands in the name of some higher truth seen to be critical for everyone.

That these activists adhere to accepted political channels explains the preponderance of the iconography of American democracy in some of these discourses. For example, the iconic script of "We the People" from the original Declaration of Independence is used as a stencil by a host of right-wing social movements, including the activist group Moms for Liberty. This archival script already signals that the politics being conducted under its banner seek to restore an imagined past. "We the People" appears on websites and social media banners. It is projected as the stage background for conventions such as "Freedom Fest." Simultaneously talisman and ornament, declaration and meme, this image authorizes the claims of whatever spectatorial politics deploys it; hollowing out the meaning of democracy, it aims to ward off accusations of being anti-democratic. Reduced to a meme, the democratic values the phrase "We the People" is intended to signal have clearly lost their foundation in a feat of nihilistic appropriation—that is, democratic values have not vanished but have become fungible, transmogrified into new values underwritten by positive desires for authoritarian rule. "We the People," when deployed as a stencil, weds the truth of the demos itself to whatever politics is conducted under its mantle. Both the demos and the truth are thus declared—whether as discourse about parental rights or about medical freedom—and now must be "restored." It is not accidental that "1776" is the other meme deployed by some of the same political movements. Unlike "We the People," it expresses a readiness to fight.

II. Politics of Exemption

Moms for Liberty asks its members to sign a pledge to protect the "fundamental rights of parents including but not limited to the right to direct the education, medical care, and moral upbringing of their children."[18] Like other parental rights groups, Moms for Liberty is ever vigilant about any civic or social encroachment on the unchecked authority of parental power. As with medical freedom movements, such an ethics of paranoia entails speaking the truth and having spoken it, arriving at a fuller understanding of one's own identity as shaped by these truths. The promised and expansive future of liberty conceived as the absence of restraint is practiced in being unafraid of giving offense in the present moment. Negative liberty of this kind has long been the aim of libertarian politics, but libertarianism as a political tendency does not quite capture all that is politically at stake for these movements. Their political rhetoric does espouse individualism as the cornerstone of libertarian thought—through notions of self-ownership, individual choice, self-sovereignty—but such individualism is overtly expressed as a concern about the social bond between parents and children and about the social relations undergirding societal reproduction. That is, all parental rights and most medical freedom groups' political rhetoric is about the nuclear family and about family values. In their concern for the social such rhetoric might not be wholly congruent with libertarian notions of freedom, but it is perfectly in line with the twin freedoms most valued by neoliberalism: traditional family and markets.

It is not accidental that so many medical freedom organizations operate under a moniker involving "Moms"—Moms for this, Moms for that. In other words, there is indeed a vision of the social, of relation, and of interdependency, at the basis of these political movements, and the "mom" has become a bearer for neoliberalism's moral charge. She is first and foremost a moral subject whose needs and wishes align with truth, and since she presumably aims at bettering the lives of her children and the children of the nation, her desires render her actions true. Her love for her children is the basis of her authority as a truth-teller. All of her demands are to be deemed legitimate because they are grounded on the truth of a mother's love. Her desire—focalized around children and family—asserts itself as a surrogate for everyone's common interest. If her desire is destructive and entails, for example, banning books from public libraries, demonizing health-care providers, subverting democratic processes or civic institutions, militating against gender-affirming surgeries, then such negativity is in the service of preserving her family, a goal legitimized by the fact of being a mom. As such, the mom inhabits a hallowed space in cultural politics: exceptional and yet representing the norm, simultaneously a privileged subject and yet one speaking for the demos. The freedom-fighting mom—who tends to refer to herself as "Warrior Mom"—is accountable only to her family, even though she seeks to govern other families' medical treatments or conditions of education. Because her actions and statements concern the family, the mom may mobilize an individualizing language of preferences, wishes, desires, and dislikes, yet even when she expresses individualist ideas, she never speaks as an individual.[19]

As Melinda Cooper has argued, contemporary capitalism produces and reinvents certain forms of kinship while demonizing others. Her analysis tracks the profound political transformations that have made the traditional nuclear family, rather than the state, the favored location of economic and moral obligation, wealth transfer, and care.[20] This shifting of values from the state to the patriarchal family entails coercive expectations of gender conformity and a renewed valorization of social-reproductive roles for mothers and wives. These roles are not passive and have become the grounds for politicizing motherhood. In his 1936 essay "Authority and the Family," Max Horkheimer noted that women's emancipation, as a project conducted under the presuppositions of the capitalist mode of production, is reduced to joining the workforce, and even this narrowed goal of freedom arrives too late for women: "for it has come at a period when unemployment has become a structural part of our present society," and so women are not welcome in the workplace.[21] Thus, he concludes, "Woman's 'vocation,' for which she is prepared in mind and feeling by her bourgeois education and character formation, drives her not behind the counter of a store nor to a typewriter, but towards a happy marriage in which she will be cared for and will be able to worry about her children."[22] Thus women are

subjected to a process of responsibilization in the patriarchal family—a
responsibilization that regularly includes work outside the home as well
as housework—a process that is confused with women's freedom. In
addition to laboring at the workplace, women are expected to organize
and regulate the domain considered "natural" to them: the mundane
details and rituals of family life. Horkheimer traces multiple displacements
in the function of the family under capitalism, by means of which the
family produces authority-bound subjects: the father must accommodate
himself to his bosses "out of love for his family," the wife—out of the same
love—defers to the father's authority, and both are thus subject to the
vicissitudes of economic necessity, an anonymous form of authority that
produces dependencies across society, and one that is invoked consistently
by the agents of capital, for whom this blind power is couched in the
language of "facts," though it resembles ancient notions of fate. Even the
putative freedom of the entrepreneur (a freedom increasingly prized in
contemporary politics) conceals what Horkheimer calls a "retrogressive
surrender of freedom"—that is, "an acceptance of the blind power of
chance."[23] Horkheimer suggests that for both the entrepreneur and the
family courting the dangerous vicissitudes of economic chance becomes
habitual. Advocates of authoritarian freedom and contemporary influencer
culture demonstrate that courting economic and political dangers need
not be a habit that is performed unthinkingly, but rather is one to be
enjoyed for the pleasures and gratifications it offers.

Fundamentally, Horkheimer's interest in the family stems from its
psychosocial significance as the site of both the production of individual
psyches as well as an index of social and collective phenomenon. The
family crystallizes the forms of authority that govern society as a whole
and, in turn, produces subjects psychically equipped for submission to
these same authorities. While Horkheimer acknowledges that the family
can be and has been organized differently in the past and in non-European
places and that it continues to contain emancipatory potential, he argues
that, in an administered society prone to economic crises, the family has
become a privileged site for practicing the surrender of freedom. It is in
the family that adaptation to the status quo becomes a habitual and
effortless practice. As himself a figurehead of authority, as both the spokesperson for and the surrogate of authorities (authorities that dominate him
in turn), the father instills in family members a sense that survival,

resilience, and success are all dependent on submitting oneself to the coercive authority of a reality principle (be it economic necessity, property relationships, etc.). Hence "universal injustice is [. . .] surrounded by the halo of necessity."[24] Decades before neoliberalism refashioned the family as an extension of what Friedrich Hayek would call the "personal protected sphere"[25] —in which the family would be treated as sacrosanct much like private property, would be rendered a kind of private firm—Horkheimer had outlined how the entrepreneur and the family, subjected to the same blind power of economic chance, are forms of life that make submission feel like freedom. The authority-bound subjectivation within the family that makes one psychically attached to the status quo also lays the psycho-social groundwork for the acceptance of more authoritarian forms of governance. Tacit in Horkheimer's analysis is a subtle distinction between a desire to submit to the status quo and a desire to demolish it, thus enabling ever-greater forms of submission, since the habitual adaptation to present realities no longer fulfills the sado-masochistic desires that adaptation had instilled. Moreover, such demolition is imagined as a restoration of an imagined past.

Today, the protections that are granted to the family which are derived from private property have become the grounds to argue for privileges and exemptions that threaten to demolish the very social order that has made such protections possible. Medical freedom movements and parental rights groups alike take up the family as the sacrosanct unit of political protection, and in their politics the family emerges as an extended zone of entitlements, especially entitlements rendered as exemptions from the law itself. "Freedom" is fantasized as limitless enjoyment of choice in a world where personal feeling can guide health decisions without interference by any other authority, a world where parents can opt their children out of values and practices, such as education about sexuality or racial inequality, arrived at through democratic processes. When medical freedom advocates express their conviction in radical (and unrealistic) individual bodily autonomy, they exhibit another form of this logic of exemption and unaccountability. Besieged and made vulnerable by a preponderance of malefactors (chemicals in the water supply, teachers unions, trans people), parental rights and medical freedom advocates express fears that slide quickly into feelings of supremacist exemption: one must fight to be exempted from all kinds of public policies. Until the law can be abolished, this logic goes, it must be exploited such that it need not apply to oneself even if it applies to others. Until a better world comes to pass, legal exemptions are among the forms of enjoyment on offer. Thus the politics of exemption align with the imaginaries of racial entitlement, of white exceptionalism, even when practiced by non-white subjects. Being exempted and being exceptional feels like freedom; on the face of it at least, exemptions offer a reprieve from the blind power of fate.

Standing in for the norm, the new phantasmatic family wishes, in a feat of juridical perversity, to exempt itself from normative requirements.[26] Researching legal exemptions, organizing protests, advocacy and lobbying, picketing and rallying—these responsibilized forms of enjoyment entail soliciting the force of the state to curtail the actions of a host of others: trans people, teachers, racial minorities, abortion clinics. These social elements are fated for elimination in the political imagination of parental rights advocates. Now the basis for undermining everything from public health ordinances to public education, "parental rights" is the secret sharer in the history of "family values," which always indexed a tension between freedom and necessity, choice and obligation. Melinda Cooper quotes Gary Bauer, Ronald Reagan's advisor, as squaring this circle: "only in a society that allows individual freedom can family members exercise the initiatives and responsibility that makes for strong family life."[27] Personal liberty is thus paradoxically derived from responsibility to the family. In the decades since Reagan's administration such liberty has become a matter of revealing the truth, the responsibility to which is indissociable from capitulating to the authority of the traditional family. It is because advocates for parental rights and medical freedom assume a discourse of responsibility to the truth—a discourse whose ultimate subject is the rights of self-sovereignty variously extending to the family unit—that their destructive aspects (banning books, disrupting medical facilities, etc.) feel to their advocates like a practice of freedom. The discourse of responsibility—whether to children and family or to the distribution of "personal choice" for medical treatments—aids their subjectivation as subjects of entitlement because their concerns are cast as moral, and moral subjects entitle themselves to act out their responsibilities. That such acting out entails violating public health orders, opting out of certain educational emphases (especially on race and gender) arrived at through democratic deliberation, or harassing librarians and public school teachers does not trouble the activists for parental rights and medical freedom, since these actions are cast as responsible to a higher authority. Such acting out entails a break from the law in order to restore it, and the family has become the hallowed ground for justifying such practices.

III. Escaping from Freedom

As it is conceived and theorized in psychoanalysis, the family is in many ways the appropriate location for political contestation around freedom and truth, since it is where one learns how to live with given constraints—in short, where one is trained in reality principles and prohibitions. As such it is the testing ground for the most primary acts of freedom. The family is the vehicle for instilling prohibitions, and therefore, the family also constitutes free or unfree subjects. For psychoanalysis the family is a privileged site of formative childhood experiences, where one learns and negotiates the unsaid, the repressed, the secretive, and the prohibitive. Love's destructive and corrosive effects are first endured in the family, before being repressed. In the family, freedom and truth are thus interwoven. It is the site where the problem of truth (whether of desire, or some shared yet unspoken or disavowed secret) becomes a matter of critical import for subjectivation.

For Erich Fromm, as for Max Horkheimer, the family crystallizes and refracts social processes larger than the family unit itself. Even before his ultimate break from psychoanalysis, Fromm had already considered the Freudian emphasis on family relations to be a reflection of social relations and larger social orders. Reading psychoanalysis itself psychoanalytically, Fromm understood the pressures of social formations and political-economic realities to be conditioning fundamental experiences for families. Since psychoanalytic categories are derived from the structure and organization of families, these categories already suggest theoretical insights into social reality. Not locatable in a particular person, the law of the father is, for Fromm, the displacement of a law that governs the social field : "The authority that the father has in the family is not a coincidental one last 'supplemented' by the social authorities, but rather the authority of the father himself is ultimately grounded in the authority structure of society as a whole. True, the father is for the child (in terms of time) the first to transmit social authority, however, (in terms of meaning) he does not model authority but rather imitates it."[28] Representing "the social character of their society or class," parents transmit "the psychological atmosphere or the spirit of a society." Therefore, Fromm concludes the family "may be considered to be the psychological agent of society."[29]

As such, in Fromm's reading, Freudian concepts, including the topography of the id, the ego, and the superego are sublimates of social realities, even as they carry significance for individual family situations and experiences. Since the superego is the psychical agency by means of which authority in the form of leaders, laws, and prohibitions is internalized, and which governs notions of responsibility and compliance, its operations are crucial for understanding the psychosocial aspects of authoritarian freedom. Theodor Adorno considered the theory of the superego to be an account of how one becomes a *zoon politikon* (political animal).[30] However, the superego does not merely bring one in line with societal and familial injunctions. It generates wishes beyond this task. While the superego might seem to curtail the subject's freedom, it is intimately tied to forms of pleasure and desire, since it is born out of their renunciation. Becoming a political animal in no way implies that one simply adheres to the putative rationality of the political realm; instead, this rationality is itself a psychosocial consequence, one subject to crises and internal contradictions. Consider, for example, sex panics against queer or trans people or the latest collective hysteria about pedophilia, expressed in accusations of "grooming" young people. These panics do not merely call out for moral correction but are in themselves forms of enjoyment.[31] Key to sex panics is a paranoid scrutiny of social relations intermixed with fear, and the condemnation that is meant to identify and root out deviance is licensed by a superegoic appeal to morality. These condemnations are as pleasurable as the paranoid fears they never quite relieve. Parental rights and medical freedom groups base their politics on varieties of moral panics, including sex panics.

It is because the superego entwines morality with enjoyment that authoritarian freedom activists can condemn what they perceive as surplus forms of enjoyment while at the same time excessively enjoying their own destructive actions. This is an example of what Melanie Klein referred to as the strange combination of "over-indulgence and excessive severity" of superegoic operations.[32] Unlike Freud, for whom the superego is precipitated through an identification with the father that resolves the Oedipus complex, Klein understood the superego as emerging from an earlier identification with the mother. For Klein, it is the mother who inaugurates the agency that will henceforth regulate pleasure and punishment. As such, Klein is attuned to the prelinguistic or pre-symbolic place of the mother in what will come to be experienced as law. Well before the law of the father is internalized, Klein argues, the pre-verbal child has already experienced the withdrawal of the breast as a kind of punishment because the child had sought to devour and destroy it. Identifying with and introjecting the breast (imagined by the child as vengeful) installs a maternal superego from whom punishments are to be expected: "the superego becomes something which bites, devours, and cuts."[33] Crucially, biting, devouring, and cutting had been the forms in which the child's own pleasure had been expressed. Thus, the child's own destructive instincts, projected onto the mother's body, become introjected as a severe and vengeful agency. This is the result of the baby having to be weaned—that is, of a primary dependence having to be overcome for the sake of a future freedom. Yet this overcoming is at the same time a loss, and weaning installs a lack. This lack animates fantasies of restoration and of satiation, which become significant for future psychical positions. Weaning does not end once and for all. When a person gives up the securities of the family to become autonomous, the process is repeated.

Understood psychoanalytically, then, freedom requires giving up on primary satisfactions whose libidinal attractions never fully disappear. The mother is herself a mark of renounced desires. Militating for authoritarian freedom, the figure of the Warrior Mom is a phantasmatic figure, without whom no restoration (of impossible plenitude, of unending jouissance) would be possible. In his engagement with Klein's concept of the maternal superego, Lacan understands weaning as the basic template for other kinds of losses and renunciations, such that it is maternal plenitude that is the template for "the nostalgias of humanity": "a perfect assimilation of totality to being. . . ; the metaphysical mirage of universal harmony; the mystical abyss of affective fusion; *the social utopia of totalitarian dependency—all derived from the longings for a paradise lost before birth and from the most obscure aspirations for death.*"[34] In contemporary cultural politics, even as the Mom promises to deliver everyone from fear—including herself—such deliverance is inseparable from the surrender of freedom.

For both Klein and Freud, the superego entwines wish with fear, an imbrication through which all kinds of future relations to authority will be experienced: the fear of the formidable power invested in authorities combined with a wish for their approbation. The superego operates according to unconscious logics that impute excessive and unrealistic powers to the authorities now internalized by the self. That is, once an authority or law is internalized, it operates according to psychical demands, not real or legalistic ones. Crucially, the desire to destroy the powerful external authority transforms into a fear of it once the authority is internalized. Although diverted from its aims, such a desire nevertheless persists and can form the basis of sadistic impulses. Having internalized authorities whose love and approbation is desired even as their power is feared, the originary identification that installs the superego reorganizes one's own desire such that new satisfactions become possible, including the satisfaction of complying with superegoic demands. Yet obeying the superego's demands proliferates them, and the demands may well be contradictory. Since it marks the point at which the subject gave up on his or her desire, its hold on the subject is as seductive as it is compulsive. The desires given up lose none of their intensity in spite of being diverted or displaced onto new objects. Superegoic demands do not have to feel pleasurable because they seek to channel pleasure so as to divert its aims while simultaneously gratifying these aims through substitutive satisfactions. Hence Lacan writes, "Nothing can force anyone to enjoy except the superego. The superego is the imperative of *jouissance*—Enjoy!"[35] The key element in Lacan's understanding is the coercive nature of the superego: force, imperative, and conscription are the fundaments of the enjoyments it makes available, and instead of detracting from pleasure, such compulsion can intensify and focalize it. The superego is more intimate with the pleasure principle than the reality principle, which is the domain of the ego.[36] Freud even considered it to be derived from the id itself.

The development of individual conscience can lead to a process of masochistic responsibilization and self-reproach. Just as masochism is sadism practiced on the self, the conscience can also require the sadistic demolition of some aspects of the social order in order to bring it in line with internalized values that have the force of authority. Hence unconscious superegoic wishes can result in a host of deleterious social violations, lending credence to Klein's formulation of the superego as a libidinally charged expression of the death instincts. Superego formation continually renews itself in light of additional transferences and so is subject to historical vicissitudes. First parents, then heroes and leaders, and then eventually, according to Freud, "the last figure in the series beginning with the parents is that dark supremacy of Fate, which only the fewest among us are able to conceive of impersonally."[37] What Horkheimer had referred to as the "blind power" of economic necessity has the authority of fate, which, Freud reminds us, is also associated with a variety of surrogates for parental authority: Providence, God, Nature. These are remote and implacable powers to which the superego binds one libidinally, and the fear of them is itself a correlate of the fear of death.[38] Derived from the originary authority of the parents, fate, necessity, and inexorability are the forms in which one is delivered to finitude, or what Lacan called "obscure aspirations for death." Death is the logical endpoint of the need for punishment, which Freud said has key significance in "unconscious guilt."[39] The fear of such mortal punishment is at the same time a wish for it, given the superego's channeling of the death drive.[40] Such fear-wishes can take the form of fighting for ivermectin, which can only cure COVID in doses so large that they would kill the person consuming them.

This is why the superego is not reducible to "conscience," which at most indicates the ego's displacements and ideations concerning superegoic demands, while the superego's contents are ultimately unconscious and not always available for egoic interpretation. According to Max Horkheimer, "conscience" operates to individualize self-reproachment, which prevents the understanding that some personal failures are the result of social causes, not personal ones: "The bad conscience that is developed in the family absorbs more energies than can be counted, which might otherwise be directed against the social circumstances that play a role in the individual's failure."[41] Horkheimer is describing a process by means of which an unjust social order sustains itself, in which the destructive energies of the superego manifest as self-reproachment rather than social critique. By making people economically, politically, and psychically responsible for injuries and dam-ages they sustain as a result of an unjust social order, neoliberal techniques depend on the operations of superegoic self-reproach. Under neoliberalism, such self-reproach manifests as a form of self-betterment and self-improvement, necessarily subtended by the fear of a less-than-optimized self. As such, neoliberal responsibilization makes a tacit claim to truth—namely, that the individual self is to blame. A politics of disinhibition responds by rejecting responsibility, engaging in all manner of offenses, and breaking civil norms, which feels like freedom. Those fighting (responsibly) for the ideals of authoritarian freedom arrive at the same juncture. For each, self-reproach is experienced as an outwardly directed sadism.

Privileging the family and morality, contemporary discourses on parental rights and medical freedom can be understood as an intensification of the superego's operations, which casts the punitive effects of neoliberalism in a new light. Where once morality had arisen as a desexualizing of the primary love object, Freud wrote that "in moral masochism morality becomes sexualized afresh" and this regression is "to the advantage neither of the person concerned nor of morality".[42] A kind of moral masochism can be recognized in expressions and practices of authoritarian freedom. While the Mom is increasingly the subject who empowers herself through moral masochism, she is also joined by consumers in the wellness industry eager to optimize their bodies, medical freedom advocates fearful of plots to divest them of bodily sovereignty, and trans-exclusionary feminists (TERFs) suspicious of encroachments on cis-female freedom.

Derived from liberal protections for private property, the "personal protected sphere" has been extended to the family and has intensified around problems of individual embodiment and finitude, but having become the basis to argue for exemptions from the law, the "personal protected sphere" has also changed. More than a disturbance or subversion of democratic law, it now directs law-making itself toward punishment. Endowed with rights against the state and against society, the family thus becomes the locus of limitless enjoyment and new social powers. "Do not comply!"—the battle cry for medical freedom activists—does not only beseech disobedience, but also anticipates a world in which new orders of compliance might be possible. Authoritarian freedom entails a controlled demolition of existing social arrangements, and such demolition begins with a moral practice of truth-telling. This could take the form of voicing aggression against racial or sexual minorities. Grounded in personal feelings, this aggression is authorized as a form of personal expression. At other times such aggression is deemed a necessary response in light of some unavoidable truth often arrived through the classic formulation of conservatism-by-proxy—a fantasy of triangulation at hand in situations where presenting one's unacceptable beliefs meets social pressure—as the viewpoint of some silent majority, imagined necessity, or bureaucratic exigency. Giving voice to offensive statements as a kind of repressed truth aligns the speech with freedom even, and especially, when it violates social mores. Far-right female influencers normalize extreme political positions and politicize heretofore neutral online spaces: for example, a reel on how to fold fitted sheets also serves as a warning against vaccines, or a cooking video becomes an occasion for opining against minorities.[43] Incitement to personal expression is virtually an imperative of liberal democratic freedom in its American variant, from which authoritarian freedom draws its energies. The sense that one speaks for some unquestionable authority (whether imagined as silent majority, the family itself, or economic necessity) makes freedom manifest as a truth act.

In political terminology no other word hits on the conjuncture of surplus enjoyment with superegoic compulsion quite like the word *freedom*. It promises a state of felicity even in formulations that mediate freedom through its (supposed) opposite, necessity. Necessity—whether in the form of reality principles, responsibilities, prohibitions, or rules—is, in any case, caught in the game of (superegoic) enjoyment. It is no wonder that freedom has historically served as a signifier for widely divergent kinds of aspirations. Despite its myriad historical formations and meanings, *freedom* has always indicated a horizon of expectation or aspiration. Overzealous pride in freedom already achieved is a sure sign of ideological mystification, as in nationalist discourse in general and Western Cold War discourse in particular. The long history of freedom's entanglement with domination only underscores its allure as an unfinished process (freedom shares this processual aspect with democracy), and so it is perpetually available to political imagination as promise or as wish. It should not be surprising therefore that the word *freedom* often articulates the wish for another world. Whether fascist utopia or progressive emancipation, calls for freedom have always been, at the same time, injunctions to transform or put an end to one world in the service of building another one. Hence its availability for many different kinds of political imaginations, including apocalyptic ones.

In this frame otherwise perplexing social symptoms begin to make sense. For example, the seamless ideological transit of yoga practitioners, alternative health seekers, and consumers in the wellness industry toward medical freedom and other authoritarian and far-right political positions can now be understood as based on practices of renunciation (rejecting the present world and its corruptions) that, over time, sediment the sense of one's own (supremacist) proximity to truth. Similar transits have been

made by erstwhile progressive media personalities like Christopher Hitchens, David Horowitz, Naomi Wolff, Glen Greenwald, Max Blumenthal,
Matt Taibbi, and Robert F. Kennedy, Jr., who all drifted toward authoritarian politics in the name of freedom. What Quinn Slobodian and
William Callison have called "diagonalism"—a political phenomenon in
which small business owners and putatively "leftish" people form coalitions
that value civil freedom over and above equality or justice—is similarly
animated by the frisson of knowingness and moral sovereignty.[44] Truth-
freedom has become its own reward, and like all forms of enjoyment, it
makes possible the pleasures of self-mutilation or self-destruction.

So it becomes possible for the leading light of anti-trans feminism, J.K.
Rowling—who considers herself to be progressive—to find common cause
with the Christian Right. Trans people, assumed to be a threat to the
traditional family, are opposed by all parental rights groups and many
medical freedom groups. TERFS, attached to their unshakable notion of
cis-women's vulnerability, have found allies among these other social
movements in their fight for women's freedom. For anti-trans feminists
wedded to their beliefs in the truth of gender, the scene of a trans person's
scandalous enjoyment is expressed most often in two fantasies: a trans
woman winning against cis women in sports, or a trans woman using a
female-designated bathroom. These fantasies are compulsively magnetizing
to anti-trans feminists, who indulge and develop them as a basis for an
exclusionary feminism seeking cis women's freedom. Moms for Liberty,
Moms for America, and similar groups seek to eradicate the world of trans
people by taking the family as the fundamental site of political intervention:
parental authority and some forms of medical freedom would make it
impossible for trans children to receive gender transition treatments. In
the United States, by the end of 2023, 22 states had passed some form of
anti-trans legislation, mostly targeting children. A keynote speaker at a
Moms for Liberty summit in the summer before his reelection, Trump
issued multiple executive orders targeting trans people immediately after
regaining office, from withholding life-saving medical care from trans
youth to criminalizing educators who might support trans students. Taken
together, the wellness industry, trans-exclusionary feminism, medical
freedom, and parental rights movements all rely on superegoic solicitations,
but their supremacism is keenly aware of the subject's embeddedness in
the social, from which the subject must be freed.

But if one is to be freed from the social, then what new social arrangement is one freed into? For medical freedom advocates opposing the "biomedical security state" or "medical tyranny," a new social order is anticipated in which responsibility is privatized and one is accountable for one's own medical choices. Medical freedom activists wish to distribute the freedom of choice and self-ownership to others. This freedom is delimited, however: for this movement, "my body, my choice" does not include the choice to have abortions or gender transition surgery, choices they insist the state take away, since these choices are considered unnatural, abusive, and immoral. Indeed, abortion and trans children are eventualities that parental rights and medical freedom groups most fear as the ultimate signs of the crises of the family.

Moms for Liberty and TERFs proffer alternate ideals for the social order, and setting aside immediate gratification, they comport their statements and political actions in the service of these ideals. These substitutive satisfactions provide, nevertheless, their own kinds of pleasure, and if truth-telling therefore becomes a form of enjoyment, it is *because* it risks offending sensibilities, norms, rules, and laws.[45] At the same time, Moms for Liberty and TERFs never pass up the opportunity to *be* offended, since taking offense sustains the feeling of embattlement and grievance so critical for binding libidinal pleasure to the superego's appetite for destruction. The danger that attaches to truth-telling is persistently invoked and narrated as a part of the truth being told, and anti-trans feminists in particular revel in such danger as a condition for their ethics of freedom-as-truth-telling. As activist Abigail Shrier, who runs an Substack called *The Truth Fairy*, explained to students at Princeton University, "What's it like to be on a GLAAD black list? What's it like to have top ACLU lawyers come out in favor of banning your book? What's it like to have prestigious institutions disavow you as an alum? [. . .] what's it like to be the target of so much hate? *It's freeing.*" Shrier's remarks to her young audience repeat the same line over and over: "take back your freedom." By rejecting "gender ideology," she argues, students can be like her and experience "the exquisite joy of not being anyone's subject" and, like her, stand "the chance of leaving the world better than I found it."[46] Shrier prescribes traditional heterosexual relationships and raising a family as a practice of freedom. This entwinement of truth with freedom, in the libidinal economy of anti-trans discourse, turns risk and danger into their own forms of enjoyment, and desublimation (the breaking of norms and the voicing of offense) takes the form of sublimation (capitulation to patriarchal gender expectations).

Recall that the superego is forged out of a primary identification through which one's desire can be given up even if not entirely vanquished, and as Melanie Klein reminds us, "the tyranny of a superego which devours, dismembers and castrates . . . is formed from the image of the father and mother alike."[47] Freud develops his notion of primary identification through his elaboration of Charles Darwin's conjecture about the earliest forms of human community—of society as it existed before the foundation of law, morality, culture, and the like. In this account the primal father enjoys sexual pleasure with all of the women and hoards them from the band of brothers who, resenting this father who creates prohibitions without himself being subject to them, take it upon themselves to kill him collectively and devour his body.[48] Yet upon his death the brothers are afflicted with guilt, and so they deify the primal father, whom they honor in certain festivals, and they lay down new laws and rules that become the basis of religion, governance, and morality. These civilizational achievements emerge from murderous rage, and the specter of the primal father who is exempt from the prohibitions he lays down continues to haunt the social order that arises after him, since that social order is oriented toward venerating his powers. As Herbert Marcuse noted, even though he is murdered, the primal father ultimately wins, since liberation from him only installs him all the more deeply into the institutions and laws that govern society. Such institutions and laws constrain individual liberty, which is why Freud notes that the "liberty of the individual is no gift of civilization."[49] Calls for liberty under the constraints of civilization might indicate a "revolt against some existing injustice, and so may prove favorable to a further development of civilization." But calls for freedom can also "spring from the remains of [human community's] original personality, which is still untamed by civilization and may thus become the basis in them of hostility to civilization."[50] A psychoanalytic understanding of freedom requires accounting for its destructive aspects. The law is haunted by the phantasm of an entity to whom it need not apply, and the lure of this phantasm persists, sometimes in the form of demagogues and authoritarian leaders, with whom one might identify to share in primal enjoyments. For medical freedom fighters and parental rights advocates the slippage between wanting to *be* the authority and wanting to please some authoritative injunction—that is, the slippage between ruling and submitting—is key to their espousal of freedom, a freedom that is, simultaneously, an exemption from the law and the instantiation of a higher normative law, which restores the law in its purest force. Thus, authoritarian freedom is conceived as an escape from freedom.

Yet when they seek exemptions and exploit loopholes, medical freedom advocates also apprehend something rotten in the law itself—namely that laws always apply differentially across the populace, punishing some while exempting others. As a stark example, abortion bans harm women of color and poorer women disproportionately. Not only do wealthy and white women have access to better medical care, but also they can travel to get abortions. Wealth and whiteness, then, exempt one from the law *even as* both wealth and whiteness are often presumed as incarnations of the norm. While such exemptions might seem to operate at the level of the individual, they systemically favor some populations over others.

Exempt from the regulations of the law, from coercion by the state, and from responsibility to the social, new fantasies of freedom nevertheless seek to endow the "personal protected sphere" with the sanctity of myth—making the family great again—returning to a time outside history when the family reigned supreme and when parents' absolute authority was buttressed by agreed-upon conventions and even by the powers of the state. Thus, such desires for radical exemptions are oriented toward restoring forms of submission. In 1943, Max Horkheimer described a similar political imagination: "Their [the Nazis'] concept of history boils down to the veneration of monuments. There is no such thing as history without that utopian element which . . . is lacking in them. Fascism, by its very exaltation of the past, is anti-historical. The Nazis' references to history mean only that the powerful must rule and that there is no emancipation from the eternal laws which guide humanity. When they say history, they mean its very opposite: mythology."[51] A similar mythologizing obtains in the new authoritarian discourses of freedom, in which the family has become the subject of eternal laws over and against society, and the Warrior Mom calls out for patriarchal authority to deliver her jouissance.

A fundamental sense of vulnerability, of finitude, and of being subject to Fate's undiscriminating power underwrites these freedom movements that, in turn, seek to proliferate vulnerability for others. The freedom these movements offer promises self-mastery even as it requires the installation of an implacable authority (whether family or moral law, or family upheld by moral law) that would ensure the exposure of others to violence or illness. Destruction of others and of the self are, of course, intertwined in the freedom on offer by those who consider themselves exempt. The new movements for medical freedom and parental rights share a fantasy similar to other death-driven politics, from preppers to accelerationists: they imagine world catastrophe as a cleansing process, in which one's own survival is secured through an assumed exemption. Such is the psychosocial afterlife of individual autonomy, which liberal democracy offers but cannot make real. So, it returns as a wish for large-scale catastrophe that is to be welcomed rather than avoided, enjoyed rather than feared. The law need not apply to oneself, and yet the law—whatever form it takes—is both necessary and iron-clad. Freedom's embrace of its cherished truths (about ivermectin, about parental rights, about the dangers of pharmaceutical research) is, at the same, time, a wish to outlive the coming catastrophe by hastening it.

4

Hysteria

I. Border Politics in an Expanded Field

Previous chapters concerned forms of adducing truth that are not governed by a regime of truth—so far as they constitute variously paranoid publics—and the truth at issue has been about ideas, whether of harms caused by vaccines, the sinister nature of political power, or the alleged aspirations of minority populations to replace the majority. This chapter will shift the focus from ideation to somatic experiences. I take up the emergence of mysterious bodily symptoms in two different populations that have good reasons to be paranoid: asylum seekers in Sweden and American spies and diplomats abroad. As in previous chapters, the games of truth deployed to demystify these embodied symptoms—whether played by scientists, lawyers, patients, government agencies, journalists, or doctors—will be treated as themselves expressive of social symptoms. Within the discourse of these social actors, truth appears near at hand yet is subject to continual dislocation. This chapter aims not to solve the mystery of these ailments, but to analyze the games of truth that play out where the body, the psyche, and the sociopolitical environment overlap. In investigating mystery illnesses, I am guided by the fissures—moments of displacement, crises of interpretation, or contortions of meaning—that somatic experiences can reveal in discourses that seek to make sense of them.

Moving geographically from the United States to international contexts, this chapter looks closely at populations who likewise cross national borders and then become afflicted with symptoms. Perhaps no place is as laden with psychopolitical significance as a national border. For self-professed "patriots," the border is earthly yet transcendent—a physical reality with psychosocial significance and consequence, signifying not only a legal or juridical boundary, but also a spiritual and moral order. Borders authorize degrees of belonging to the country: who is inside or outside, included or excluded, native or stranger. All these aspects are enfolded within what I will gloss as "border politics"—the primary political discourse assumed and analyzed in what follows.

The juridical assessment of citizenship—and its regime of truth—only imperfectly aligns with the popular and collective imaginary of nationality as racial purity or cultural heritage. During the so-called War on Terror, with the advent of Immigrations and Customs Enforcement (ICE), the Department of Homeland Security, and a host of new spy agencies, US statecraft fused national security with the collective fantasy of national purity through institutional apparatuses. Accordingly, a perceived need to police the border of the nation becomes a salient justification for doing violence to those deemed not to belong. Letting some people die or exposing them to danger, in turn, becomes a grounding rationality for the nation's social reproduction. Contemporary right-wing politics, in the United States and elsewhere, calls for a punishing form of authority that would, once and for all, deliver total national security by achieving total national purity. Not incidentally, one of the common symbols for American military personnel, police force members, and far-right sympathizers is the Marvel Comics vigilante figure the Punisher, whose decal is often brandished on their person or vehicle. This display asserts hostility toward "others," while constituting a community with like-minded and right-leaning people.

The geographical border might exist at the edge of the country, but the border is always somewhat dematerialized. Borders demarcate not only the physical and geographical limits of nation-states, but also signify a host of cultural, linguistic, and racial limits, governing libidinal relations inside and outside the nation. To build walls or demolish them means to engage with these supplementary and seemingly dematerialized forms of the border. This expanded field of border politics includes psychosocial, material, somatic, political, and economic realms. Borders, then, are more than a geographic location: the *nomos* they mark leaves its trace across the socius.

In some countries, this border logic has resulted in governmental policies explicitly targeting those deemed to be outsiders. As British Prime Minister Theresa May put it in a 2012 interview with *The Daily Telegraph,* "The aim is to create here in Britain a really hostile environment for illegal migration," finally naming a set of policies that had been evolving under Labour, coalition, and Conservative governments.[1] By requiring employers, landlords, health services, and banks to demand evidence of citizenship before offering housing, employment, healthcare, or financial services, these hostile measures sought to make living in Britain as difficult as possible for immigrants without legal status. Over time, access points for the fundamentals of life became quasi-checkpoints, extending the authority of border enforcement by recruiting new agents into its regime of truth. What Walter Benjamin had once called "law-preserving violence"[2] became an expanded threat endowed with a kind of police power conferred on banks, landlords, human resources departments, and hospitals.

Britain is hardly alone in adopting such an expansive purview of immigrant surveillance. It merely exemplifies a pattern of anti-immigration and anti-minoritarian policies also taking shape in other places, including the United States, France, Scandinavia, Hungary, and India—a global drift toward cultivating the homeland as a hostile environment for outsiders. With their insistence on "fairness" and enforcement, such policies claim moral grounds. Like the spectral "welfare queen" of Ronald Reagan's America, the undocumented immigrant is assumed to be an immoral person feeding off the largesse (however diminished) of public services and employment opportunities. Trump's second administration has added new dimensions to this kind of moral panic by making a repressive definition of antisemitism central to its revocation of student visas and its attacks on universities. "Hostile environment" is a bureaucratic and legalistic phrase, one that crops up in situations as disparate as military combat and espionage, workplace management ("hostile work environment"), neoliberal economics (by describing all conditions detrimental to the free movements of capital), and sexual harassment.[3] In most discourses, a hostile environment is something to be avoided and accounted for—or, if unavoidable, negotiated and managed through combat, harm reduction, or accountability. Where migrants or minorities are concerned, countries actively seek to turn themselves into hostile environments for particular people.

The dynamics of narcissism, aggression, and collective assertion of cultural identity are abundantly clear in majoritarian and patriotic politics that call for a punishing form of authority. These border politics shore up a regime of exposure, a regime that scrutinizes and polices immigrant communities even as it produces the (racial) majority population as vulnerable to danger. Theresa May's policies, while aiming to create a hostile environment for some, assumed that Britain was already a hostile environment for majoritarian populations, whose forms of enjoyment might be threatened by migrants seeking legal status. The political unconscious of these and similar policies aligns with the paranoid politics of racial conspiracy theory. Insofar as a hostile environment designates a conflict or a danger, one that resolves into a subject facing off with another entity in a drama of aggression, its invocation is always to some extent a matter of sovereignty—personal, national, or some combination of the two. For their part, migrants and refugees naturally respond with heightened vigilance and paranoia, since they are being targeted by both official policy and popular sentiment.

People who cross borders can manifest the force of border politics quite acutely. These populations must remain cognizant of the dangers and possibilities of border crossing. Diplomats and spies negotiate border politics wherever they go. They are powerful insiders when at home, yet outside of their home country's borders, all environments are potentially hostile environments for them. If they are spies, they have transgressed a foreign border to gather information. Spies are necessarily combating enemies and are themselves enemies to the governments or group they surveil—always potentially exposed (CIA training includes a course on "hostile environments")—and paranoia becomes an occupational necessity. For these state employees, the juridical exemptions or inclusions entailed in living abroad, the lived realities of expat enclaves, and the psychosocially produced sense of one's identity are all continuous. Similarly, asylum seekers and undocumented people also carry the border with them. They are juridically, culturally, and socially marked as *not* belonging to the country in which they are living. Should a refugee be permitted to apply for asylum (since not all refugees qualify), then the border between the country of origin and the country of possible asylum becomes all the more charged through a legal process which tries to ascertain the truth of the threat posed to the asylum seeker in their home country. The psychosocial experience of the border for refugees is simultaneously a juridical and institutional reality, as with diplomats, but with a critical difference: for diplomats, this institutional reality ensures protection, while for refugees, it restricts or questions state protection. In these contexts, authority sutures the psychosocial to the juridical. This suturing, moreover, is a bodily matter: assessments of belonging and nationhood govern what kinds of bodies are deemed insiders or outsiders, and borders leave their marks on bodies themselves.

In recent years, strange mystery illnesses have emerged in American diplomats and spies serving abroad, and among specific communities of asylum seekers in Sweden. These illnesses—and the truth claims underlying the means for treating them—are instructive for understanding the expanded field of border politics. Border politics have always extended to the body, which is most evident in the kinds of care national authorities extend to their citizenry, but materialize more subtly and mysteriously in the interfaces across psyche, soma, and the environment. Border politics shape and mark the body not only on its surfaces, but also in its internal processes—from a mind's rational thought to the forms of consciousness that condition thinking itself. This chapter takes up limit cases—unusual phenomena among very small populations—because their anomalous status makes them fertile for understanding the operations of truth in border psychopolitics.

II. Havana Syndrome

In March 2017, Tina Onafur, an employee in the American Foreign Service Office at the recently opened American Embassy in Havana, Cuba, stood at her kitchen sink doing dishes when she felt attacked. As a foreign service employee, she was aware of being under surveillance by the Cuban government, which had stationed guards near the residence complex for American staff. In her description of the incident years later, she recalls:

> . . . all of a sudden, with no reason or explanation, I felt like I was being struck with something. It was nothing tangible. It was just a

sensation. And it was an overwhelming sense of anxiety, pressure completely inexplicable, and then pain that I have never felt before in my life or hadn't at that point. Mostly in my head and in my eyes. . . . It's like I'd been seized by some invisible hand and I couldn't move.[4]

The next day Onafur had trouble reading the text on a cereal box when serving her kids breakfast. Disorientation, fatigue, headaches, and visual disturbances became, over time, chronic symptoms. She was neither the first, nor the only, American stationed in Havana to experience these symptoms. The illness afflicted men and women alike. When the symptoms began, many patients recalled hearing a piercing sound, or feeling as if they were standing in some kind of energy beam. While the symptoms would usually abate when they "got off the X" (in military parlance, moved away from the area of attack), some suffered chronic symptoms similar to concussions: ongoing or periodic disorientation, fuzzy thinking, fatigue, blurred vision, and migraines.

Patient zero, a CIA agent, was stationed in Cuba soon after Barack Obama reestablished diplomatic ties with the country in 2016. His symptoms began after Donald Trump was first elected president and announced that he would be rolling back Obama's diplomatic initiatives in Cuba. Fidel Castro had recently died, and the future of the embassy, as well as the future of Cuba, seemed briefly to hang in the balance. One night, the CIA agent was in his apartment when he heard a piercing sound and felt pressure in his head, which lead to a debilitating headache and disorientation. He moved away from the "X," as his CIA training on hostile environments had taught him, and the pressure subsided, but the symptoms never quite went away. Over time, the symptoms proved chronic, and he had to retire early. Regarding the relatively small outpost of the American embassy in Havana in 2017, journalist Adam Entous reported that "almost everybody" was affected, and when the ambassador openly informed all employees of these incidents, even more employees came forward with accounts of having suffered similar incidents.[5]

In March 2023, the CIA and six other intelligence agencies released a report concluding that the US State Department employees and CIA agents who experienced what the report called "Anomalous Health Incidents" (AHIs)—symptoms of which were popularly known as the "Havana

Syndrome"—were *not* being attacked by a foreign adversary, and their medical conditions were *not* the result of a directed energy weapon.[6] Just days after this report, the Defense Department issued a press release explaining that it would, nevertheless, continue its research into AHIs, keeping open the possibility that a weapon targeting US personnel abroad might be involved. The Pentagon would plan to develop "defenses" against AHIs, which eventually afflicted over a thousand American spies and diplomats since their first emergence in Havana in 2016.[7]

The cluster of symptoms that initially coalesced under the name Havana Syndrome were the following: a relatively sudden onset of pressure in the head, disorientation, vertigo, tinnitus, visual impairment, and, in some cases, vomiting. A handful of these early patients (including Tina Onafur) were sent to University of Pennsylvania for medical assessment. The Cuban government expressed concern and explained that they were not responsible for any attacks on US personnel. A Cuban investigation into the phenomena analyzed the ringing sound recorded by patient zero when he first felt the symptoms, concluding he had recorded the mating call of the Indies short-tail cricket—among the loudest cricket calls in the world.

American personnel in Havana live in highly fortified communities that are impermeable except to Cuban intelligence agents, whose techniques of spy-craft have long been admired and feared by the CIA. Spies expect to be under surveillance, and the truth of their activities is always subject to discovery. Embassy employees in "hostile" countries are used to arriving home to find signs of intrusion: a toilet unflushed, a cigarette snuffed out in an unusual place. Such signs are reminders of being watched, indicating the presence of an authority other than the protective authority of the United States.[8] These signs are understood as a shared language: by demonstrating a breach, they call for continued vigilance; by creating an ultimately harmless disturbance, they signify a code of honor among spies. Foreign service personnel report growing used to such intrusions.

Since no credible motive could be found for Cubans to target American personnel with directed weapons, US spy agencies settled on Russia and perhaps China as likely culprits. Still, guided in part by ever-vigilant Cold Warriors in charge of the State Department and the CIA, and with an increasing number of US diplomats and spies experiencing AHIs, Trump's administration closed the US embassy in Cuba in 2018. Some Trump officials argued that whatever caused AHIs should be taken as an act of war. The embassy did not re-open until January 2023, under Joe Biden's presidency.

The University of Pennsylvania doctors, who treated the first patients returning from Havana in 2016, found their brain imaging results so anomalous they did not know what to call the illness. Doctors and patients referred to it as "The Thing." The brain scans corroborated concussion-like results but, notably, without the biomarkers of physical injury that accompany scans of concussed brains. Doctors sometimes referred to the illness as the "immaculate concussion." The study the doctors published in the prestigious medical journal JAMA would be widely discredited by other scientists, and the journal's editorial board distanced itself from the study due to its questionable and somewhat wishful methodology.[9]

In June 2022, the Biden administration granted the suffering agency employees upwards of $100,000 in compensation—thanks to the Helping American Victims Afflicted by Neurological Attacks (HAVANA) Act, which passed both the House and the Senate with a unanimous vote, a miraculous feat in 2022. Symptoms had spread among American foreign service staff across the world: since 2016, AHIs have occurred in China, Russia, Colombia, India, Vietnam, Australia, the United Kingdom, Poland, Taiwan, Kyrgyzstan, Uzbekistan, Austria, and in the US (on the White House grounds). AHIs mostly affect American diplomats and spies—with some scattered cases among Canadian diplomats.

Each time a fact about AHIs is established by a medical or governmental report, it is quickly contested by additional reports. In the more than ten years since the first cases of AHIs—with over a thousand people affected (accurate estimates not being possible since doctors cannot agree on diagnoses of all susceptible cases)—there is still no consensus across, or within, these games of truth.[10] The lack of consensus—and the penumbra of mystery regarding this phenomenon—provides some explanation for the overly nebulous label, Anomalous Health Incidents. That designation seems to indicate with certainty what makes these health incidents "anomalous." We might ask, though, against the background of what kinds of normative illnesses are these health incidents "anomalous"? Also, if AHIs concern "incidents" rather than a syndrome, the label suggests that the anomaly attaches to an event rather than to a person. It also suggests that for anyone experiencing symptoms, that experience does not persist over time as it would for a syndrome or a disease but has the piercing character of a singular incident. As with any diagnostic label, "AHI" is an interpretation with its own coercive force. Those who suffer from ongoing symptoms designated as AHIs regularly complain of governmental cover-up. Regardless, this phenomenon is one whose fundamental facts are repeatedly thrown into crisis.

Medical claims surrounding AHIs are conflicting. Usually, the claims are so qualified they can hardly be called claims at all. The only medical fact that can be established with certainty is the suffering of the presenting patients. These subjects consistently fail the most basic tests of cognitive skill and proprioception; experience extreme headaches; and suffer tinnitus, blurry vision, and brain fog. The FBI's behavioral unit deemed the phenomenon a "mass psychogenic illness," but when the agency was criticized for relying on transcripts of patient testimony without examining the patients' bodies, the report was retracted. Scientists ruled out the possibility that a sonic weapon—an initial hypothesis—could cause brain injury or be directed in such a surgical manner.

A recent study by the National Academies of Sciences, Engineering, and Medicine (NASEM), however, concluded that it is plausible that "directed, pulsed radio frequency energy" could have caused the symptoms.[11] As it happens, the Pentagon itself has been developing a pulsed frequency energy weapon since the 1990s, and a patent was issued for such a device. The United States, therefore, could conceivably have and use such a weapon, but intelligence agencies report that China and Russia do not have this technology. The same NASEM report also does not rule *out* the possibility that this phenomenon could be an example of mass psychogenic illness, noting that the committee was "not able to reach a conclusion about mass psychogenic illness as a possible cause of the events in Cuba or elsewhere."[12] We are left to assume, then, that it remains an open question.

There is strenuous opposition among patients and doctors to the assessment that this could be mass psychogenic illness, because to them, the diagnosis suggests that the suffering is unreal and merely imagined—though this judgment misunderstands psychogenic illnesses. What is at stake is the truth of the suffering, so the search for "hard facts" and biomarkers continues apace. Yet, this positive evidence remains as elusive as the existence of an energy beam weapon that might plausibly zap American personnel in fortified houses, hotel rooms, and even on the Ellipse on the

White House grounds (a case reported, then contested). In addition, established facts have proven difficult for several reinforcing reasons: governmental agencies operate secretively among themselves; those afflicted by an AHI have committed to various forms of secrecy; and diagnosis of an illness evades institutionalized medicine. Some cases were later attributed to food poisoning or migraines, and other cases previously rejected were diagnosed as AHIs as diagnostic criteria evolved.

Scientists have not yet been able to determine with certainty what causes this cluster of symptoms, and it is possible that some combination of environmental or extra-subjective causes for illness might still be found. Yet, a stark opposition—between physiological and psychological explanations for illness—has structured journalistic, governmental, and medical discourses. Not only is this opposition untenable, it also turns on a deleterious moralizing tone and an implicit judgment. If illness has a psychological component, then it must not be fully physiological, and therefore those suffering from it are merely malingering, which renders them immoral subjects undeserving of sympathy, resources, and attention.

A former CIA agent afflicted by Havana Syndrome when stationed in Moscow, and a public advocate for those suffering from it, Marc Polymeropoulos speaks about "the moral injury that a lot of us suffered when you're not believed, you know you're physically hurt yet people are not believing you."[13] Neurologists, patients, governmental agencies, and journalists might disagree about AHIs, but their games of truth assume that a psychological etiology is morally dubious and, consequently, that a psychogenic illness is "unreal." Advocates for the victims suffering from the syndrome, in turn, argue for exclusively physiological origins, claiming an unshakable belief in the division between psyche and soma.

The psyche is not some abstract miasma that hovers over the body, however, but inheres in the body itself. Additionally, bodies themselves are also, to use feminist theorist Elizabeth Wilson's language, "strange matter." Citing "biofeedback [and] neurofeedback training," even Marc Polymeropoulos has noted, "There's the *softer side of medicine* and that, for the special operations community, for traumatic brain injury, has really helped."[14] Polymeropoulos is one of the staunchest supporters of "hard" physiological etiology, but he concedes that "softer" therapies, which address the interface of the psyche with the body, have alleviated the victims' suffering. If "softer" therapies alleviate the symptoms of AHIs, it suggests that bodies are not merely passive and inert matter at the disposal of psychical processes—the mind in full control of bodily matter—but instead, bodies are engaged with, and honed by, psychic, environmental, and somatic processes with more wayward effects. A socially inflected psychoanalysis would have to consider bodily symptoms as not only representations of psychical realities, but also as efforts to resolve a disturbance that interfaces across these three interconnected poles of psyche, soma, and environment. Following the tracks of such psychoanalytic games of truth, while adjusting them to the parameters of this situation, bodily symptoms could be seen as more than mere ciphers of psychic conflict: they also mark a biopsychosocial solution to a given situation.

For the exposed and persecuted American spies in Havana, the adversary was both invincible (because Cuban intelligence is known to be among the most skilled in the world) and shapeless (because Cuban intelligence could be a proxy for Russian or Chinese intelligence). With the election of Donald Trump and the death of Fidel Castro in the same year, the opening of the embassy felt even more precarious to the staff: a mood of uncertainty, a sense of persecution, and the pressure of constant scrutiny pervaded their lives. Crucially, the persecuting agencies multiplied: alongside the usual foreign adversaries to whom one must impute advanced powers, one's own government had become hostile, threatening one's professional advancement by shutting down the embassy. The environment became unpredictable both inside and outside, its demands increasingly conflicted. How to comport oneself when the malevolent force is not locatable? For these subjects, exposure was a mood that became so inescapable that even the body committed to it.[15]

The invisible hand that reaches from somewhere in the environment—and trespasses into the body—might be explained as a stress response or as the biopsychosocial manifestation of an aspect of reality. These explanations ring true, yet they are not fully satisfactory. "Stress" is too generic an explanation for this limit case, and the body is not merely reflecting a social reality like a mirror. The body is, we might say, continuous with that social reality. But how so? The conceptual field that psychoanalysis offers about the interface of soma and psyche helps to develop this claim of the body's continuity with social reality—as a part, indeed, of the expanded field of border politics. But mind you, psychoanalysis does not settle the matter either.

III. Hysteria

Psychoanalysis assumes a continuous relation between the mind and body, which challenges problematic Cartesian assumptions about their separation. Many medical specialists and academic scholars have sought to overcome Cartesian dualism since it leads to many fallacious judgments—not the least of which that physiological problems are authentic and true ("hard"), while other kinds of suffering are unreal or somehow under the control of the sufferer ("soft"). The insistence on the inadequacy of Cartesian formulations is necessary, but it can risk ignoring a third element at play alongside the body and the mind: the environment in which the body-mind organism lives. Critiques of Cartesian dualism seek to dismantle the wall between body and mind, but they can, nevertheless, share the Cartesian assumption that consciousness is a matter of dual (if entwined) entities. Medical assessments about AHIs and similar illnesses are likewise split between those that adduce purely physiological origins and those that emphasize the interaction of the psyche with the body ("Functional Neurological Disorder" and "Mass Psychogenic Illness").

"Psychogenic" suggests the origin (genesis) of the ailment is psychical. However, not all specialists who use the term "psychogenic" emphasize that psyches are socially conditioned. This fact is critical to parsing mystery illnesses, which are not infectious like pathogenic illnesses although they can be communicated socially yet selectively. These maladies are mimetically reproduced neither consciously nor intentionally. They wander not only across the imagined border between psyche and soma, but also traverse the permeable fabric of social relations. Psychic distress takes somatic form and originates in the history of interactions with people, things, institutions, and structures. The world, the environment, and exterior reality are not givens—not merely inert backdrops to life. Taken together, these comprise heterogenous social relations, environmental factors, forms of authority, and political-economic processes, any of which might become salient in the interface between consciousness and the world.

Even when it challenges Cartesian thinking, clinical psychoanalysis has paid too little attention to social and political processes that make up the environment that mind-bodies inhabit. This non-Cartesian psychoanalytic understanding of consciousness is focalized most sharply in its discourse on hysteria—an early preoccupation for Freud, one that even predates the word "psychoanalysis." Hysteria, that much maligned illness, has always indicated the struggles of integration across body and mind, the world and time. Simply put, the classic psychoanalytic formulation of hysteria articulates how a physical symptom (a facial twitch, a paralyzed limb)—for which no physiological cause can be determined—can be understood as the effect of an unfulfilled unconscious wish. Prevented by the ego from becoming conscious yet still carrying its emotional charge, this wish persists and changes modalities to appear as a physical expression on the body. Contemporary diagnostic language retains this expressive form. In the most recent edition of the *Diagnostic and Statistical Manual of Mental Disorders* (DSM-5), hysteria is now called a "conversion disorder."

Freud observed how the delusional thoughts of the paranoid mind and the bodily symptoms of the hysteric share analogous psychical structures. The difference, as he succinctly explains, is that a paranoiac's delusional fantasies have become conscious while the hysteric suffers from an unconscious fantasy. The hysteric's bodily symptom expresses a rebus, a puzzle, for a fantasy out of conscious reach.[16] Freud's overly symmetrical opposition, however, obfuscates more than it illuminates. A paranoid fantasy might be delusional, but the conscious articulation of this delusion in no way suggests that one has become conscious of the motivating desire at the heart of the fantasy. Whether it is the divine rays that penetrate the body of Schreber or the life-giving adrenochrome in children's blood that serves as the repast for an evil cabal, as imagined by some QAnon adherents, fantasies that appear conscious nevertheless conceal the terms of social and psychical disturbances. This suggests, then, that paranoia can be *continuous* with hysteria. Rather than the conscious or unconscious status of the fantasy itself, the decisive difference between the two is the conscription of the body's "strange matter" in the service of fantasy.

In his analysis of the Schreber case, Freud expresses the distinction between hysteria and paranoia by specifying that "paranoia decomposes just as hysteria condenses."[17] This suggests that hysterical symptoms, like dreams, are forms of symbolization—a means for the organism to express and channel psychic pain, conflict, or desire. With its persistent disturbance of the body, hysteria led to Freud's conceptions about unconscious processes and to a "talking cure." Language would not dispel the mysteries of the body, but it would become a means for mobilizing the body's receptivity.

That is, Freud's treatment aimed at reaching the bodily symptom by means of language. By attaching words to freely associated thought, language might provide resolution that anatomy on its own had not been able to provide. Such an assumption takes it as given that both language and the hysterical symptom are forms of symbolization, and insofar as symbolization presumes an addressee, each is a social phenomenon. Whether as spoken language or embodied hysterical symptom, symbolization is not merely representation—passive and reflective of a reality occurring elsewhere—but an active component embedded in a social process. While Freud does not emphasize this important social aspect of hysterical symptomology, its indications are abundant in the case studies he examined: Dora (Ida Bauer) and Anna O (Bertha Pappenheim), for example, suffer from different kinds of hostile environments in which malevolence and distress take the form of an expectation of a woman's readiness to be a caregiver or sexual object.

Hysterical symptoms can effect transformations in the body that exceed ordinary anatomical capacities. The anatomical body and the hysterical body, according to Freud, are distinguished by different logics and processes: "the lesion in hysterical paralyses must be completely independent of the anatomy of the nervous system, since *in its paralyses and other manifestations hysteria behaves as though anatomy did not exist or as though it had no knowledge of it.*"[18] Hysteria remains ignorant of how the anatomical body is arranged—as an assemblage of muscle, ligaments, nerves, and blood vessels—and what kinds of pathways and signals are required for its function: "It takes the organs in the ordinary, popular sense of the names they bear: the leg is the leg as far up as its insertion into the hip, the arm is the upper limb as it is visible under the clothing."[19] Hysteria maps the body through experiential, tactile, and visual perceptions, not through the logics of the anatomical mechanisms of the body. In Jacques Lacan's words, the hysterical body is composed of "an imaginary anatomy."[20]

In other words, the critical distinction here is not between psychological or physiological origin of illness. Rather, what hysteria reveals are the capacities of the fantasied body itself. What gives hysteria a wondrous, magical, or monstrous aspect is this disarticulation of bodily symptoms from anatomical limits. A kind of thinking that happens in the unconscious—"primary process thinking," as Freud named it—transits across qualitatively diverse modalities. Contradictory ideas can exist simultaneously since there is no negation in the unconscious. One idea can represent a different idea, or a host of different ideas, or can itself be displaced across other ideas. Concepts, images, and memories converge and transform into each other. Hysterical symptoms share the logic of primary process thinking, which is why they can vary and switch so easily, and why they confound scientific explanations.

If contemporary understandings of hysteria designate an ailment for which no physiological origin can be found, they depend on a fundamental category error, according to psychoanalyst Juliet Mitchell: "it is not that hysteria is necessarily organic or non-organic, but that our definition always demands a distinction between the two."[21] Mystery, magic, and wonder are the surplus products when the hysterical symptom escapes the game of truth that sought to apprehend it. As the object targeted by a game of truth, hysteria tends to wander past its own terms (hence the difficulties of naming the ever-shifting clusters of symptoms), just as the logic of primary process thinking facilitates the wandering of an idea across heterogenous modalities. It is such wandering that psychoanalysis has sought to follow through its procedures of adducing the truth of the hysterical symptom.

Consider how Sandor Ferenczi referred to hysteria as a "materialization phenomenon" by which the body aids a process of adaptation to one's environment—an attempt to become adequate to one's reality.[22] Hysterical materialization manifests when "the organism does not yet endeavor to adapt to reality by a modification of the external world, but by that of its own body—by magic gestures," Ferenczi wrote," and the hysterical language of gesture may indicate a regression to this stage."[23] Hysteria produces "magic gestures" for two reasons. On the one hand, these gestures stand in for a change that is wished for in the environment but is, instead, modified and enacted on the body. On the other hand, since the hysterical body does not coincide with the anatomical body, hysterical symptoms can manifest as mysterious bodily (in)capacities. Its mysteries originate, however, in relation to an obdurate reality. Why would one not try to modify the external environment rather than modify one's own body? Ferenczi does not answer this question directly, but one might assume a variety of reasons: one is helpless in the face of a hostile environment which imposes itself as a crisis; one is so self-aggrandizing or dissociative that a modification of oneself is presumed as modification of the world; one masters the ambient anxiety of one's environment by attempting to remake oneself. The significance of a specific hysterical symptom cannot be decisively settled, and psychoanalytic discourse on hysteria remains unsettled by it. In short, hysteria is the originary scene of psychoanalysis while also remaining one of its unresolved mysteries.

Like Freud, Pierre Janet was a student of Jean-Martin Charcot. For Janet, one of the central components of hysterical symptomatology is that consciousness reduces its perceptual input by taking in less stimuli while making more of what it admits. Through this retraction of consciousness, Janet argued, hysteria keeps psychological phenomenon from being assimilated to one's personality.[24] He lists this as one of the fundamental "stigmata" of hysteria, invoking the word's archaic medical sense of a pathology's distinguishing mark. Stigmata are simultaneously marks on the surface of a body, but also openings into it. These marks indicate the operations of another entity or process, so they also signify receptivity and relationality, especially where opprobrium or honor hang in the balance (a double meaning accentuated most clearly in Christ's stigmata).

Janet noted in his 1906 lectures at Harvard Medical School that hysterics were once considered to be divinely inspired or possessed:

> Is it not such persons who have always excited the religious admiration of peoples, whether sibyls, prophets, pythonesses of Delphi or Ephesus, or saints of the Middle Ages, or ecstatics, or illuminates? Now they were considered as worthy of admiration and beatified, now they were called witches or demoniacs and burnt; but at the bottom, they always caused astonishment and they played a great part in the development of dogmas and creeds.[25]

What holds these historically diverse and differentially valued instances together is the "astonishment" caused by the visionary, the sibyl, the witch, or in our case, the AHI-afflicted bureaucratized patient, whose MRI scans show the results of concussion without the biomarkers of physical injury.

As with the historically shifting nature of the hysteric's significance to society, the symptomology of hysteria, too, shifts over time. Janet notes how Charcot "described a type of hysterical which disappeared with him," concluding that all hysterical phenomenon "are ephemeral." To draw the corollary, hysterias are subject to the social relations of their time, and as such, hysterical symptoms encode historical change. Departing from Freud's "vaguely mental explanation" prioritizing the psyche over soma,

Janet considered the assemblage of the two without assuming in advance the priority of the psyche.[26] If, for Janet, hysteria is a historically variable phenomenon, for Ferenczi, historical variegation is due to the means of adaptation to environmental realities. Neither give priority to individual psychology as the origin of hysteria, but they foreground, instead, history and social environment as dynamically integrated by bodily matter. Hysteria is an engagement with, rather than a rupture from, history and reality.

I am tracking the itinerary of discourses on hysteria advisedly, because the diagnosis has had a checkered and relatively nonlinear history: considered long ago to be an exclusively female disorder of "wandering wombs" [27]; repudiated for being imprecise; reclaimed for its analytical capaciousness; critiqued for its misogynistic deployment by Freud and others; valued for its insights into the shape suffering can take under patriarchy; waned as an object of study with the rise of non-psychoanalytic methods; haunted those methods in the form of citation, anecdote, negation, or mockery. As a clinical diagnosis, the diminution of hysteria does not mean its cluster of symptoms have disappeared. If hysteria indicates a fundamentally unruly form of embodiment, rendering the body wayward with respect to social and biological demands, its own diagnostic application has been unruly, or at best, imprecise. Yet the problems it sought to name persist in new names: "Mass Psychogenic Illness," "Functional Neurological Disorder," and the qualifier "psychosomatic" all describe phenomena that evoke hysteria.

"Hysteria has not, then, disappeared from [. . .] the world," Juliet Mitchell explains, "it is rather that this world manifests a hidden hysteria and is not recognizing this."[28] Culturally, hysteria has shifted from a clinical diagnosis to an invective wielded at others. In its clinical history, hysteria has also carried the charge of an insult, leveled at the female patient whose suffering could be dismissed as her feminine nature—or, what amounts to the same thing, a figment of her imagination. Whether by disqualifying or diminishing women's suffering, these practices have outlived the strictly medical diagnosis of hysteria. At the outset of the nineteenth-century medicalization of hysteria, Charcot, Freud, and Janet had insisted on examples of male hysteria, but the category "hysteria" retained its feminizing implication. As a clinical diagnosis, the gradual disappearance of hysteria over the twentieth century, as Mitchell argues, was because the masculinity of soldiers in the First World War had to be

sheathed in diagnoses like shell shock or schizophrenia—protected from
the taint of femininity.

Likewise, maladies such as *anorexia nervosa*, Borderline Personality
Syndrome, and Histrionic Personality Syndrome would become associated
with women over the course of the twentieth century.[29] The symptomology
of all these illnesses overlaps with diagnoses of hysteria. As supposed forms
of illnesses, "female maladies" with new names could take over from hysteria
precisely because they are deemed minor by established medicine. Hysteria's
disappearance hardly marks the elevation of women and women's health
in institutionalized medicine. These maladies—and their forms of treatment—constitute "the softer side of medicine," to use the description Marc
Polymeropoulos had ready to hand when discussing treatments for AHIs.

As ever, hysteria is an opprobrious term, and it simultaneously carries
the mark of femininity *as well as* misogyny. Its categorical repudiation can
resemble a refusal to engage this double-bind encoded in the word's history.
The term *hysteria*, much like the body that channels hysterical symptoms,
designates a mystery, even as that term (and that body) remain the only
available condition for understanding that mystery. As a mark of both
femininity and misogyny, hysteria already points to a political and social
reality in which it appears as a form of (social) suffering as well as a demand.
In the rest of this chapter, I retain the word *hysteria*, because the knotted
problems within discourses on hysteria have not gone away: neither cap-
tured by purely psychical nor anatomical accounts, what capacities of the
body does hysteria reveal through its magic gestures? How do mind, body,
and environment interface? To be clear, it is neither my aim nor my
expertise to diagnose AHIs or the "mystery illness" introduced in the next
section as forms of hysteria. My analysis offers, instead, a framework to
continue a line of psychopolitical inquiry that the diagnosis of hysteria
was originally intended to answer.

IV. Magic Words

In the early aughts or the late nineties, depending on how one counts the
cases, a strange illness emerged among children of asylum seekers in
Sweden. The children gradually withdrew from activities, becoming listless
and inactive. Eventually they had trouble keeping their eyes open, and as
the illness progressed, their bodies seemed to give up altogether: they laid

back with their eyes shut, and they entered a seemingly catatonic state, their bodies reduced to the involuntary functions of breathing, digestion, and excretion, a state considered to be fatal unless the child was manually fed.[30] For some children this illness lasted for more than a year, and for others even longer. It affected boys and girls equally.

This cluster of symptoms eventually resolved into a new medical diagnosis—dubbed *"uppgivenhetssyndrom,"* or Resignation Syndrome (RS)—although the social malaise in Sweden that conditioned the rise of RS remains as yet undiagnosed. No matter their ideological, scientific, or journalistic commitments, most accounts of RS linger in detail over the images of children in its grip: descriptions of a child visited by a writer or gleaned through medical accounts; a doctor applying a common test by pressing on the fingernails of an unresponsive boy; unfluctuating vital signs of a girl whose bare stomach was exposed to ice; nonexistent reactions to intubation; the stillness of a body that merely breathes. Photographer Magnus Wennman's image of two sisters—Roma refugees from Kosovo—won the

Photograph by Magnus Wennman.

first prize in the 2018 World Press Photo competition, and the image exemplifies the scene of this illness.

The girl on the right was bed-ridden for two-and-a-half-years and the one on the left for more than six months, in Horndal, Sweden.[31] With expressionless faces, closed eyes, and feeding tubes emerging from their nasal cavities, the sisters seem to have retreated to a place where the camera cannot find them. The camera encounters, instead, presences that are only barely present: incontinent and incapable bodies with minimal consciousness. Frequently referred to as Sweden's "mystery illness," RS involved not just the children, but also institutions, discourses, and ideological battles over the soul of Sweden. These faded presences crystallize a profound and expansive conjuncture of soma and psyche, of medical and juridical scrutiny, of multifarious forms of the Swedish border. RS exposes the contiguity of detention and habitation, insecurity and asylum. Insofar as symptoms are a means of symbolization, there may be no better somatic mimicry of detention's root sense: *detinere*—to hold off, keep back. Here, life itself is detained, suspended.

As with Havana Syndrome, the facts of RS pointed to additional mysteries. For example, given that children arriving from Syria never fell ill, experiences of war did not result in RS. This puzzled clinicians and researchers, because if RS were a response to trauma, it was precipitated by a different kind of trauma than war. There were demographic complications as well. The ages of those affected ranged from seven to sixteen. Children from various parts of Africa did not develop RS. Almost all children exhibiting symptoms came from minority communities in their countries of origin, and Roma, Uyghur, and Yazidi children seemed particularly susceptible.

The clinical profile of the susceptible child resolved into a handful of loose correlations that included a history of persecution in the home country, acute trauma within the family before arrival in Sweden, and the loss of hope stemming from their denied asylum status in Sweden. Scans showed that the children were conscious yet remained unresponsive to stimuli. The truth of the children's symptoms was already encoded in the Resignation Syndrome diagnosis. In the face of psychically insurmountable difficulties, their bodies gave up altogether. Some doctors noted that many children's symptoms were triggered by the news that their family's asylum claim had been denied. Having picked up Swedish faster than their parents, they were often the first to read the mailed asylum decision. A Swedish investigation found that this illness was not occurring in the children's countries of origins. Authorities were dealing with a mystery unique to Sweden.

The journalist Gellert Tamas's 2009 book *The Apathetic* blamed politicians, journalists, and doctors for making matters worse for the children due to their own xenophobic approach to asylum policies.[32] From the opposite ideological camp, Dr. Thomas Jackson published two books— *Veritofobi* (Truth Phobia) and *Copycatbarnen* (Copycat Children)—claiming that children were merely simulating their symptoms under pressure from parents. The liberal milieu in Sweden, he insinuated, was silencing truth-tellers like himself.[33] Jackson would go on to join the far-right *Svenskarnas Parti* (Party of the Swedes), which grew out of the defunct neo-Nazi party, National Socialist Front.

Treatment for RS entailed training families on protocols for tube-feeding and other care tasks. Each family was asked to ensure as secure, safe, and hopeful a household as possible for the children. Ensuring hope and security is surely an impossible prescription for parents at the mercy of extended juridical processes they can barely control. Their capacity and their authority to cultivate hope had been taken from them as parents, ultimately residing in the hands of legal authorities whose decision to deny asylum had nullified hope. How can a parent make their household feel like a refuge to their child when the surrounding environment had already handed down a hostile decision that refused their family sanctuary? For asylum seekers, the border exists as a strangely dematerialized psychical reality, in which the asylum seeker is cast outside of the border, even if they are geographically within it. Juridical authority can, nevertheless, grant a safe refuge, often through protracted asylum processes. For asylum seekers the games of truth entailed in the asylum process inflate the psychosocial presence of juridical authority—along with the dread and anxiety of its felt omnipotence. This precarious situation heightens the possibility that a seemingly hospitable environment had been hostile all along.

After he recovered from RS, one boy told a journalist that, in the months when he was bedridden, he felt he was in a glass box with very thin and fragile walls deep under the ocean. If he spoke or moved, any vibration threatened to shatter the glass, so he had to remain very still and silent.[34] Self-preserving vigilance—so crucial to everyday life when one is a refugee—becomes a kind of self-annihilation in the form of RS. The kids carry the experience of helplessness their parents cannot afford to carry by somatizing it.[35]

As if the illness spread by means of news media, eventual reports of RS appeared across Scandinavia and in Australian detention centers in Nauru. Medical specialists are divided, however, about whether any of the cases outside of Sweden can be classified as Resignation Syndrome. In Sweden, if the asylum decision was reversed and the family were granted residency permits, many children gradually recovered. Starting in 2006, when Sweden made its asylum process more lenient, cases of RS declined. Yet more confounding, there was evidence of an opposite trend: the tightening of migration laws correlated with lower incidences of RS. Cases of Resignation Syndrome have steadily declined, from its height of about 400 cases in 2004–2006 to 67 cases in 2019.[36] This decline in cases is as mysterious and fraught as is their initial emergence.

Sociologists, doctors, medical historians, and government agencies have relied on a battery of heuristics to try to understand the truth of RS, and the consensus increasingly converges on "sociocultural factors" as a primary explanation. In this vein, neurologist and writer Susanne O'Sullivan explains that the story of the children afflicted with RS "has been impacted by poor social circumstances, poor nutrition, epigenetics, abusers, authority figures, politicians, parents, doctors and the media. Without the correct combination of these, resignation syndrome would not exist."[37] She concludes that the children are "*unconsciously* playing out a sick role that has entered the folklore of their small community."[38] O'Sullivan invokes "sociocultural factors" for each of the "mystery illnesses" analyzed in her book, *Sleeping Beauties*. She is not alone in simply pointing to such factors without analyzing them.[39]

"Sociocultural factors" are rarely enumerated or analyzed, which speaks both to the disciplinary limits of the researchers as well as to the analytical challenges of making sense of overdetermined phenomena. These factors are understandably taken to have an almost transcendent analytic power: they indicate the origin of the illness, name its mechanism of operation, and by implication, point to its cure. An analytic feat in its own right, even if unintended, O'Sullivan's account treats sociocultural factors as a kind of pharmakon—a symptomatic solution where cause and cure are one and the same—but since her investigation seems to elide clinical research and

clinical practice, its explanatory power is limited. The truth game, in other
words, is blocked from the truth it seeks. Taking "sociocultural factors"
fully into account, then, would require that RS be considered a phenomenon that straddles group psychology and individual psychology, because
its symptoms materialize in a social milieu that has increasingly politicized
migration.

Sweden has steadily expanded its migrant detention and deportation
infrastructure since the 1990s. In the past twenty years, its immigration
policies have undergone constant revision and change, becoming more
and more restrictive. In 2016, Sweden's "Reception of Asylum Seekers Act"
(LMA) was amended to legally withdraw access to public services, including
housing and social benefits, from undocumented immigrants or from
asylum seekers whose claims have been denied.[40] In the same spirit of
Britain's more aggressive "hostile environment" measures, proposed by
Theresa May and described at the beginning of the chapter, this amendment sought to make living in Sweden intolerable for undocumented
immigrants.

By abandoning state protections—hoping immigrants would thereby
become responsibilized economic subjects and pursue their self-interests
in their countries of origin—the state assumed people would voluntarily
seek deportation. As in Ireland, Norway, the Netherlands, and Switzerland,
where similar neoliberal measures were already in place, the amendment
made undocumented people more destitute and exploitable.[41] This amendment materialized Swedish state power's growing emphasis on extreme
exclusion and containment of immigrants. Backed by the imprimatur of
Swedish lawmakers, the accelerated political tendency toward mass panic
in anti-immigration discourses must be read in relation to RS—part of the
same symptomatologic frame as the resigned and biologically vegetative
child's body. RS added fuel to preexisting anxieties about immigration,
about the purity of the Swedish nation, and about the nation's imperiled
social reproduction. It is undecidable whether RS should be understood
to result from such panics, or whether this agitated mass has found in RS
a new way to denigrate migrants, or whether one process reinforces the
other. What is clear is that aggression against migrants is itself enjoyable
for those concerned about migration.

Sweden has not been immune to the wave of right-wing movements
that has swept the globe in the last decade. Emerging from the Neo-Nazi

movement, Sweden Democrats is a far-right party that eventually won 18 percent of the voting population. This marks a steady increase in popularity since 2010—the first time they won any seats in parliament, with 5.7 percent of the vote. At that time, ten thousand people participated in a "sorrow march against racism" to mark solidarity with immigrants.[42] Since 2015, Sweden has enforced tighter immigration restrictions on asylum seekers, and in 2022, based on a largely anti-immigration platform, the Sweden Democrats won 20 percent of the vote in the general election. The week of the 2022 election, Rebecka Fallenkvist, a media personality and a Swedish Democrat candidate in the Stockholm city council, drunkenly declared *"Helg seger,"* raising her arm in salute. *Helg seger* means "weekend victory," but it also invokes *"Hell seger,"* Swedish for *"Sieg Heil."* Fallenkvist later disavowed the reference to the Nazi salute, explaining this was simply a verbal slip.[43] She did not offer explanation for her body's spontaneous gesture: raised twice, seemingly of its own accord, her arm synchronized to *"Helg seger"* as she drunkenly stumbled through the phrase. This bodily automatism appears fueled not by distress but by elation, and while her bodily gesture seems an involuntary spasm of jouissance released by the phrase *"Helg seger"/"Hell seger,"* the fantasy that underwrites it is not unconscious at all since her political party actively campaigns for a racially purified notion of Sweden. Indeed, this notion has become central to mass hysteria about migration in Sweden.

"Mass hysteria," an imprecise and overly general phrase, nevertheless indicates the fusion of emotional agitation with a misapprehension of reality. Although this group phenomenon must not be confused with a psychoanalytic understanding of hysteria as I have described it in this chapter, "mass hysteria" or mass panics do operate through general processes of displacement and libidinal pulsion. Such panics about migration should be considered among the "sociocultural factors" impacting the phenomenon of RS. Mass panic does not cause RS, strictly speaking, but it creates the field of fantasy from which RS emerges. From a psychoanalytic point of view, the question of causality is not resolved by indicating "sociocultural factors," but must be pursued through a consideration of fantasy: both the unconscious fantasy on the part of the child that results in RS symptoms, as well as the force of collective Swedish fantasies about national purity. As with AHIs, part of RS's mystery turns on how the illness is not purely social nor strictly biological nor entirely psychical. While historically and socially situated, the work of fantasy moves across all of these registers.

In 2019, Swedish television aired an explosive interview with twenty-year-old Anahit Arkelyan, who recounted how she was made to lie down and pretend she was ill. Widely taken to expose RS as an instance of migrant cunning, people argued that all cases of RS were similarly fallacious.[44] Government agencies played their part in this game of truth by increasingly associating child abuse with RS. To those ready to think the worst of refugees, Anahit's truth-telling became evidence of refugee corruption, an occasion to express sympathy toward abused children, and an opportunity to traffic in anti-immigration sentiment. Among this group, the more moderate and centrist voices sought to raise awareness of child abuse within refugee communities, combining pleas to save the children with a commitment to deport them.[45] Saving the children, so this logic went, necessitated closing the borders.

The challenges RS poses to clinical psychoanalysis, the so-called "talking cure," are all too literal. Although linguistic speech acts, like the asylum decision, may have triggered the symptoms, the patient retreats not only out of language but out of range of all communicative possibility. Because this poses such a profound challenge for analysts, the necessarily diverted paths of their games of truth are illuminating.

Overseeing the care of many RS cases early on, Göran Bodegård proposed a psychodynamic theory: many refugee families were, in his view, "dysfunctional," with desperately unhappy mothers who wished to care for their children in extremely precarious circumstances. An unconscious interplay had developed, he argues, between mother and child whereby the child conformed to the mother's fantasies that the child is helpless and dying. On his account, this unconscious fantasy provides the mother a twofold psychic benefit. It enables her to fulfill her task of care, otherwise made impossible by the conditions of refugee precarity, and at the same time, she can rid herself of her own need to be consoled and cared for, projecting those needs onto the child.[46] Bodegård's explanation of what he called "lethal mothering" aligns with the dubious psychiatric tradition of targeting the mother as the source of familial and societal ills, and other researchers pointed out the mothers of children with RS seem no more afflicted with unhappiness than the mothers of children who do not suffer from RS. Alternative psychoanalytic accounts have been proposed. For instance, Daniel Butler reads RS as a zone of nonbeing imposed on all subjects considered abject and outside the fold of a particular community. For Butler, children suffering from RS suffer from the psychopolitics of anti-Blackness: "asylum seeking (if not simply migration) is a racialized and racializing process that carries the trace of blackness."[47] Rachel Peltz's account of RS assumes that these children retreated into themselves to protest a hostile environment.[48] While Butler and Peltz's analyses are based on hasty assumptions—that the taint of Blackness extends to children suffering from RS, and that these children are engaged in a protest—and Bodegård's analysis reaches a questionable conclusion, these three explanations still raise important questions even if the authors themselves do not pose them. If a child introjects a parent's affective demands, what of the introjection of social demands that condition parenting? No doubt, given their linguistic and cultural immersion, children with RS were in the process of assimilating to Sweden—at least culturally, if not juridically. So, while it is reductive to read RS as a problem to do with Blackness—not least because Black children in Sweden have not been diagnosed with RS—how does the problem of minoritization and assimilation feature in this phenomenon? Likewise, though Peltz assumes rather than argues for it, can RS actually be understood as form of protest? Moreover, if such interventions take involuntary forms, how does this change our understanding of protest?

Doctors and researchers in Sweden have wondered whether their treatments are themselves part of the problem. In the words of Dr. Karl Sallin, "The appeal to culture-bound psychopathology raises an ethical dilemma. [If] cultural sanctioning contributes to the generation of specific kinds of behavioral patterns, [it] implies that by offering treatment, to which there is no alternative, we are also, on another level, causing new cases."[49] Treatment—in the form of medical, institutional, or even juridical care— connects a cluster of symptoms to a beneficial result. This formation might embed RS into what the medical historian Edward Shorter has called a "symptom repertoire—a range of physical symptoms available to the unconscious mind for the physical expression of psychological conflict."[50] If it is the case, as Ian Hacking has argued, that diagnoses are "a way to be a person, to experience oneself, to live in society,"[51] then treatments for RS necessarily risk becoming part of the disease. Indeed, Ian Hacking's own analysis of the phenomenon of RS argues that, to express their own distress, the children imitate cases heard in the news or via gossip. Over time, he concludes, they genuinely "acquire" a "new psychic state."[52] In cases of RS, medical authority is both cure and disease. The truth it adduces about the patient is not mere description, but potentially creates the demands it seeks to address. If a hysterical illness spreads by means of mimetic replication, it also enlists medical authorities in its schema.

This symptomology led Michel Foucault to refer to hysterics as "the true militants of antipsychiatry," because their symptoms could not be resolved by psychiatry's game of truth—"the asylum game"—to which the hysteric responds by "pursuing a game such that when one wants to fix her illness in reality, one can never manage to do so." Shifting readily and prone to simulation and imitation, the symptoms do not permit "madness" to be "fixed in reality," because the knowledge of the illness yields only a simulation of it. The hysteric, then, destabilizes the power dynamics between patient and doctor.[53] The hysteric emerges in Foucault's account as endowed with political agency.[54] Yet the agency at work in hysterical materialization is disconnected from intention. In Foucault's reading of hysteria, the symptom exceeds the very game of truth that identified it and so requires a different one. Unsettling certainties like this, hysteria and its treatment require again and again a new epistemological ordering through which to ascertain truth and falsehood.

V. Hysterical Demand

In psychoanalytic discourses on hysteria, it is a common assumption that the hysteric requires another person to participate in the hysterical situation, whether a caregiver or a companion who shares symptoms. Hysteria requires relationality for the symptoms to do their work. In Sweden, asylum-seeking children who are in the country alone do not develop RS. By assuming an audience, the hysteric creates a social relationship, in which the symptom emerges as a kind of demand.

Elisabeth Hultcrantz, a doctor with years of experience of working with families suffering from RS, describes a case of two brothers from an undocumented family in the Balkans. The brothers' father hid the knowledge that their asylum claim had been denied. The family had been in Germany before their arrival in Sweden, and in the husband's absence, their mother had suffered repeated rapes from German policemen, who threatened her with death if she told her husband: "Everything was done in complete silence so that the children, who slept in the same room, would not wake up."⁵⁵ The mother held on to the hidden truth of her sexual assaults, and the father to his secret of the denied asylum claim in Sweden. When the brothers went to the local Swedish school, they were told that they were permitted to attend the school, but that they would not be permitted to eat school lunch due to Sweden's own "hostile environment" measures for undocumented migrants.

This is how the brothers learned of their "illegal" status. The signal did not come from the nuclear family, but from a social policy and a public institution. Rather than coming home ravenous and starving, the elder brother began to eat less and less even at home. This was the initiating symptom. Over time, he became listless, still refusing food, and took to his bed. He was eventually admitted to a hospital where he was intubated and fed. The younger brother followed suit. Their eventual recovery entailed both parents divulging their traumatic secrets to each other. Helped by Dr. Hultcrantz and others to re-apply for asylum, given the life-threatening nature of RS, the family eventually obtained residency permits.⁵⁶

In this instance, the social policy of refusing school lunch to undocumented children becomes somatized by the elder brother. His symptom is both a form of compliance and a demand—or compliance as a form of defiance. By refusing food at home, as he had been refused school lunch, the boy's undocumented status is a traumatic revelation in two senses: the revelation is epistemic, because the school policy gives away his father's secret and usurps his authority, and it is experiential, because the starvation casts him outside of the national fold—now revealed as a formation to which he does not belong. He tends toward a state of consciousness that resembles sleep—where he was when his mother was raped, which haunted the family as an unspoken secret. In this state, only a short step from death, the gendered violence visited on his mother is out of reach of consciousness. RS preserves his innocence as a form of ignorance of the truth and, in turn, his symptoms demand the intervention of familial and social authorities for constant care.

While Ian Hacking considered RS patients to be replicating or mimicking other cases, this example shows there is more than one kind of mimicry at work. A bodily mimicry of a social reality—losing one's appetite altogether when a social policy denies one a school lunch—is at the same time a tacit demand made to whomever feels addressed by the symptom. Psychoanalysis reads mimesis as the basis of hysteria's creative and innovative moments. Symptoms do not merely and automatically replicate something elsewhere but are instead a moment in which demands and compulsions find an expression that, in turn, transforms these very demands. The demand that underwrites the symptom is necessarily multifaceted—like the meanings behind a dream image—and expressed in a register not immediately readable or assimilable to the social order. The truth of the symptomatic demand, in other words, is not ultimately resolvable once and for all.

Medico-juridical specialists often debate whether cases of RS are instances of "malingering" (intentionally pretending to be ill), "factitious disorders" (pretending without awareness that it is a pretense), or genuine illness (a combination of involuntary somatic and psychological disturbance).[57] Malingering for the purpose of obtaining a residency permit would constitute a criminal act, while understanding RS as a variety of factitious disorder would render the patient somewhat more innocent. Nevertheless, among these gradations, the fact of not-knowing, of acting without intent or consciousness, or of being passively overtaken by the illness are all grounds for medico-juridical exemption. The child's innocence is conditioned on an appraisal of the genuinely unconscious or involuntary nature of the symptoms. Some lack of consciousness or intent is required by these medical and juridical authorities. In legal and medical judgements, the unconscious persists in the strange form of an apparition—transparent and insubstantial, to be sure, but still capable of generating profound mystery. This mystery does not necessarily impede medico-juridical assessments about whether a case of RS constitutes malingering, factitiousness, or genuine illness. Sweden has deported children and their families even when the child remains unconscious. The medico-juridical taxonomy is aimed, ultimately, at assessing the measure of force that will be applied by state authorities. If the difference across these taxonomic designations indicates a tacit acceptance of unconscious processes, it also indexes the level of aggression the state permits itself with respect to any case of RS.

VI. The Law Is the Law

That RS constitutes a kind of demand is tacitly acknowledged in medical and juridical accounts, yet the demands of children suffering from RS are, crucially, unvoiced and unspecified. One girl, after her recovery, was asked by her doctor, Elisabeth Hultcrantz, "What do you remember about the time before you became ill, do you remember anything about what happened?" The girl responds, "I remember the letter. I read the whole letter and then everything became a blank screen."[58] This letter is not just any kind of language, but authoritative language that carries psychological import and performative force, which demands that the child and their family leave Sweden. It is also quite literally the language that triggered her symptoms.

Before rendering an ultimate decision, juridical processes aim to resolve the very social tensions that they themselves protract, demonstrate, and perform. Extending over many years, asylum processes are adversarial and are oriented toward disproving the cases presented in applications. This juridical game of truth's double-bind is written into the scrutinizing procedures of asylum cases, which assume that the subject before the law has something to hide. While the cases are processed, refugee families are housed in dormitories or detention centers with other refugees. Over time, younger refugee children often master the Swedish language more quickly than other family members, often becoming a liaison between lawyers and the parents, and they are usually the first to read the asylum decision. "Everything became a blank screen," Hultcrantz's patient says, as if in a video game, where a blank screen signifies annihilation—the game is over. The ensuing symptoms resemble death, but because the symptoms demand care, they might signify a wish for a livable or less hostile world. Still, the demand is, again, a form of compliance: facing an injunction that the child go away, consciousness retreats.

These retreats of consciousness take the law at its word. As such, the law is revealed to be obscene, but in the way that Ferenczi describes the operations of obscene words: they stand apart from ordinary language. An obscene word "has the peculiar power of compelling the hearer to imagine the object it denotes, the sexual organ or function, *in substantial actuality*,"[59] he writes, and it "possess[es] the capacity of compelling the hearer to revive memory pictures in a regressive and hallucinatory manner. . . . [with]

attributes which all words must have possessed in some early stage of psychical development."⁶⁰ This primal magic attaches to obscene words and endows them with a power of materialization: obscenity makes possible the wandering of bodily substance. In this light, obscenities share a weak and formal homology with hysteria, which permits the wandering of substance across multiple registers. Additionally, obscene words are taboo— determined by sociocultural authorities that sort the acceptable from the unacceptable—and this regulative force of authority endows obscenity with its powers of immediacy, hailing us as children, who, in Freud's words, "treat words as objects."⁶¹

In obscenity one confronts the force of authority *as* a magical power of materialization—in short, a curse. RS stages denial, rejection, and retreat precisely as form of compliance to the curse that passes as a legal deci- sion—rendered by seemingly omnipotent authorities. In a feat of literalism the child escapes their intolerable situation. The in-between state of detention and habitation, in which the family had been living, converges now in the child's body and mimics that very reality. In the face of a hostile environment, the body resigns itself fully to care; the child obeys the asylum decision, and the wishes of those who would have migrants leave the country, and "goes away." RS is a form of somatic compliance, defiance, and breakdown, all at once. Falling into RS is, at the same time, an exit from, and an extreme embrace of, the situation.

As with AHIs, the symptomology of RS is a veridical discourse with two kinds of veridiction entwined: what the symptom signifies in the psychic economy of the child and its family, and what it might signify in Swedish cultural politics. In the case of AHIs, the paranoid practices at the heart of secretive spy and diplomatic work result in the assumption of a perse- cuting agency for whom, now, all kinds of persecution have become possible. The spies and diplomats suffering from AHIs assumed there was a real attack from an ideal and inchoate enemy. The fixed idea of having been attacked stabilizes the fantasy into a world of layered certainties. In turn, Trump's administration seized on AHIs to repeal Obama's policies, which it had no intention of honoring in any case, and some in the administration called for war, if only they could find the culprit.

Hysterical symptoms are corollary to delusions. In this case, delusion does not designate a proposition or belief, but rather somatic compliance to a command or belief—one that is itself unavailable to consciousness.

In its stead, the bodily symptom presents itself as kind of (social) demand: with both AHIs and RS, the anxiety produces, and is produced by, the conversion of a seemingly safe environment into a hostile one—animated by a keen sense of being scrutinized and exposed—and the symptomatic demand turns on the conversion of their social situation. While it is incontestably true that US spies and diplomats are not living in the same kind of precarious circumstances as many asylum seekers in Sweden, they are trained to assume they are being watched at every turn (and usually they are). One common-sensical function of anxiety is to ready oneself for danger—where escaping a malevolent force can put an end to anxiety—but as AHI-afflicted spies demonstrate, even though their training to work in hostile environments mitigates anxiety, it also produces it. In a way, they had been preparing all along for the energy beam that finds them.

Freud theorized anxiety as having "an unmistakable relation to *expectation*: it is anxiety *about* something. It has a quality of *indefiniteness and lack of object*."[62] Realistic anxiety ensues in response to known dangers in one's environment, according to Freud's distinction, while neurotic anxiety—whose presence is indicated by reactions far exceeding the necessity of preparedness for real danger—arises in response to unknown dangers. Neurotic anxiety can, nevertheless, be activated by any number of *real* dangers, aiming to avoid the slightest of threats. At stake in all experiences of anxiety is the feeling of intolerable helplessness, Freud contends, a feeling whose primal and pre-linguistic form harkens back to the disturbance of the fetal environment around the moment of birth.

This is the *biological* and pre-psychic prelude to the *psychosocial* object relation with the caregiver who, in satisfying the child's needs, becomes central to later experiences of anxiety. Experiences of anxiety, then, involve relations to some authority: a protective authority that might shield oneself, or a punishing authority whose wrath is imminent. Since early infantile and childhood experiences are grounds for later experiences of anxiety, for Freud, experiences of anxiety have a regressive quality—displacements of these primal forms of helplessness and danger: "Anxiety is therefore on the one hand an expectation of a trauma, and on the other a repetition of it in a mitigated form."[63] The helplessness of birth remains the template for anxious feeling, an often inexplicable and automatic phenomenon, and the latter object-relation with a caregiver gives rise to the signal-function of anxiety—a signal that aims to protect the self against danger.[64]

The biological and the social are, thus, bound in Freud's understanding of anxiety, and the helplessness that anxiety both marks and foretells has biological and social implications. This might help us to clarify the symptomatically perceived threats—real and imagined—in our case studies. An early sufferer from an AHI reported being "seized by some invisible hand." The precise nature of this invisible hand remains mysterious. We might, nevertheless, speculate that it is the malevolent hand of an outlaw whose attack transgresses the norms and laws of diplomatic protections with such force that the American embassy in Cuba must quickly shut. In this case, the perceived transgression of the law is symptomatically expressed as a felt attack. For the children suffering from RS, the legal decision itself is the malevolent force. This legally sanctioned hostile environment is, to illustrate again, an example of Benjamin's "law-preserving violence," casting the children and their families beyond the border and outside the purview of the law's protection but—crucially—within the crosshairs of its performative force. As with all law-preserving or law-transgressing forms of violence, including police violence, it contains a whiff of the obscene origins of the law itself—an originary act of violence that tautologically authorizes and legitimates itself—expressed neatly in Kafka's phrase from *The Trial*, "The law is the law." In either of our case studies, the law figures as a central psychosocial dimension of these respective symptoms.

Placing AHIs and RS, two mystery illnesses, alongside each other forces us to consider the borders between psychological truth and historical truth, or psychic realities and the reality principles to which psyches must adapt. Asylum processes can lapse into outright persecution, but even if they do not, the ever-present possibility that asylum will be denied creates a felt persecutory element to routine asylum procedures. The persecutory force of asylum hearings is all too real for those waiting for asylum decisions, but the directional energy beam targeting US operatives has yet to be historically established. On the one hand, in the form of the verifiable reality of a negative asylum decision, the truth of RS is the result of psychosocial dynamics amid mass panics over immigration. On the other hand, in the form of an unverifiable reality of an invisible and malevolent hand, the truth of AHIs creates its own psychosocial disturbances and knots in the social fabric that condense a host of meanings: the unfulfilled promises of a social contract, the death-driven projects of social reproduction as national security, and the literal and figurative disorientation about America's place in the world.

Although precipitated by the locatable and concrete event of a legal decision, RS is more readily understood by researchers as a psychogenic phenomenon. In contrast, while the precipitating cause of AHIs is unknown—not yet sedimented into a stable medical explanation—there is a discursive injunction, backed by considerable funding, to read it as a purely physiological phenomenon. Perhaps a feminizing diagnosis of psychogenic illness is politically easier to attribute to supplicants like asylum seekers, whereas it may be corrosive to the image of American power abroad. Just as directional high-frequency microwaves are not visible, except in their effects on the surfaces where they land, it is also true that hysterical conversions are not visible except as a symptom manifested through the body.

With this surprising similarity in mind, perhaps AHIs deserve to be reconsidered. The deep mystery of the so-called Havana Syndrome lies in the fact that a group of highly protected, juridically fortified citizen-subjects—backed with the force of one of the best-funded armies in the world—feel vulnerable to weapons that may or may not be possible to build given current scientific constraints. They deserve, like anyone else, to have their symptoms taken seriously, without moral judgment or blame ascribed to their predicament. What if an AHI, whatever its etiology, also indexed a disturbance in social relations and were itself a kind of demand? How might one listen to such a demand?

The US government's label, "Anomalous Health Incidents" is far less capacious than it sounds: the label presumes US citizenship and excludes all kinds of health anomalies within US borders. For representatives of the state who suffer from it, AHIs read like a confrontation with the unbearable experience of being a representative of the United States abroad: desperately afraid of being targeted, avoiding the "X" as much as possible, treating all environments outside of the US border as hostile. The symptoms consolidate a sense of national belonging, but they do not express the self-aggrandizing feeling of patriotic prowess. They are felt as a shock to the system. The energy beam delivers a keen but debilitating sense of national identity. AHI patients speak of being personally targeted, attacked, and singled out by an unseen enemy, and this fixed idea assumes, as well, that one has been chosen. The painful symptoms that ensue from contact with the energy beam, therefore, make good on long-held wishes that were simultaneously corrosive fears: the existence of advanced weaponry; an exit from ambient persecution anxiety, because the "attack" makes concrete an inchoate threat; a call for protection and care from an authority who might provide it; or a call for an authority who might punish the attacker through demonstrations of law-preserving violence. All of this is, tragically and painfully, all *too* real, and the body suffers for it.

In addition, those suffering from AHIs have felt abandoned by the protective authority of the United States. The mother country can find neither a physiological or environmental cause nor a hostile agent to explain their symptoms. Unmoored and unfixed from agreed-upon realities, they pursue political demands to assimilate a shared reality. As activists have sought compensation for the ill health that ensued in their line of work—compensation they deserved and were owed—they, nevertheless, have overwritten the far more mysterious demand that issues from their bodies, displacing that unbearable and unspoken demand onto a struggle for recognition and care. In this respect, it is telling that once the state met their demands with the passage of the "Havana Act"—compensating all victims of AHIs financially—the demands did not cease. When the government released its findings that AHIs were not caused by a hostile foreign power or a targeted weapon, some AHI sufferers returned to the media spotlight to condemn these findings, insisting on their original explanations of advanced weaponry and a physiological basis for their symptoms. The wandering demand of this libidinal pulsion continues apace. Likewise, AHI symptoms—though scanned and investigated by the most advanced medical machinery and the best doctors—continue to elude medical understanding.

Even when authorities resolve the meaning of the bodily symptoms on the basis of governmental action—whether through compensation in the case of US foreign service personnel, or by deportation or granting residency in the case of asylum seekers—these actions are based on games of truth that, nevertheless, fail to name the significance of the symptom. As a cipher of something unknown, part of the truth wanders past them. No doubt the unconscious demand is multivalent, but in the checkered forms in which it appears, the demand calls out for protection—for the state to make good on promises spoken and unspoken, and for the law to be the law. Those who experience AHIs symptomize the insecurity that allegiance to a nation is intended to relieve. Yet this interpretation does not exhaust the significations of AHI symptoms, just as a reading of RS as a demand for a livable world does not explain the phenomenon entirely. Asylum-seeking children suffering from RS and US foreign service personnel suffering from AHIs inhabit bodies that have become—for all their helplessness— autonomous in the root meaning of the term: they give themselves a law, but not in a voluntarist or conscious way. Their bodies behave in accordance with rules and principles inaccessible to conscious thought.

For RS as for AHIs, the audience conscripted into the drama of the symptom is an entire social and political apparatus prone, in turn, to forms of mass panic. For the families suffering from incidences of RS, the panicked withdrawal of security and protection exacerbates their affliction. For the spies and diplomats with AHI symptoms, the promised state protections can never quite repress the helplessness they intend to remedy. Both illnesses, therefore, test the limits of the social contract, and in both instances, hysteria is a figure for the mimetic nature of sociality—of address, promise, and demand—operating both at the level of creaturely life and within the conscious and unconscious layers of contemporary politics. Rather than dispel the mystery—the complex interface between the social and the somatic—in two very different instances of border illnesses discussed here, we can only trace the psychopolitical outlines of the mystery itself. In this way, we can better circumscribe what remains unknown about the body and its receptivity to the social. Tracing the edges of these mysteries invites deeper unknowns—a ready demonstration of how I understand psychoanalytic hermeneutics.

Coda

Psychopolitical considerations of our contemporary historical juncture entail reading for seemingly unreadable phenomena. For example, the workings of paranoid ideation suggest something of the unrepresentable, especially in figures such as the deep state or the evil cabal. Ostensibly serving as an explanation for conspiracy theory, such figures are nevertheless insufficient for the conspiracist who must continually embroider additional lurid details, obsessively document extraordinary deceptions to find new patterns in the same set of facts, forcing patterns to yield a meaning that has already been presumed. These varied repetitions suggest there is something that escapes narrative, language, or the symbolic, and must escape it if paranoia is to flourish. As Alenka Zupančič puts it, "the moment conspiracy theories turn out to be right, they also turn out to be wrong, since the (successful) deception is over."[1] In conspiracy theory, the libidinal attachment to a deceptive and powerful figure delivers a form of enjoyment that combines identification with unsurpassed power with the twinned pleasures of deception and truth-telling.

The cultural and political itineraries of paranoia are far more varied than conspiracy, though. Moms for Liberty and medical freedom movements, for example, might borrow from conspiracy theories but their political purchase and their forms of enjoyment involve fantasies of freedom. These fantasies might be conditioned on conspiratorial notions of existing bondage to omnipotent forces, but they also anticipate a new political era in which their truth claims (about traditional morality and radical bodily autonomy, for example) will be enforced by a new and different all-powerful authority. Freedom means, paradoxically, to be exempt from existing laws and to anticipate stringent future laws. While not in itself paranoiac, whistleblowing lays bare the epistemic and affective grounds for paranoia. By confirming what is widely suspected in any case, it extends the reach of suspicion and distrust by opening up the possibility that the governmental or institutional malfeasance runs deeper than any isolated whistleblower can expose. What all these examples have in common is an overriding preoccupation with exposure—an ambient mood and biopolitical rationality that privileges truth-telling—whether it is the ceaseless exposure of an evil cabal or the denunciation of unwarranted governmental or corporate power.

Foucault raised the stakes of any investigation into truth by demonstrating how truth was a matter not just of knowledge but of politics and ethics. Psychoanalysis after Foucault requires understanding politics and ethics as themselves matters of and for psychical truths. The psyche, like politics, struggles with truth, and these struggles modify politics. *Paranoid Publics* has traced games of truth that are not necessarily enforceable by power (whether state power, popular support, scientific consensus, or juridical decision) and yet are politically consequential. These symptomatic games illuminate the social order from which they emerge, and this book offers starting points for understanding these psychopolitical phenomena in which distinctions among a fact, a hallucination, a lie, and a wish blur so readily. Psychoanalysis is helpful in analyzing games of truth because, in presupposing the unconscious, its own game of truth is always conducted provisionally, ever in relation to the unthought and the not fully knowable. Michel Foucault characterized the opacity of psychoanalysis's form of veridiction as "what is there and yet is hidden, [that which] exists with the mute solidity of a thing, or of a text closed in upon itself, or of a blank space in a text."[2] Such an epistemological orientation opens psychoanalysis to non-representational or not wholly represented processes and elements that nevertheless affect social relations.

Orienting an analysis of politics toward the unconscious has profound implications since it discloses politics as a domain far larger and stranger than that conceived by sociology or political science. The language of interests, class, party affiliation, or inequality itself encodes an oft-ignored psychical dimension, and investigation of the psychopolitical makes available additional complexities that elude these terms. Psychopolitics, in turn, also necessarily challenges concepts offered by psychoanalysis. The social realities and the expanded notion of the political that psychoanalysis opens up to critical thought demand that psychoanalytic concepts themselves must be reinvented. In my account of hysteria, for example, psychoanalysis's game of truth reaches an impasse, not because the body necessarily escapes language or representation (although it might), but because Havana Syndrome and Resignation Syndrome mark the conjuncture of social disturbance with bodily being, a conjuncture that in no way resolves the fundamental mystery of these illnesses.

While considering such mysteries, one must bear in mind the equally strange mystery of witnessing public incidents whose import, despite being clearly manifest, is nevertheless publicly contested. In Chapter One, I detailed the scene of Trump's 2017 press conference in which the paperwork on display was meant to prove that Trump had separated his business interests from the office of the Presidency, and yet this press conference was clearly itself one of the tools of corruption. The press conference's spectacle of disavowal encouraged its audience to participate in disavowal. In other examples, Swedish politician, Rebecka Fallenkvist, slurred words that sounded like "Sieg Heil" while raising her arm in what looked like a Nazi salute (see Chapter Four), and later claimed her words came out wrong because she was inebriated. Speaking at Trump's 2025 inauguration, days before he would proceed to dismantle government agencies, Elon Musk pressed on his audience the historically consequential nature of Trump's win. While thanking the audience, he slapped his right hand on his chest and extended his arm upwards. He then turned around and repeated the gesture to the onlookers behind him. There was much debate about whether this was a Nazi salute—some German newspapers said it was, while the Anti-Defamation League, longtime campaigners against anti-Semitism, judged it to be merely "an awkward gesture in a moment of enthusiasm."[3] Major American newspapers equivocated in their interpretation, yet American neo-Nazi groups were thrilled. A psychopolitical understanding of Musk's salute and of Fallenkvist's words and gesture would understand the manifest appearance as significant and layered even when its meaning seems obvious. What appears as a sign of regressive fascism is actually a sign of regressive fascism, but this same manifest sign also stands in the way of understanding the emergent social order and the forms of exposure it will produce. The real concern, therefore, is not the sign's latent meaning, but the collective investments guided by it. Such guidance includes the full range of affective response, from enthusiastic acceptance to anticipatory obedience to outright opposition; only an analysis attuned to psychopolitics can illuminate such social realities.

Acknowledgments

This book began with my own sense of shock whose early peak (there would be others) was the 2017 Unite the Right rally in Charlottesville, Virginia. An invitation in 2018 from the English Institute to speak on the topic of truth-telling was my first foray into this material, and eventually it became my main preoccupation as I paused work on another book. Many friends and colleagues have assisted me in making sense of seemingly unprecedented and disorienting events across the globe, helping me maintain my sanity while pushing me toward more precise conceptual formulations. There are too many people to list here, but a few deserve a special mention for their pivotal role in moving this book along. Thanks to Sangeeta Ray (and to the English Institute) for the invitation to speak and for the care she took as an editor in developing the article that would eventually become the first chapter of this book. Camille Robcis's generous readings and her formidable expertise as an intellectual historian have taught me a great deal, and I am in her debt. David Eng's astute feedback on an early draft of Chapter Four, "Hysteria," helped me find my way into a difficult topic. Eliana Rozinov's comments in a writing workshop helped me to improve it further as did Brooke Holmes's insightful reading and Alex Colston's editorial assistance. Ben Conisbee Baer's feedback sharpened Chapter Two, "Paranoia," in ways I had not realized it needed; Gayle Salamon's incisive reading of the introduction did the same. I am also grateful to Ben for finding the artwork that became the book's cover.

Thanks to the Estate of Nancy Reddin Kienholz and L.A. Louver for the use of this image. Thanks, as well, to Magnus Wennman, for his generosity in permitting the use of his prize-winning photograph. A special thanks to Dr. Elizabeth Hultcrantz and Dr. Karl Sallin for their time and generosity in engaging my non-clinical approach to understanding Resignation Syndrome; their work continues to inspire me. Aaron Carico came to the rescue in later stages of the manuscript's preparation and helped me untangle longstanding conceptual and writerly knots with impressive ease; this book is significantly improved as a result. Thanks to Thomas Lay, editor extraordinaire, who has made every step of this book's process seamless and transparent.

I spent 2023–24 at the Institute of Advanced Study in Princeton, and the intellectual community there was pivotal for sharpening my conceptual framework, especially Wendy Brown and Joan Wallach Scott. Wendy Brown took time to help me to clarify and raise the stakes of Chapter Three, "Freedom"; her intellectual generosity is as inspiring to me as is her paradigm-shifting work. Joan Scott encouraged me to pursue the problem of paranoia as a political reality when she invited me to contribute an article to *History of the Present*. That article would become the basis for Chapter Two, and it was her critical acumen as an editor that helped me see that gamification is the conceptual center of my argument there. Generously, she continued as an interlocutor for other chapters after that point, a generosity she extends without compromising her honest, rigorous, and precise readings. I am humbled by the many worlds of thought Joan has opened through her own work, in conversations about my work, and even in brief engagements in seminar responses to others' work.

Robyn Wiegman worked through with me many of the ideas I have written about in their earliest inchoate form and continued to help me shape them as they developed, all the while encouraging me to write at the very limit of what I think I know about my object of study. The rigor she brings to concepts as much as to matters of style is invaluable; our writing retreats were key to this book's progress, and I am grateful for her wisdom and her friendship.

This book is dedicated to John Wood without whose steady love and support it would not be possible at all to write about the disorientations of contemporary life, let alone bear them.

Notes

Introduction. Psychopolitics of Truth

1. Accounts of neoliberalism have proliferated recently. For the best accounts of its cultural and economic effects, see Wendy Brown, *Undoing the Demos: Neoliberalism's Stealth Revolution* (New York: Zone Books, 2015); Wendy Brown, *In the Ruins of Neoliberalism: The Rise of Antidemocratic Politics in the West* (New York: Columbia University Press, 2019); Melinda Cooper, *Family Values: Between Neoliberalism and the New Social Conservatism*, Near Futures (New York: Zone Books, 2017); Quinn Slobodian, *Globalists: The End of Empire and the Birth of Neoliberalism* (Cambridge, MA: Harvard University Press, 2018).

2. The chapter on paranoia will discuss influencer culture in light of QAnon

3. At one point in the exhibition, information about one's cell phone was displayed on a public screen, picked up by surveillance equipment installed nearby.

4. This term has a checkered history, but its most sustained and well-known account was written by former Congressional staffer Mike Lofgren in a 2014 article, "Anatomy of the Deep State," that became the basis for a longer book. See Mike Lofgren, "Anatomy of the Deep State," *BillMoyers.Com* (blog), February 21, 2014, https://billmoyers.com/2014/02/21/anatomy-of-the-deep-state/.

5. For the best discussion of disavowal and climate catastrophes, see Alenka Zupančič, *Disavowal*, (Polity, 2024).

6. For an insightful discussion on the relation between disavowal and historical truth, see Nadia Abu El-Haj, "'We Know Well, but All the Same . . . ':

Factual Truths, Historical Narratives, and the Work of Disavowal," *History of the Present* 13, no. 2 (October 1, 2023): 245–64, https://doi.org/10.1215/21599785 -10630149.; Also see Lisa Wedeen, *Authoritarian Apprehensions: Ideology, Judgment, and Mourning in Syria,.* (University of Chicago Press, 2019).

7. Or perhaps even earlier, when Nixon, speaking in the spirit of post-truth, declared "I am not a crook." One of the many problems with the term "post-truth" is that it becomes impossible to locate a golden age of truth. I discuss the limits of this designation in the chapter, "Exposure."

8. David Remnick, "Making a Case," accessed August 29, 2023, https://www .newyorker.com/magazine/2003/02/03/making-a-case; Ezra Klein, "Mistakes, Excuses and Painful Lessons From the Iraq War," *Bloomberg.Com*, March 19, 2013, https://www.bloomberg.com/view/articles/2013-03-19/mistakes-excuses -and-painful-lessons-from-the-iraq-war.

9. Tony Judt, "Bush's Useful Idiots," *London Review of Books* 28, no. 18, September 21, 2006.

10. Eva Cherniavsky offers a subtle analysis of the political economy of derealized politics, under whose sway the second Iraq war was launched. This is a politics aimed not at producing normative dispositions that support a dominant bloc, but "the art of running simulations" Eva Cherniavsky, *Neocitizenship: Political Culture after Democracy* (New York University Press, 2017), 160.

11. Hannah Arendt, *Between Past and Future* (New York, NY: Viking Press, 1961), 239. Arendt also warned of "organized lying" taking hold of the public sphere, which she thought could be countered by institutions such as universities and the courts. As the last vestiges of truth in all its fragility, Arendt presciently noted the dangers that attend them.

12. Slobodian, *Globalists*; Pankaj Mishra, *Age of Anger: A History of the Present* (Juggernaut Publication, 2022); William Davies, *Nervous States: Democracy and the Decline of Reason*, Reprint edition (W.W. Norton & Company, 2020).

13. James Bridle, *New Dark Age* (Verso, 2018); Davies, *Nervous States*; Richard Seymour, *The Twittering Machine* (Verso, 2020).

14. Nicolas Guilhot and Samuel Moyn, "The Trump Era Is a Golden Age of Conspiracy Theories—on the Right and Left," *The Guardian*, February 13, 2020, https://www.theguardian.com/commentisfree/2020/feb/13/trump-era -conspiracy-theories-left-right. Elsewhere, Nicolas Guilhot has a more subtle and insightful analysis of QAnon and the January 6, 2021 insurrection and theme of apocalypticism he takes up there is also key to my argument in the chapter on paranoia. See Nicolas Guilhot, "Bad Information," *Boston Review*, August 23, 2021, https://www.bostonreview.net/articles/bad-information/.

15. In an incisive critique of such explanations, Jacques Rancière writes, "A political people is not the expression of a sociological people that pre-exists it. It is a specific creation: the product of a number of institutions, procedures and forms of action, but also of words, phrases, images and representations that do not express the feelings of an existing people but create a particular people, by creating a specific regime of affects for it." See "The Fools and the Wise," Verso blog, accessed August 20, 2024, https://www.versobooks.com/blogs/news/4980 -the-fools-and-the-wise.

16. Enzo Traverso, *The New Faces of Fascism: Populism and the Far Right* (London: Verso, 2019), 19.

17. This misunderstanding is common among journalists and academics. See Charles Taylor, "Foucault on Freedom and Truth," *Political Theory* 12, no. 2 (1984): 152–83; Michiko Kakutani, *The Death of Truth: Notes on Falsehood in the Age of Trump* (New York: Tim Duggan Books, 2018), https://catalog .princeton.edu/catalog/10898879; Carole Cadwalladr, "Daniel Dennett: 'I Begrudge Every Hour I Have to Spend Worrying about Politics,'" *The Observer*, February 12, 2017, https://www.theguardian.com/science/2017/feb/12 /daniel-dennett-politics-bacteria-bach-back-dawkins-trump-interview; Hilary Putnam, *Reason, Truth and History*, Reprint Used edition (New York: Cambridge University Press, 1981); Lee McIntyre, *Post-Truth* (The MIT Press, 2018).

18. Notably, Foucault conceives of games of truth later in his career, when his conceptual focus shifts to practices of subjectivation and self-cultivation.

19. For the best account of how Foucault conceives of the relations between games and regimes of truth, see Daniele Lorenzini, *The Force of Truth: Critique, Genealogy, and Truth-Telling in Michel Foucault*, (University of Chicago Press, 2023), 33–53. My own account of this distinction is indebted to his analysis.

20. The word "regime" not only keeps in view the political and juridical connotations of the mechanism by which truth is adduced, but it also links up Foucault's later discussion of truth to his earlier lectures on state rationalities like liberalism and neoliberalism, and the differing relationship of each to biopolitical regulation.

21. Michel Foucault, *On the Government of the Living: Lectures at the Collège de France, 1979–1980* (Hampshire, England: Palgrave Macmillan, 2014), 97.

22. Foucault, 97.

23. Foucault, 97.

24. Michel Foucault, *The Politics of Truth*, ed. Sylvere Lotringer (Los Angeles, CA: Semiotext, 2007), 44.

25. See Colin Koopman, "Genealogical Pragmatism: How History Matters for Foucault and Dewey," *Journal of the Philosophy of History* 5, no. 3 (January 1, 2011): 533–61, https://doi.org/10.1163/187226311X599943; Lorenzini, *The Force of Truth*.

26. Michel Foucault et al., *Security, Territory, Population: Lectures at the Collège de France 1977–1978*, ed. Michel Senellart, trans. Graham Burchell,. (Picador, 2009), 199.

27. Rebecca Morin and David Cohen, "Giuliani: 'Truth Isn't Truth,'" POLITICO, accessed December 31, 2019, https://politi.co/2Bo8FIq.

28. Theodor W. Adorno, *Critical Models: Interventions and Catchwords*, trans. Henry Pickford, Annotated edition (New York: Columbia University Press, 2005), 199.

29. In an interview Foucault said, "If I had been familiar with the Frankfurt School, if I had been aware of it at the time, I would not have said a number of stupid things that I did say and I would have avoided many of the detours which I made while trying to pursue my own humble path—when, meanwhile, avenues had been opened up by Frankfurt School." Gérard Raulet, "Structuralism and Post-Structuralism: An Interview with Michel Foucault," *Telos* 1983, no. 55 (March 20, 1983): 200, https://doi.org/10.3817/0383055195.

30. There's a common understanding that Foucault's thought and psychoanalysis are fundamentally incompatible because of Foucault's critique of psychoanalysis as a discourse that aims at normalization and adaptation. This has been challenged most convincingly by Amy Allen and Joan Scott. Pointing to Foucault's valorization of psychoanalysis in *The Order of Things* as a counter-science that permits a more critical and reflective relationship to the human sciences, Scott explains that for Foucault the value of psychoanalysis lies in its rethinking of the place of knowledge: "that knowledge has to do not with empirical information, but rather with that which cannot be known." Joan Wallach Scott, *The Fantasy of Feminist History* (Durham, NC: Duke University Press Books, 2011), 15. Amy Allen adds that Foucauldian genealogy as a form of critique is itself methodologically similar to psychoanalysis because both "rework the past with the aim of opening up or transforming problems and crises in the present in the direction of a non-teleological, open-ended future. Both are ways of doing the history of the present." Amy Allen, *Critique on the Couch: Why Critical Theory Needs Psychoanalysis* (New York: Columbia University Press, 2020), 181.

31. These include William Mazzarella, Amy Allen, Sheldon George, Joan Scott, David Eng, Anne Cheng, Eric Santner, Jacqueline Rose, Elizabeth Wilson, Lee Edelman, David Marriott, Todd McGowan, and Stephen and Lara Sheehi. See William Mazzarella, *The Mana of Mass Society* (University of Chicago Press, 2017); Amy Allen, *Critique on the Couch*; Sheldon George,

Trauma and Race: A Lacanian Study of African American Racial Identity, Reprint edition (Waco, TX: Baylor University Press, 2021); Joan Wallach Scott, *The Fantasy of Feminist History;* David L. Eng and Shinhee Han, *Racial Melancholia, Racial Dissociation: On the Social and Psychic Lives of Asian Americans* (Durham, NC: Duke University Press Books, 2019); Anne Anlin Cheng, *The Melancholy of Race: Psychoanalysis, Assimilation, and Hidden Grief* (Oxford University Press, 2001); Eric L. Santner, *My Own Private Germany: Daniel Paul Schreber's Secret History of Modernity* (Princeton University Press, 2001), http://www.jstor.org/stable/10.2307/j.ctt7sq33; Jacqueline Rose, *Sexuality in the Field of Vision,* Reprint edition (Verso, 2020); Elizabeth A. Wilson, *Psychosomatic: Feminism and the Neurological Body* (Durham, NC: Duke University Press, 2004); Lee Edelman, *No Future: Queer Theory and the Death Drive* (Durham, NC: Duke University Press, 2004); David S. Marriott, *Lacan Noir: Lacan and Afro-Pessimism,* (Palgrave Macmillan, 2021); Todd McGowan, *Capitalism and Desire: The Psychic Cost of Free Markets* (New York: Columbia University Press, 2023); Lara Sheehi and Stephen Sheehi, *Psychoanalysis Under Occupation,* (New York, NY: Routledge, 2023). See also, Camille Robcis's valuable account of institutional psychotherapy and the politics of psychoanalysis itself in Camille Robcis, *Disalienation: Politics, Philosophy, and Radical Psychiatry in Postwar France,* (University of Chicago Press, 2021).

32. Sophia Rosenfeld's *Democracy and Truth* exemplifies this latter tendency, and although it is one of the best liberal analyses of the contemporary crisis, detailing the *longue durée* of truth demolition in the history of liberal democracy, it does little more than assert that democracy relies on truth that is verifiable and is collectively agreed upon. See Sophia Rosenfeld, *Democracy and Truth: A Short History* (Philadelphia: University of Pennsylvania Press, 2018).

33. On algorithmic radicalization, see Yochai Benkler, Robert Faris, and Hal Roberts, *Network Propaganda: Manipulation, Disinformation, and Radicalization in American Politics* (New York, NY: Oxford University Press, 2018).

34. Bill Clinton's telecommunication bill of 1996 included a provision, section 230, which deemed that internet platforms are not to be treated as publishers and so cannot be held liable for their content.

35. Shoshana Zuboff, *The Age of Surveillance Capitalism: The Fight for a Human Future at the New Frontier of Power* (New York: PublicAffairs, 2019).

36. The subfield of critical data science, though trafficking at times in technological determinism, nevertheless offers valuable insights into the social production of technological development in its analyses of racial biases encoded in data technologies, increasingly fine-tuned possibilities of surveillance, and ingenious strategies of data capture. McMillan Cottom, "Where Platform Capitalism and Racial Capitalism Meet: The Sociology of Race and Racism in Digital Society" *Sociology of Race and Ethnicity* 6, no. 4, 441–449; Safiya Umoja

Noble, *Algorithms of Oppression* (New York University Press, 2018); Ruha Benjamin, *Race after Technology (Polity, 2019)*. Also see: Angela Xiao Wu and Harsh Taneja, "Platform Enclosure of Human Behavior and Its Measurement: Using Behavioral Trace Data against Platform Episteme," *New Media & Society* 23, no. 9 (September 1, 2021): 2650–67, https://doi.org/10.1177/1461444820933547; Jenna Burrell and Marion Fourcade, "The Society of Algorithms," *Annual Review of Sociology* 47, no. 1 (2021): 213–37, https://doi.org/10.1146/annurev-soc-090820-020800.

37. Freud theorizes paranoia early in his career as a form of defense, in "Draft H" and "Draft K," both from 1892. See Sigmund Freud, *The Standard Edition of the Complete Psychological Works of Sigmund Freud (1914–1916)*, vol. XIV (London: Hogarth Press and the Institute of Psycho-analysis, 1953). These early speculations inform his later analysis of Schreber. See Sigmund Freud, "Psycho-Analytic Notes on an Autobiographical Account of a Case of Paranoia (Dementia Paranoides)," in *The Standard Edition of the Complete Psychological Works of Sigmund Freud*, ed. James Strachey (London: Hogarth Press, 1978), 1–82.

38. See "Notes on Some Schizoid Mechanisms" in Melanie Klein, *The Collected Works of Melanie Klein, vol. 3* (London: Hogarth Press, 1955).

39. On the paranoic nature of all knowledge see chapters 2, 3, and 17 in Jacques Lacan, *Écrits: The First Complete Edition in English*, trans. Bruce Fink, (New York, NY: W.W. Norton & Company, 2007). Paranoia was one of Lacan's abiding concerns, from his doctoral thesis on paranoic psychosis to his later work in the 1970s. Also see Jacques Lacan, *The Sinthome: The Seminar of Jacques Lacan, Book XXIII*, (Cambridge: Polity, 2018).

40. Adorno and Horkheimer indicate something similar in "Elements of Anti-Semitism" when they write, "In a certain sense, all perception is projection" Theodor W. Adorno and Max Horkheimer, *Dialectic of Enlightenment*, (Stanford University Press, 2007), 154.

41. Santner, *My Own Private Germany.*

42. While they explain that "in a certain sense, all perception is projection," they argue that to make critical use of one's projective capacities it is important to be able differentiate between one's own "thoughts and feelings and those of others" and thus "a distinction emerges between outer and inner, the possibility of detachment and of identification, self-consciousness and conscience." This "controlled form of projection" entails mediation and reflection, including self-reflection. Adorno and Horkheimer, *Dialectic of Enlightenment*, 155.

43. Adorno and Horkheimer, 157.

44. Adorno and Horkheimer, 157.

45. See Freud, "Psycho-Analytic Notes on an Autobiographical Account of a Case of Paranoia (Dementia Paranoides)" in *The Standard Edition of the Complete Psychological Works of Sigmund Freud*, vol. 12.

46. See "Toward the Gothic: Terrorism and Homosexual Panic" in Eve Kosofsky Sedgwick, *Between Men: English Literature and Male Homosocial Desire*, 30th anniv. ed. (New York: Columbia University Press, 2015). Also see "(Gay) Panic Attack" in Eng and Han, *Racial Melancholia, Racial Dissociation*.

47. Theodor Adorno, *Introduction to Sociology*, (Stanford University Press, 1999), 113.

48. See Eng and Han, "(Gay) Panic Attack."

49. In literary studies debates about paranoia inspired by Eve Kosofky Sedgwick's famous essay, "Paranoid Reading and Reparative Reading" have led many critics to value reparative readings. This turn toward the reparative has both conflated paranoia with critique and sidelined the necessity of thinking more carefully about paranoia precisely at a time when paranoid publics are on the rise. See Eve Kosofsky Sedgwick, *Touching Feeling: Affect, Pedagogy, Performativity*, Illus. ed. (Durham, NC: Duke University Press Books, 2003). Some anthropologists and social scientists, on the other hand, have embraced the affinities between paranoia and critique as themselves worthy of critical analysis. See Joseph Masco and Lisa Wedeen, eds., *Conspiracy/Theory* (Durham, NC: Duke University Press Books, 2024).

50. See James H. Jones, *Bad Blood: The Tuskegee Syphilis Experiment, New and Expanded Edition*, Revised edition (Free Press, 1993); Eric J. Bailey, *Medical Anthropology and African American Health:*, Reprint paperback edition (Praeger, 2002).

51. Patricia Turner, *I Heard It Through the Grapevine: Rumor in African-American Culture* (Berkeley: University of California Press, 1993), 232.

52. An account of his beliefs is available in his book (written under a pseudonym), Jacob Angeli, *One Mind At A Time: A Deep State of Illusion* (Independently published, 2020).

53. William Callison and Quinn Slobodian, "Coronapolitics from the Reichstag to the Capitol," *Boston Review*, January 5, 2021, https://bostonreview .net/politics/william-callison-quinn-slobodian-coronapolitics-reichstag-capitol.

54. See Jane Mayer, *Dark Money: The Hidden History of the Billionaires Behind the Rise of the Radical Right* (New York: Random House, 2016).

55. Hannah Arendt, *The Origins of Totalitarianism* (New York, NY: Houghton Mifflin Harcourt, 1976), 333.

56. Brown, *In the Ruins of Neoliberalism*.

57. To take just one example, scholars have demonstrated how putatively liberal populations and politicians have proactively expanded the prison system

in the United States. See Michelle Alexander, *The New Jim Crow: Mass Incarceration in the Age of Colorblindness*, 10th anniv. ed. (The New Press, 2020); Naomi Murakawa, *The First Civil Right: How Liberals Built Prison America* (Oxford University Press, 2014).

58. See "The Meaning of Working Through the Past" in Adorno, *Critical Models.*

1. Exposure

1. In light of Donald Trump's overt calls for foreign involvement in American elections at the same time he was being investigated for such calls, Judith Butler offers a fascinating psychoanalytic account of the intermingling of the death drive with shamelessness. See Judith Butler, "Genius or Suicide," *London Review of Books*, October 24, 2019, https://www.lrb.co.uk/the-paper/v41/n20/judith-butler/genius-or-suicide.

2. Paul Mozur, "A Genocide Incited on Facebook, With Posts From Myanmar's Military," *The New York Times*, October 15, 2018, https://www.nytimes.com/2018/10/15/technology/myanmar-facebook-genocide.html; Christopher Wylie, *Mindf*ck: Cambridge Analytica and the Plot to Break America* (New York: Random House, 2019).

3. Palantir has mobilized its data integration capacities to deploy artificial intelligence (AI) for "predictive policing," surveillance, and for AI-generated kill lists in war zones, including Gaza. In 2025, Google dropped its pledge not to use AI to develop weapons, yet the company has been developing such weapons all along.

4. Michiko Kakutani's book in particular, *The Death of Truth*, makes a simple-minded causal link connecting French post-structuralism and the rise of Trump. Michiko Kakutani, *The Death of Truth: Notes on Falsehood in the Age of Trump* (New York: Tim Duggan Books, 2018), https://catalog.princeton.edu/catalog/10898879.

5. Michel Foucault, *On the Government of the Living: Lectures at the Collège de France, 1979–1980* (Hampshire, England: Palgrave Macmillan, 2014), 1.

6. Foucault, *On the Government of the Living*, 2.

7. Foucault is notoriously critical of psychoanalysis, though he gave Freud (along with Nietzsche) a privileged place in the modern episteme's self-understanding, in *The Order of Things*. Deploying psychoanalytic insights alongside Foucault's insights on power and truth means to work in the face of Foucault's own theoretical blind spots, and also, in turn, refunction psychoanalysis in light of Foucault's insights. See Penelope Deutscher,

"'Foucault for Psychoanalysis': Monique David-Ménard's *Kind of Blue*," *philoSOPHIA* 5, no. 1 (June 7, 2015): 111–27.

8. Lacan notes that "as soon as the subject who is supposed to know exists somewhere there is transference." Jacques Lacan, *The Four Fundamental Concepts of Psycho-Analysis (Book X1)*, rev. ed. (W.W. Norton, 1998), 232.

9. Philip Mirowski has astutely analyzed the phenomenon of fake news and post-facts as direct results of a confluence between technological change and the practice of neoliberal doctrines. In a chilling analysis, he demonstrates how the incapacity to distinguish fact from fiction was a long-standing goal for neoliberal theorists such as Leo Strauss, Ronald Coase, George Stigler, and James Buchanan. Such a goal has been facilitated by the amplification of fake news by online bots, the dominance of ad networks that finance news platforms, and the de-skilling of journalism itself, such that some semblance of click-baiting now governs all news. Philip Mirowski, "Hell Is Truth Seen Too Late," *Boundary 2* 46, no. 1 (February 1, 2019): 1–53, https://doi.org/10.1215/01903659 -7271327.

10. Tarek El-Ariss, *Leaks, Hacks, and Scandals: Arab Culture in the Digital Age*, (Princeton University Press, 2019), 176, http://www.jstor.org/stable/10.2307 /j.ctv346n75.

11. Slavoj Žižek, "Good Manners in the Age of WikiLeaks" *London Review of Books*, January 20, 2011, https://www.lrb.co.uk/the-paper/v33/n02/slavoj-zizek /good-manners-in-the-age-of-wikileaks.

12. Scholars have argued that the devalued public sphere is both condition and symptom of a transformation in the nature of representative democracy under neoliberalism. Eva Cherniavsky makes a compelling argument, in a wide-ranging book, that the liberal-democratic state has increasingly abdicated its representative function and taken on a corporatist managerial role, and among the many outcomes of this transformation is "the dissolution of normative political cultures," a proliferation of "decontextualized narrative fragments, trigger points for a repertoire of intense but *dissociated* feeling," and the disappearance of "a common, given world." Eva Cherniavsky, *Neocitizenship: Political Culture after Democracy* (New York University Press, 2017), 140–42.

13. Hal Foster, "Père Trump," *October* 159 (January 1, 2017): 3–6, https://doi .org/10.1162/OCTO_a_00277; Peter Sloterdijk, *Critique of Cynical Reason*, (Minneapolis: University of Minnesota Press, 1987). Also see Alenka Zupančič, *Disavowal* (Hoboken, NJ: Polity Press, 2024).

14. Brown discusses Trumpian politics as disinhibited in Wendy Brown, "Neoliberalism's Frankenstein: Authoritarian Freedom in Twenty-First Century 'Democracies,'" *Critical Times* 1, no. 1 (April 1, 2018): 60–79, https://doi.org/10

.1215/26410478-1.1.60; Wendy Brown, "Apocalyptic Populism," Eurozine, accessed December 28, 2019, https://www.eurozine.com/apocalyptic-populism/; Wendy Brown, *In the Ruins of Neoliberalism: The Rise of Antidemocratic Politics in the West* (New York: Columbia University Press, 2019).

15. Brown, *In the Ruins of Neoliberalism*, 167.

16. Brown, 171.

17. Foucault, *On the Government of the Living*, 17.

18. Wendy Hui Kyong Chun and Sarah Friedland, "Habits of Leaking: Of Sluts and Network Cards," *Differences: A Journal of Feminist Cultural Studies* 26, no. 2 (2015): 16, https://doi.org/10.1215/10407391-3145937.

19. Tarek El-Ariss, "Scandal," in *Oxford Research Encyclopedia* (Oxford University Press, 2020), https://doi.org/10.1093/acrefore/9780190201098.013.1039.

20. Shoshana Zuboff, *The Age of Surveillance Capitalism: The Fight for a Human Future at the New Frontier of Power* (New York: PublicAffairs, 2019).

21. "User" in digital media lexicon refers, of course, to the end user of digital platforms but "user" is a dispersed category in this mediascape, as data collected by digital platforms is itself variously put to use by known and unknown entities. A cultural and political genealogy of the word "user"— its replacement of the word "consumer," its association with the realm of intoxication, its false assumption of a liberal subject endowed with instrumental reason—has yet to be written.

22. Bernard Harcourt has detailed the social consequences of this kind of exposure. See Bernard E. Harcourt, *Exposed: Desire and Disobedience in the Digital Age* (Cambridge, MA: Harvard University Press, 2015).

23. Computer scientists have been sounding the alarm on "information exposure," data mining, and covert data collection. See Arvind Narayanan and Vitaly Shmatikov, "De-Anonymizing Social Networks," *2009 30th IEEE Symposium on Security and Privacy*, May 2009, 173–87, https://doi.org/10.1109/SP.2009.22; Arvind Narayanan and Vitaly Shmatikov, "How To Break Anonymity of the Netflix Prize Dataset," *arXiv:Cs/0610105*, November 22, 2007, http://arxiv.org/abs/cs/0610105; Wolfie Christl, "Corporate Surveillance in Everyday Life," 2017, 93; Hooman Mohajeri Moghaddam et al., "Watching You Watch: The Tracking Ecosystem of Over-the-Top TV Streaming Devices," in *Proceedings of the 2019 ACM SIGSAC Conference on Computer and Communications Security—CCS '19* (the 2019 ACM SIGSAC Conference, London, United Kingdom: ACM Press, 2019), 131–47, https://doi.org/10.1145/3319535.3354198; Jingjing Ren et al., "Information Exposure From Consumer IoT Devices: A Multidimensional, Network-Informed Measurement Approach," in *Proceedings of the Internet Measurement Conference on—IMC '19* (the Internet Measurement Conference, Amsterdam, Netherlands: ACM Press,

2019), 267–79, https://doi.org/10.1145/3355369.3355577; Dan Goodin, "More Android Phones than Ever Are Covertly Listening for Inaudible Sounds in Ads," *Ars Technica*, May 5, 2017, https://arstechnica.com/information-technology/2017/05/theres-a-spike-in-android-apps-that-covertly-listen-for-inaudible-sounds-in-ads/."

24. In Spring 2018, whistleblower Christopher Wylie provided evidence that Cambridge Analytica had harvested an immense amount of user data from Facebook's platform, algorithmically assessed the most susceptible users, targeted them with propaganda, and mobilized them to vote. Cambridge Analytica did this during the Brexit vote and also during the Trump campaign. They honed their skills through similar election interference via weaponized data in Trinidad, Nigeria, and Kenya. See Wylie, *Mindf*ck*.

25. Samuel Gibbs, "Facebook Apologises for Psychological Experiments on Users," *The Guardian*, July 2, 2014, https://www.theguardian.com/technology/2014/jul/02/facebook-apologises-psychological-experiments-on-users.

26. Chun, "Habits of Leaking."

27. These risks include having no benefits, no sick pay, no rights and protections, no break time, etc.

28. My account of gig work is indebted to Colin Crouch's insightful analysis in Colin Crouch, *Will the Gig Economy Prevail* (Medford, MA: Polity Press, 2019). Also see Ilana Gershon, *Down and Out in the New Economy: How People Find (or Don't Find) Work Today*, (University of Chicago Press, 2017).

29. Michel Foucault, *The Birth of Biopolitics: Lectures at the Collège de France, 1978–1979*, (New York: Picador, 2010), 32.

30. On racial capitalism, see Cedric J. Robinson, *Cedric J. Robinson: On Racial Capitalism, Black Internationalism, and Cultures of Resistance* (London: Pluto Press, 2019), https://www.jstor.org/stable/10.2307/j.ctvroqs8p.

31. Quinn Slobodian, *Globalists: The End of Empire and the Birth of Neoliberalism* (Cambridge, MA: Harvard University Press, 2018), 169.

32. These important arguments have been made by a number of scholars— see Safiya Umoja Noble, *Algorithms of Oppression: How Search Engines Reinforce Racism* (New York University Press, 2018), http://www.jstor.org/stable/10.2307/j.ctt1pwt9w5; Ruha Benjamin, *Race after Technology: Abolitionist Tools for the New Jim Code* (Medford, MA: Polity, 2019); Lisa Nakamura, *Digitizing Race: Visual Cultures of the Internet* (Minneapolis: University of Minnesota Press, 2008). On "algorithmic citizenship" see James Bridle, "Algorithmic Citizenship," *Exposing the Invisible*, accessed December 30, 2019, http://exposingtheinvisible.org/films/algorithmic-citizenship/."

33. Michel Foucault, *"Society Must Be Defended": Lectures at the Collège de France, 1975–1976* (New York: Picador, n.d.), 256.

34. Foucault, 256.

35. Foucault was the first to analyze neoliberalism as a subjectivation technique for the making of new kinds of subjects: *homo economicus* is no longer a participant of exchange, but an entrepreneur of him or herself, for whom consumption and production occur in the same act. Foucault, *The Birth of Biopolitics*, 226–30. For an interesting extension and expansion of Foucault's thinking in the context of new technologies, see Ilana Gershon, "Un-Friend My Heart: Facebook, Promiscuity, and Heartbreak in a Neoliberal Age," *Anthropological Quarterly* 84, no. 4 (November 19, 2011): 865–94, https://doi .org/10.1353/anq.2011.0048; Ilana Gershon, "'Neoliberal Agency,'" *Current Anthropology* 52, no. 4 (2011): 537–55, https://doi.org/10.1086/660866.

36. Jonathan Flatley, "Reading for Mood," *Representations* 140, no. 1 (November 1, 2017): 147, https://doi.org/10.1525/rep.2017.140.1.137.

37. On December 14, 2012 Adam Lanza shot 26 people—including 20 children—at Sandy Hook Elementary School in Newtown, Connecticut.

38. Alex Jones, "Free Speech Systems LLC Media Press Kit," accessed August 20, 2024, https://static.infowars.com/ads/mediakit_public.pdf.

39. Nick Srnicek, *Platform Capitalism* (Cambridge, UK: Polity, 2016).

40. I have avoided using the language of precarity here because the problem of precarious life, as elaborated by Judith Butler, has to do with bodily vulnerability, with the finitude of life itself. Precarity does not address the problem of truth and veridiction as part and parcel of the operations of power. I am interested in precarity or vulnerability but would like to emphasize how the subjection of others to vulnerability, and the cultivation of one's own precarious aspects are linked together by a similar game of truth. See Judith Butler, *Precarious Life: The Powers of Mourning and Violence* (New York: Verso, 2004).

2. Paranoia

1. Robert A. Pape, "Opinion: What an Analysis of 377 Americans Arrested or Charged in the Capitol Insurrection Tells Us." *Washington Post*, April 6, 2021, http://www.washingtonpost.com/opinions/2021/04/06/capitol-insurrection -arrests-cpost-analysis/.

2. As Richard Hofstadter noted in his 1964 analysis of what he called "paranoid style" in American politics, paranoia has a life outside the sphere of psychology, as a tendency of political thought. Hofstadter draws too sharp a distinction, however, between the pathological and nonpathological, and his designation of "paranoid style" as an explicitly pejorative term assumes liberalism (and moderation) as a grounding and normative principle. See

Richard Hofstadter, *The Paranoid Style in American Politics* (New York: Vintage, 2008).

3. QAnon was banned by mainstream platforms soon after the insurrection of January 6, 2021, and fragmented across alt-tech platforms such as Gab and Telegram, among others. Starting in 2022, QAnon-style political positions started to emerge again on all social media platforms, and with Elon Musk's purchase of Twitter formerly banned Q-influencers reclaimed their positions.

4. Robyn Marasco, "Toward A Critique of Conspiratorial Reason," *Constellations* 23, no. 2 (2016): 238, https://doi.org/10.1111/1467-8675.12222.

5. For details on who Schreber was and what his paranoid delusions consisted of, see my discussion in the Introduction.

6. Sigmund Freud, "Psycho-Analytic Notes on an Autobiographical Account of a Case of Paranoia (Dementia Paranoides)," in *The Standard Edition of the Complete Psychological Works of Sigmund Freud, vol. 12*, trans. James Strachey (London: Hogarth Press, 1978), 69–70.

7. Fredric Jameson has read conspiracies as attempts to solve the aesthetic-political problem of representing an increasingly complex social totality Fredric Jameson, *The Geopolitical Aesthetic: Cinema and Space in the World System* (Bloomington, IN: Indiana University Press, 1995), 3. Following on his provocation, Timothy Melley reads conspiracy as a manifestation of what he calls "agency panic," a malaise specific to late modernity's processes of post-industrialism and the intensification of automation and control technologies. Agency panic imputes motives to nebulous or shadowy agents to explain the lack of control one experiences or registers unconsciously. Such panic results from the persistence of liberal individualist attachments to fantasies of individual autonomy and rationality, in the face of realities that challenge precisely these assumptions. Timothy Melley, *Empire of Conspiracy: The Culture of Paranoia in Postwar America* (Ithaca, NY: Cornell University Press, 2000), 14. For both Jameson and Melley, conspiracy represents a solution to an impossible problem: representation of social totality (Jameson) or the apprehension of individual autonomy (Melley).

8. See "Opinion Delusion Society" in Theodor W. Adorno, *Critical Models: Interventions and Catchwords*, trans. Henry Pickford, annotated ed. (New York: Columbia University Press, 2005).

9. Adorno, 105.

10. Sigmund Freud, *The Standard Edition of the Complete Psychological Works of Sigmund Freud, vol. 1* (London: Hogarth Press, 1966), 226.

11. A May 2021 poll found that 15 percent of Americans believe that a cabal of Satan-worshipping pedophiles are in control of the world, and 20 percent

believe that a cataclysmic storm will wipe out these evil elites. QAnon beliefs have become as popular as some religions Giovanni Russonello, "QAnon Now as Popular in U.S. as Some Major Religions, Poll Suggests," *The New York Times*, May 27, 2021, https://www.nytimes.com/2021/05/27/us/politics/qanon -republicans-trump.html.

12. It is notoriously difficult to assess how many people are adherents of QAnon. Stef W. Kight, "Poll: One-Third of Americans Are Open to QAnon Conspiracy Theories," Axios, accessed February 12, 2021, https://www.axios .com/poll-qanon-americans-belief-growing-2a2d2a55-38a7-4b2a-a1b6-2685a 956feef.html.

13. Commentators have increasingly noted the resemblance between QAnon participation and role-playing games. See "QAnon: A Game That Plays People," January 21, 2021, https://think.kera.org/2021/01/21/qanon-a-game-that -plays-people/; Reed Berkowitz, "A Game Designer's Analysis Of QAnon," Phil Davis, accessed February 11, 2021, https://www.thestreet.com/phildavis/news/a -game-designers-analysis-of-qanon; "QAnon Resembles the Games I Design. But for Believers, There Is No Winning," *The Washington Post*, accessed August 21, 2024, https://www.washingtonpost.com/outlook/qanon-game-plays -believers/2021/05/10/31d8ea46-928b-11eb-a74e-1f4cf89fd948_story.html. These analyses miss that LARPing is a generalized phenomenon not specific to QAnon but part of an emerging cultural and political logic.

14. What Johan Huizinga in his classic 1938 study, *Homo Ludens*, referred to as the "consecrated spot" or "temporary worlds within ordinary worlds" in which the rules of the game obtain, is no longer distinguishable as such for a politics of the LARP J. Huizinga, *Homo Ludens: A Study of the Play Element in Culture* (Beacon Press, 1950), 10.

15. *The Standard Edition of the Complete Psychological Works of Sigmund Freud*, vol. 18 (London: Hogarth Press, 1955), p.127.

16. See "Freudian Theory and the Pattern of Fascist Propaganda" in Theodor W. Adorno, *The Culture Industry: Selected Essays on Mass Culture*, ed. J.M. Bernstein, 2nd ed. (Routledge, 2001).

17. Theodor W. Adorno, *The Psychological Technique of Martin Luther Thomas' Radio Addresses* (Stanford University Press, 2000), 80.

18. For the classic account of de-individuation and group psychology, see Gustave Le Bon, *The Crowd: A Study of the Popular Mind* (London: Dover, 2002).

19. NBC Staff, "Armed Man Threatened Violence Against DC Mayor in Texts to Family, Friends: Feds," *NBC4 Washington*, accessed February 12, 2021, https://www.nbcwashington.com/news/local/armed-man-threatened-violence -against-dc-mayor-in-texts-to-family-friends-feds/2540682/.

20. Paul P. Murphy and Elizabeth Joseph, "All Lives Matter protesters re-enacted George Floyd's Death as a Black Lives Matter march went by," CNN," June 11, 2020.

21. *Q: Into the Storm*, documentary, 2021.

22. D.W. Winnicott, "The Use of an Object," *International Journal of Psychoanlysis* 50 (1969): 712.

23. Freud, "Psycho-Analytic Notes on an Autobiographical Account of a Case of Paranoia (Dementia Paranoides)," 62–63.

24. Thanks to Ben Conisbee Baer for suggesting this neologism. The corporate scandals of WeWork and Theranos involved LARPing tendencies that have become increasingly normalized for start-ups.

25. F.A. Hayek, *Law, Legislation and Liberty, Volume 2: The Mirage of Social Justice* (University of Chicago Press, 1978), 71.

26. Hayek, 108.

27. Hayek, 71. Seemingly unaware of the affinities between deluding and playing, and the resulting contradiction between truth and gamification, Hayek deludes both himself and his adherents.

28. Hannah Arendt explains that the hostile relationship between truth and politics is an ancient conflict, explained by qualities intrinsic to each: the work of politics requires a reduction of truth, and truth requires impartial investigation free of self-interest. See "Truth and Politics" in Hannah Arendt, *Between Past and Future* (New York: Penguin Books, 2006).

29. Roger Caillois, *Man, Play and Games*, Reprint edition (Urbana: University of Illinois Press, 2001), 23.

30. Sigmund Freud, "Inhibitions, Symptoms and Anxiety," in *The Standard Edition of the Complete Psychological Works of Sigmund Freud*, vol. 20 (London: Hogarth Press, 1978), 79.

31. Sigmund Freud, "The Unconscious" in *General Psychological Theory: Papers on Metapsychology* (New York: MacMillan, 1963), 128

32. Sigmund Freud, *The Standard Edition of the Complete Psychological Works of Sigmund Freud*, trans. James Strachey, vol. 18 (London: Hogarth Press, 1955), 404.

33. Franz L. Neumann, "Anxiety and Politics," *tripleC: Communication, Capitalism & Critique. Open Access Journal for a Global Sustainable Information Society* 15, no. 2 (June 27, 2017): 619, https://doi.org/10.31269/triplec.v15i2.901.

34. See Freud, *The Standard Edition of the Complete Psychological Works of Sigmund Freud, vol. 18*.

35. Adorno, *The Culture Industry*, 142.

36. Adorno, 148.

37. Neumann, "Anxiety and Politics," 618

38. Benedict, Anderson, *Imagined Communities: Reflections on the Origin and Spread of Nationalism* (Verso, 1991), 11.

39. Anderson, *Imagined Communities* 12.

40. Alenka Zupančič calls this the "delirium of interpretation"; she analyzes QAnon's forms of enjoyment via Lacan's notion of *joui-sens*, a play on the word *jouissance* to mean "enjoy-meant," in which the stranger and more incredible the conspiratorial claim, the more it fascinates those who believe themselves to be in the know—the outlandish element in the claim becomes a criterion of its truth. See Alenka Zupančič, "A Short Essay on Conspiracy Theories," in *Objective Fictions: Philosophy, Psychoanalysis, Marxism*, ed. Adrian Johnston (Edinburgh University Press, 2021), 232–49.

41. Adorno, *Critical Models*, 98.

42. See Chapter Three, "Freedom."

43. Adorno, *Critical Models*, 98.

44. Adorno, 99.

45. Melanie Klein, *The Collected Works of Melanie Klein, Volume 3* (London: Hogarth Press, 1955), 4. Klein's most sustained discussion of projection is her essay, "Notes on Some Schizoid Mechanisms" in this volume.

46. Klein, *The Collected Works of Melanie Klein, Volume 3*, (London: Hogarth Press, 1955) 8.

47. W.R. Bion, *Experiences in Groups*, (London: Routledge, 1968), 178.

48. Bion, *Experiences in Groups*, 189.

49. For an insightful account of conspiratorial apocalypticism, see Nicolas Guilhot, "Bad Information," *Boston Review*, August 23, 2021, https://www.bostonreview.net/articles/bad-information/. Guilhot's argument that the QAnon Shaman seeks to rebuild a destroyed world resonates with my argument here, though Guilhot and I differ on our assessment of psychosocial explanations.

50. For recent accounts of the resurgence of fascism, see Harry Harootunian, "A Fascism for Our Time," *The Massachusetts Review*, January 6, 2021, 1–26; Alberto Toscano, *Late Fascism: Race, Capitalism and the Politics of Crisis* (Verso, 2023).

3. Freedom

1. https://www.wtphealthcare.com.

2. https://momsforamerica.us/moms-for-america-groups/.

3. "Prescription for Freedom," *This American Life*, accessed June 6, 2024, https://www.thisamericanlife.org/805/the-florida-experiment/act-one-5.

4. Medical freedom advocates seek to ban what is known as "gain of function" research, in particular. This is a research practice whereby scientists

alter a virus to make it more virulent in controlled environments, in order to devise treatments against it.

5. As Joan Scott warned three decades ago, "The evidence of experience, whether conceived through a metaphor of visibility or in any way that takes meaning as transparent, reproduces rather than contests given ideological systems." Joan W. Scott, "The Evidence of Experience," *Critical Inquiry* 17, no. 4 (Summer 1991): 778.

6. "Prescription for Freedom."

7. For an elaborated account of contemporary nihilism see Wendy Brown, *Nihilistic Times: Thinking with Max Weber* (Cambridge, MA: Belknap Press, An Imprint of Harvard University Press, 2023).

8. See Wendy Brown, *In the Ruins of Neoliberalism: The Rise of Antidemocratic Politics in the West* (Columbia University Press, 2019); Melinda Cooper, *Family Values: Between Neoliberalism and the New Social Conservatism*, Near Futures (New York: Zone Books, 2017).

9. Wendy Brown, "What Is Left of Freedom?," in *Power, Neoliberalism, and the Reinvention of Politics: The Critical Theory of Wendy Brown*, eds. Amy Allen and Eduardo Mendieta (The Pennsylvania State University Press, 2022), 33.

10. Kay Gabriel, "Inventing the Crisis," *n+1* (blog), April 10, 2024, https://www.nplusonemag.com/issue-47/politics/inventing-the-crisis/.

11. Brown, "What Is Left of Freedom?," 18–19.

12. Tyler Stovall, *White Freedom: The Racial History of an Idea* (Princeton University Press, 2022).

13. Aziz Rana, *The Two Faces of American Freedom*, Reprint edition (Harvard University Press, 2014); Jefferson Cowie, *Freedom's Dominion: A Saga of White Resistance to Federal Power*, Reprint edition (New York: Basic Books, 2024).

14. Brown, "What Is Left of Freedom?," 31.

15. Alberto Toscano, *Late Fascism: Race, Capitalism and the Politics of Crisis* (Verso, 2023), 58.

16. I am echoing Freud's analysis of totems in *Totem and Taboo*. See Sigmund Freud, *The Standard Edition of the Complete Psychological Works of Sigmund Freud, vol. 18* (Vintage, 2001).

17. Erich Fromm, *Escape from Freedom*, (New York: Holt Paperbacks, 1994), 166.

18. "STAND WITH PARENTS, SIGN THE PLEDGE. | M4L National—USA |," Moms for Liberty, accessed August 21, 2024, https://portal.momsforliberty.org/pledge/.

19. When progressive thinkers like William Davies and Naomi Klein argue that the erosion of state protections and the rise of digital media have led to

new forms of radical and dangerous individualism, their critique—though starting from and aiming at a very different set of values—overlaps with critiques of individualism emerging from the newly emergent "tradwives" culture that condemns individualism in favor of traditional wifedom, the superiority of husbands, and the sanctity of the nuclear family. In turn by reducing a host of extremist politics to individualist tendencies, one misses the collective and social nature of these tendencies. See Naomi Klein, *Doppelganger: A Trip into the Mirror World* (Picador, 2024); William Davies, *Nervous States: Democracy and the Decline of Reason*, Reprint edition (W.W. Norton & Company, 2020).

20. See Cooper, *Family Values.*

21. Max Horkheimer, "Authority and the Family," in *Critical Theory* (New York: Continuum Publishing Company, 2002), 122.

22. Horkheimer, 122.

23. Horkheimer, 82.

24. Horkheimer, 93. Wilhelm Reich makes a similar point about the family being critical for producing what he calls "acquiescent subjects," and refers to the family as "the authoritarian state in miniature" and *"political reaction's germ cell."* See Wilhelm Reich, *The Mass Psychology of Fascism.* Trans Theodore Wolfe (New York: Orgone Institute Press, 1946), 47, 109. Italics in original.

25. F.A. Hayek, *The Constitution of Liberty: The Definitive Edition*, ed. Ronald Hamowy, The Collected Works of F.A. Hayek edition (University of Chicago Press, 2011), 207.

26. This is akin to what Penelope Deutscher, in her analysis of the *Dobbs v. Jackson* Supreme Court ruling, has called a "qualifying disqualification"—it is an exemption from criteria imposed on people who are less fully enfranchised. See Penelope Deutscher, "Revocability, Exception, Disqualification: Grammars of Power after *Dobbs.*" *Critical Times* 7, no. 1 (April 2024).

27. Cooper, *Family Values*, 72.

28. Erich Fromm, *Fromm Forum 24: Erich Fromm's Early Writings. Dietrich, Jan, Rainer Funk and Hel*, eds. Jan von Dietrich, Funk Rainer, and Helmut Johach (Tübingen, Germany: International Erich Fromm Society, 2020), 19.

29. Fromm, *Escape from Freedom*, 285.

30. Adorno, *Notes on Sociology*, 114.

31. For an account of how sex panics articulate with state power, see Roger N.N. Lancaster, *Sex Panic and the Punitive State*, (Berkeley: University of California Press, 2011).

32. Melanie Klein, "Early Stages of the Oedipus Conflict," *International Journal of Psychoanalysis* 9 (1928): 168.

33. Klein, 168.

34. Jacques Lacan, "Family Complexes in the Formation of the Individual," trans. Cormac Gallagher (Unpublished Manuscript, 1938), 21 (emphasis added).

35. Jacques Lacan, *The Seminar of Jacques Lacan: Book XX: Encore (1972–1973)*, eds. Jacques-Alain Miller and Bruce Fink, (W.W. Norton & Company, 1999), 3.

36. Todd McGowan provides a compelling account of the authoritarianism that underwrites superegoic forms of enjoyment in Todd McGowan, "Superego and the Law," in *Routledge Handbook of Psychoanalytic Political Theory* (New York: Routledge, 2020), 139–50. However McGowan downplays both Melanie Klein's contributions to a theory of the superego as well as the role of the maternal imago in superegoic operations.

37. Sigmund Freud, *Collected Papers*, International Psycho-Analytical Library; v. 7, Etc. (London: Hogarth Press and the Institute of Psycho-Analysis, 1953), 198.

38. Freud, 198–99.

39. Freud, 199.

40. Eva Cherniavsky has argued that for groups militating against public health measures, expressions of self-interest become a means for channeling the death drive: "To live in the inevitable grip of one's own best interests is to lose oneself, to have lost oneself—to become, like the zombie, the evacuated form of a compulsion." Eva Cherniavsky, "Immortality Is Not a Civil Right: Self-Interest, the Death Drive, and the State" (n.d.), 10.

41. Horkheimer, "Authority and the Family," 109.

42. Freud, 200.

43. For an analysis of such content see Eviane Leidig, *The Women of the Far Right: Social Media Influencers and Online Radicalization* (New York: Columbia University Press, 2023).

44 William Callison and Quinn Slobodian, "Coronapolitics from the Reichstag to the Capitol," *Boston Review*, January 5, 2021, https://bostonreview.net/politics/william-callison-quinn-slobodian-coronapolitics-reichstag-capitol.

45. Michel Foucault grasped this kind of enjoyment in his discussion of the incitement to discourse about sexuality (*History of Sexuality, vol. 1* (New York: Vintage, 1990)), but in his later accounts of *parrhesia*, truth-telling emerges first and foremost as a problematic about the self's subjection to punishment. But what Michel Foucault called the "game of truth" also generates new forms of enjoyment.

46. Abigail Shrier, "What I Told the Students of Princeton," June 3, 2023, https://www.thetruthfairy.info/p/what-i-told-the-students-of-princeton.

47. Klein, "Early Stages of the Oedipus Conflict," 75.

48. See "Totem and Taboo" in Freud, *The Standard Edition of the Complete Psychological Works of Sigmund Freud*, vol.13.

49. Sigmund Freud, *Civilization and Its Discontents*, eds. James Strachey and Peter Gay, Reprint edition (W.W. Norton & Company, 2010), 47.

50. Freud, 72.

51. Quoted in Martin Jay, *The Dialectical Imagination: A History of the Frankfurt School and the Institute of Social Research, 1923–1950* (University of California Press, 1996), 278.

4. Hysteria

1 James Kirkup and Robert Winnett, "Theresa May Interview: 'We're Going to Give Illegal Migrants a Really Hostile Reception'," *The Telegraph*, June 19, 2020, https://www.telegraph.co.uk/news/0/theresa-may-interview-going-give -illegal-migrants-really-hostile/.

2. Walter Benjamin, "Critique of Violence," in *Selected Writings*, eds. Marcus Paul Bullock and Michael William Jennings, vol. 1, 1913–1926 (Belknap Press, 1913), 236–52.

3. In a feat of collective repression, this bureaucratized notion tends not to refer to climate change and the all-too-real hostile environments it creates.

4. "'Seized by Some Invisible Hand': What It Feels like to Have Havana Syndrome," accessed August 31, 2023, https://www.nbcnews.com/politics/national -security/seized-some-invisible-hand-what-it-feels-have-havana-syndrome-n1281326.

5. The account I provide here of the beginnings of "Havana Syndrome" is indebted to multiple investigative reports by journalist Adam Entous. See *Havana Syndrome: American Officials Under Attack* (Cambridge, MA: Harvard Belfer Center, 2021), https://www.belfercenter.org/publication/report-havana -syndrome-american-officials-under-attack. Also See Adam Entous, "Are U.S. Officials Under Silent Attack?" *The New Yorker*, May 24, 2021, https://www .newyorker.com/magazine/2021/05/31/are-us-officials-under-silent-attack; Adam Entous and Jon Lee Anderson, "The Mystery of the Havana Syndrome," *The New Yorker*, November 9, 2018, https://www.newyorker.com/magazine/2018/11 /19/the-mystery-of-the-havana-syndrome.

6. "Intel community bats down main theory behind 'Havana Syndrome' incidents," POLITICO, March 1, 2023, https://www.politico.com/news/2023 /03/01/havana-syndrome-cia-intelligence-00085021.

7. "Pentagon still probing what caused 'Havana Syndrome,' even after spy agencies found no smoking gun," POLITICO, March 6, 2023, https://www .politico.com/news/2023/03/06/havana-syndrome-pentagon-research-00085686.

8. Adam Entous and VICE Media, "Havana Syndrome," podcast, accessed August 31, 2023.

9. Randel L. Swanson II et al., "Neurological Manifestations Among US Government Personnel Reporting Directional Audible and Sensory Phenomena in Havana, Cuba," *JAMA* 319, no. 11 (March 20, 2018): 1125–33, https://doi.org/10.1001/jama.2018.1742; Christopher C. Muth and Steven L. Lewis, "Neurological Symptoms Among US Diplomats in Cuba," *JAMA* 319, no. 11 (March 20, 2018): 1098–1100, https://doi.org/10.1001/jama.2018.1780.

10. Periodically a news report collects circumstantial evidence for one or another theory about AHIs. The most recent is a report that attributes AHIs to Russian intelligence, based on a handful of coincidences and reports that Russians have been researching energy weapons; but this a field of research in which many governments have invested, including the United States, and the fact of research is hardly evidence of attack. See Michael Weiss, Christo Grozev, and Roman Dobrokhotov, "Unraveling Havana Syndrome: New Evidence Links the GRU's Assassination Unit 29155 to Mysterious Attacks on U.S. Officials and Their Families," *The Insider*, March 31, 2024, https://theins.ru/en/politics/270425. "Unraveling Havana Syndrome" (2024)

11. "An Assessment of Illness in U.S. Government Employees and Their Families at Overseas Embassies" (Washington, DC: National Academies of Sciences, Engineering, and Medicine, 2020).

12. "An Assessment of Illness in U.S. Government Employees and Their Families at Overseas Embassies," 27.

13. *American Officials Under Attack.*

14. *American Officials Under Attack.*

15. See Chapter One.

16. ". . . hysterical symptoms are the realization of an unconscious phantasy which serves the fulfilment of a wish." Sigmund Freud, "Hysterical Phantasies and Their Relation to Bisexuality," in *The Standard Edition of the Complete Psychological Works of Sigmund Freud, vol. 9* (London: Hogarth Press, 1972), 163.

17. Sigmund Freud, "Psycho-Analytic Notes on an Autobiographical Account of a Case of Paranoia (Dementia Paranoides)," in *The Standard Edition of the Complete Psychological Works of Sigmund Freud*, vol. 12, trans. James Strachey (London: Hogarth Press, 1978), 49.

18. Sigmund Freud, "Some Points for a Comparative Study of Organic and Hysterical Motor Paralyses," in *The Standard Edition of the Complete Psychological Works*, 169.

19. Freud, "Some Points for a Comparative Study of Organic and Hysterical Motor Paralyses," 169.

20 Jacques Lacan, *The Seminar of Jacques Lacan: The Psychoses*, trans. Jacques-Alain Miller and Russell Grigg, Reprint edition (New York London: W. W. Norton & Company, 1997), 178.

21. Juliet Mitchell, *Mad Men and Medusas: Reclaiming Hysteria* (London: Basic Books, 2001), 120.

22. Sándor Ferenczi, "Stages in the Development of the Sense of Reality," in *First Contributions to Psycho-Analysis* (The International Psycho-Analytical Library, 1952), 96.

23. Ferenczi, 90.

24. Pierre Janet, *The Major Symptoms of Hysteria: Fifteen Lectures* (New York: Macmillan & Co., 1920), 15.

25. Janet, *Major Symptoms of Hysteria*, 8.

26. Janet, 18.

27. Elizabeth Wilson's reinterpretation of this problematic notion is illuminating: "[this notion] has long been considered a violence against the female body. However, before such an etiology is dismissed altogether, the question of organic wandering demands closer attention. The notion of a roaming uterus contains within it a sense of organic matter that disseminates, strays, and deviates from its proper place. *Perhaps all biology wanders.* Formulated in this way, hysterical diversion is not forced on the throat, legs, or eyes from the outside, it is already part of the natural repertoire of biological matter." Elizabeth A. Wilson, *Psychosomatic: Feminism and the Neurological Body* (London: Duke University Press, 2004), 13, emphasis added.

28. Mitchell, *Mad Men and Medusas*, 134.

29. See Mitchell, *Mad Men and Medusas*.

30. Rachel Aviv, "The Apathetic," *The New Yorker*, March 27, 2017.

31. At the request of the doctor treating the sisters I have not identified them by name.

32. Gellert Tamas, *De Apatiska: Om Makt, Myter Och Manipulation* (Stockholm: Natur & Kultur, 2009).

33. Thomas Jackson, *Copycatbarnen* (Recito, 2009); Thomas Jackson, *Veritofobi: Simulera Sjukdom!: apatister och apatiska barn* (Recito, 2008).

34. Aviv, "Apathetic."

35. I am grateful to Susie Orbach for this insight.

36. National Board of Health and Welfare, "RS Demographic Data," Powerpoint (Socialstyrelesen, n.d.), Socialstyrelsen; Anne-Liis von Knorring and Elisabeth Hultcrantz, "Asylum-Seeking Children with Resignation Syndrome: Catatonia or Traumatic Withdrawal Syndrome?," *European Child and Adolescent Psychiatry*, 2019; Karl Sallin et al., "Resignation Syndrome: Catatonia? Culture-Bound?," *Frontiers in Behavioral Neuroscience* 10 (2016): 7.

37. Suzanne O'Sullivan, *The Sleeping Beauties: And Other Stories of Mystery Illness* (New York: Pantheon Books, 2021), 37.

38. O'Sullivan, 38.

39. Karl Sallin has done some of most thorough theoretical research on RS and arrives at a similar conclusion. Karl Sallin et al., "Separation and Not Residency Permit Restores Function in Resignation Syndrome: A Retrospective Cohort Study," *European Child & Adolescent Psychiatry* 32, no. 1 (January 1, 2023): 75–86, https://doi.org/10.1007/s00787-021-01833-3; Sallin et al., "Resignation Syndrome"; Jan N.M. Schieveld and Karl Sallin, "Pervasive Refusal Syndrome Revisited: A Conative Disorder," *European Child & Adolescent Psychiatry* 30, no. 1 (January 1, 2021): 1–3, https://doi.org/10.1007/s00787-020-01685-3.

40. Annika Lindberg, *Deportation Limbo: State Violence and Contestations in the Nordics*, Political and Administrative Ethnography (Manchester University Press, 2022), 116.

41. Lindberg, 126–27.

42. Niklas Magnusson, "Swedes Protest as Anti-Immigrants Enter Parliament," *Bloomberg*, September 21, 2010, https://www.bloomberg.com/news/articles/2010-09-21/swedes-throng-streets-to-protest-against-anti-immigrant-party-in-goverment."

43. Elisabeth Asbrink, "Sweden Is Becoming Unbearable," *The New York Times*, September 20, 2022, https://www.nytimes.com/2022/09/20/opinion/sweden-democrats-elections.html.

44. "Anahit, 20, tvingades spela apatiskt barn," September 23, 2019, https://www.expressen.se/nyheter/apatiska-barnen-berattar-vi-tvingades-spela-sjuka/."

45. Ola Sandstag, "Ohörda Rop," *Filter*, November 2019.

46. Göran Bodegård, "Life-Threatening Loss of Function in Refugee Children: Another Expression of Pervasive Refusal Syndrome?," *Clinical Child Psychology and Psychiatry* 10, no. 3 (July 1, 2005): 337–50, https://doi.org/10.1177/1359104505053753.

47. Daniel Butler, "A Child Is Being Caged: Resignation Syndrome and the Psychopolitics of Petrification," *Journal of the American Psychoanalytic Association* 68, no. 3 (2020): 15.

48. Rachael Peltz, "Going to Where the World Ends: When the Bodies of Children Speak Who Is Listening?," *Psychoanalytic Dialogues* 30, no. 2 (March 3, 2020): 166–79, https://doi.org/10.1080/10481885.2020.1722571.

49. Sallin et al., "Resignation Syndrome," 14.

50. Edward Shorter, "Paralysis: The Rise and Fall of a 'Hysterical' Symptom," *Journal of Social History* 19, no. 4 (Summer 1986): 549.

51. Ian Hacking, "Kinds of People: Moving Targets," *Proceedings of the British Academy* 151 (2007): 299.

52. Ian Hacking, "Pathological Withdrawal of Refugee Children Seeking Asylum in Sweden," *Studies in History and Philosophy of Science*, Culture-

bound syndromes, 41, no. 4 (December 1, 2010): 317, https://doi.org/10.1016/j
.shpsc.2010.10.001.

53 Michel Foucault, *Psychiatric Power: Lectures at the Collège de France,
1973–1974*, trans. Graham Burchell (New York: Picador, 2003), 254. For an
excellent account of Foucault's place in a genealogy of radical psychiatry, see
chapter four in Robcis, *Disalienation*. Camille Robcis, *Disalienation: Politics,
Philosophy, and Radical Psychiatry in Postwar France* (University of Chicago
Press, 2021).

54. Interestingly, Freud's famous hysterics Ida Bauer (Dora) and Ana O
(Bertha Pappenheim) gravitated toward feminism over the course of their lives.

55. Elisabeth Hultcrantz, *Om dessa vore svenska barn. . .* (The Ethics
Commission in Sweden, 2020). Machine Translated.

56. Hultcrantz.

57. Zahid Chaudhary, Karl Sallin Conversation, Zoom, January 17, 2022.

58. Hultcrantz, *Om dessa vore svenska barn. . .*

59. Sandor Ferenczi, "On Obscene Words," in *First Contributions to Psycho-
Analysis* (The International Psycho-Analytical Library, 1952), 137.

60. Ferenczi, 137–38.

61. Ferenczi, 140.

62. Sigmund Freud, "Inhibitions, Symptoms and Anxiety," in *The Standard
Edition of the Complete Psychological Works of Sigmund Freud*, vol. 20
(London: Hogarth Press, 1978), 164.

63. Freud, 165.

64. Freud, 138.

Coda

1. Alenka Zupančič, "A Short Essay on Conspiracy Theories," in *Objective
Fictions: Philosophy, Psychoanalysis, Marxism*, ed. Adrian Johnston (Edinburgh
University Press, 2021), 241. The phenomenon Zupančič describes conforms to
the operations of Lacan's understanding of enjoyment, for which the deepest
satisfaction resides in not being satisfied enough. See William Mazzarella's
brilliant discussion of Trumpism as a politics of enjoyment: Mazzarella,
"Brand(ish)ing the Name, or, Why is Trump so Enjoyable?" in William
Mazzarella, Eric Santner, and Aaron Schuster, *Sovereignty, Inc.* (Chicago:
U Chicago Press, 2020), 113–60.

2. Michel Foucault, *Order of Things: An Archaeology of the Human Sciences*,
2nd ed. (Routledge, 2001), 408.

3. ADL [@ADL], https://x.com/ADL/status/1881474892022919403, January 20,
2025.

Index

abortion, 105
Abu Ghraib prison, 5
Adorno, Theodor, 22, 28, 58, 65, 71–75;
    Dialectic of Enlightenment, 16, 20, 21;
    "Elements of Anti-Semitism," 156n40;
    superego and, 98
Afghanistan, 79
African Americans: anti-Blackness, 134;
    paranoia of, 24–25
agency panic, 163n7
aggression, 40, 67, 77, 102, 112
AHIs. *See* Anomalous Health Incidents;
    Resignation Syndrome
AI. *See* artificial intelligence
Alexa (Amazon), 42
algorithmic radicalization, 18
algorithms, 42, 44, 69
Allen, Amy, 154n30
alternative facts, 2
Amazon, 42
American Foreign Service Office, 113
Anderson, Benedict, 72, 73
Anomalous Health Incidents (AHIs),
    114–18, 120, 124, 132, 139–44,
    171n10
Anonymous, 36
anonymous authority, 88
anorexia nervosa, 126

anti-Blackness, 134
Anti-Defamation League, 147
anti-immigration discourse, 131, 133
anti-lockdown protestors, 26, 83
antisemitism, 21, 67, 111, 147
anti-trans, 17, 84, 104
anti-vax movement, 2, 3, 27, 83–84
anxiety, 3, 70–75, 140
apartheid, 46
The Apathetic (Tamas), 129
Arendt, Hannah, 7, 27, 152n11, 165n28
El-Ariss, Tarek, 36, 42
Arkelyan, Anahit, 133
Article 8, of European Convention on
    Human Rights, 38
artificial intelligence (AI), 158n3
ashwagandha, 50
Asian Americans, 23
assault on truth, 8
asylum game, 135
asylum seekers, 25, 109, 112–13, 128–29,
    132, 141, 144
Australia, 116, 130
Austria, 116
authoritarian freedom, 94, 107
authoritarianism, 8–9, 17, 28, 169n36
authority, 71, 100; anonymous, 88; juridi-
    cal, 129

"Authority and the Family" (Horkheimer), 93
autonomy: bodily, 95; of truth, 12

Bauer, Gary, 96
Bauer, Ida, 122
"Become Ungovernable" (catch phrase), 14
Beinart, Peter, 7
belief, 7–8, 69
Benjamin, Walter, 43, 111, 141
Berlusconi, Silvio, 10
Biden, Joe, 81, 116
Big Tech, 18–19, 45
big tent conspiracy, QAnon as, 55
Bildung (self-formation), 58
biomedical security state, 105
Bion, Wilfred, 77–78
biopolitics, exposure as, 45–48
biopower, 47
bios, 34, 49
Black Lives Matter (BLM), 65–67, 80
Blackness, 134
Black paranoia, 24–25
BLM. See Black Lives Matter
Blumenthal, Max, 104
Bodegård, Göran, 133
bodily autonomy, 95
Boebert, Lauren, 69, 80
Bollas, Christopher, 33
Boogaloo Bois, 56, 77, 78
Borderline Personality Syndrome, 126
border politics, 109–13
"both sides" arguments, 27
bourgeoisie, 50
Brain Force Ultra, 50–51
Breaking Bad (TV series), 49
British Broadcasting Corporation, 36
Brogan, Kelly, 27
Brown, Wendy, 28, 39–40, 85–87
Buchanan, James, 159n9
Bush, George W., 7–8
Butler, Daniel, 134, 162n40
Butler, Judith, 158n1

Caillois, Roger, 62, 69
Callison, William, 26, 104
Cambridge Analytica, 44, 52, 161n24

Canada, 116
cancel culture, 74
capitalism, 74; data capture and, 42; family under, 94; kinship and, 93; platform, 51–52; pleasure and, 40; surveillance, 19, 45, 46, 52
Cartesian thinking, 120
Castro, Fidel, 119
Central Intelligence Agency (CIA), 32, 114, 118
Certeau, Michel de, 16
Chansley, Jacob. See QAnon Shaman
Charcot, Jean-Martin, 124–25
Charlottesville, "Unite the Right" rally in (2017), 17, 66
Chávez, Hugo, 10
Cherniavsky, Eva, 152n10, 159n12, 169n40
China, 116, 117, 119
Chun, Wendy, 41–42
CIA. See Central Intelligence Agency
citizenship, 110
climate change, 6, 14–15, 80
Clinton, Bill, 18, 155n34
Clinton, Hillary, 64
Coase, Ronald, 159n9
cognitive mapping, 32
Cold War, 31, 66–67, 79, 103, 115
"Collateral Murder" (video), 4–5, 38
collective delusions, 59
collective imagining, 72–73
collective paranoia, 62
Collège de France, 15, 33
Colombia, 116
the Coming Storm, 69
community, sense of, 62–63
compliance, 136
conscience, 100–1
consciousness, 120, 138
consent, manufactured, 36
conspiracy theories, 1, 3, 10, 35, 57, 145. See also QAnon
conspiracy thinking, 58
conspiratorial fantasy, 58
Cooper, Melinda, 93, 96
Copycatbarnen (Copycat Children) (Jackson, T.), 129
corruption, 32
Council for National Policy, 85

COVID-19 pandemic, 1, 52–53, 64, 80; diagonalism and, 26; freedom and, 82–92; ivermectin and, 82–83, 101; QAnon and, 56
Cowie, Jefferson, 87
critical attitude, 14
critical data science, 155n36
Critical Race Theory, 86
Critique of Cynical Reason (Sloterdijk), 39
cultural identity, 112
cyber unconscious, 43
cynical reasoning, 39

The Daily Telegraph, 111
dark money investors, 26–27
Darwin, Charles, 106
data capture, 42–43
Davies, William, 167n19
death, 27, 48, 101, 108
death drive, 77, 169n40
The Death of Truth (Kakutani), 158n4
Declaration of Independence, US, 91
decolonization, 46
deep state, 5, 71, 74, 145
Defense Department, US, 115
DEI. *See* Diversity, Equity, and Inclusion
delirium of interpretation, 166n40
Deliveroo, 45
delusional formations. *See Wahnbildung*
delusions, 58–59, 62, 139
demand, hysterical, 135–37
dementia praecox, 21
democracy, 13, 27, 79, 91; fascism in, 28; war on terror and, 59; whistleblowing and, 4
Democracy and Truth (Rosenfeld), 155n32
demonization, 76
DeSantis, Ron, 83–84
desire, 44
desublimation, 106
Deutscher, Penelope, 168n26
Diagnostic and Statistical Manual of Mental Disorders (DSM-5), 121
diagonalism, 26, 104
Dialectic of Enlightenment (Adorno and Horkheimer), 16, 20, 21
digital extraction, 43
digital media, 8

digital revolution, 45
Dillon, Sheri, 31
disavowal, 3, 6, 39–41, 45
disinformation, 31, 52
disinhibition, 40, 65, 90, 101
displacement, 9
Diversity, Equity, and Inclusion (DEI), 67
divine justice, 34
Dobbs v. Jackson, 168n26
double realities, 75–81
DSM-5. *See Diagnostic and Statistical Manual of Mental Disorders*
Dungeons and Dragons, 60

earthly justice, 34
Eastern despotism, 7
ego, 68, 71–72, 76–77, 101; superego, 98–100, 105, 106
"Elements of Anti-Semitism" (Adorno and Horkheimer), 156n40
emotional release, 78
Eng, David, 22–23
engagement, 44
enjoyment, 28, 63, 66, 90; freedom and, 95, 98, 100–8; hysteria and, 98–99, 112; paranoia and, 6, 19, 157; sex panics and, 98, 169n45; superegoic, 98–106, 169n35; truth and, 6, 74, 166n40
"Enjoy the Show" (QAnon dictum), 55
Enlightenment, 16, 87
Entous, Adam, 114, 170n5
entrepreneurship, 49, 162n35; and freedom, 94–95
episteme, 34, 49
"essential" workers, 53
ethics: gamification and, 69; of paranoia, 90, 92; politics and, 146; of self-enrichment, 51; of whistleblowing, 41
European Court of Human Rights, 38
evidence, 39
exemption, politics of, 92–97
exposure: as biopolitics, 45–48; as extraction, 41–45; as mood, 48–53; "plain sight" and, 31–33; as revelation, 33–41
extraction, exposure of, 41–45
"extremely online" people, 26

Facebook, 32, 41–42, 44
factitious disorders, 137
factual truth, 7
fake news, 74, 159n9
Fallenkvist, Rebecka, 132, 147
false concreteness, 71
family, 93–94, 97, 107
family values, 96
fantasy, 17, 121, 145; conspiratorial, 58; heroic action, 80; knowledge and, 35; projective, 21; social dimension of, 23
Farage, Nigel, 10
fascism, 22, 27–28, 65, 71, 107, 147
fascist freedom, 87–88
fathers, 94–95, 97
FBI. *See* Federal Bureau of Investigation
fear, 44, 99–100
Federal Bureau of Investigation (FBI), 117
femininity, 126
Ferenczi, Sandor, 123, 125, 138
fetishistic disavowal, 39–41, 45
fiction, 33
fight/flight reactions, 70, 77
First World War, 125
Floyd, George, 65–67
Foster, Hal, 39
Foucault, Michel, 11–15, 89–90, 135, 146, 153n15, 153n20, 162n35; biopower and, 47; on Frankfurt School, 154n29; on neoliberalism, 46; *On the Government of the Living*, 33–34; *The Order of Things*, 154n30, 158n7; *parrhesia* and, 37, 169n45; psychoanalysis and, 158n7; on racism, 48; "What is Critique?," 14
4chan, 61, 62, 90
France, 111
Frankfurt School, 16, 154n29
freedom, 79; escaping from, 97–108; medical, 25–26, 83, 89–91, 95–98, 102, 105–8, 145, 166n4; politics of exemption, 92–97; truth-freedom, 82–92
"Freedom Fest," 91
Freud, Sigmund, 1, 19, 100, 102, 106, 120–21, 124–25, 140; on anxiety, 70; death drive and, 79–80; on distrust, 59; on fascism, 71; hypnosis and, 64; language and, 121–22; Schreber and, 21–22, 57
Friedland, Sarah, 41–42

Friedman, Milton, 46
Fromm, Erich, 88, 97–98

Gab, 4, 90, 163n3
games of truth, 11–15, 18, 32–33, 57, 153n15
gamification, 69
GCHQ. *See* Government Communications Headquarters
gender ideology, 86, 105
Germany, 135
gig economy, 45–46
Giuliani, Rudy, 15
The Good Fight (Beinart), 7
Google, 42, 158n3
Goop, 50–51
Government Communications Headquarters (GCHQ), 38
the Great Awakening, 69
Great Replacement Theory, 25
Greene, Marjorie Taylor, 69
Greenwald, Glen, 104
grooming, 86, 98
group psychology, 71, 77–78
Group Psychology and the Analysis of the Ego (Freud), 71
The Guardian, 9
Guilhot, Nicholas, 9–10, 152n14

Hacking, Ian, 134, 136
Han, Shinhee, 22, 23
Harvard Medical School, 124
HAVANA. *See* Helping American Victims Afflicted by Neurological Attacks Act
Havana Syndrome, 25, 113–19, 128, 142, 147, 170n5
Hayek, Friedrich, 46, 68–69, 95, 165n27
healing attempt. See *Heilungsversuch*
Heidegger, Martin, 50
Heilungsversuch (healing attempt), 58, 59
Helping American Victims Afflicted by Neurological Attacks (HAVANA) Act, 116, 143
heroic action fantasy, 80
historical anxiety, 71
Histrionic Personality Syndrome, 126
Hitchens, Christopher, 104

HIV, 27
Hofstadter, Richard, 162n2
Homeland (TV series), 66–67
homo economicus, 162n35
Homo Ludens (Huizinga), 164n14
homophobia, 22
Horkheimer, Max, 16, 20–21, 28, 93–97,
    101, 107, 156n40
Horowitz, David, 104
hostile environment, 111–12, 131
Huizinga, Johan, 164n14
Hultcrantz, Elisabeth, 135, 138
Hungary, 111
Hussein, Saddam, 7
hypnosis, 64–65
hysteria, 25, 120–25; border politics and,
    109–13; Havana Syndrome and, 113–19;
    magic words and, 126–35
hysterical demand, 135–37

"I Can't Breathe" (slogan), 80
ICE. *See* Immigrations and Customs
    Enforcement
idealization, 76
identity, cultural, 112
I Heard it Through the Grapevine
    (Turner), 24
immigrants, 1, 131–33
Immigrations and Customs Enforcement
    (ICE), 32, 110
income inequality, 49
India, 111, 116
individual choice, 92
individual freedom, 82
individualism, 92, 167n19
inequality, 49, 80
influencers, 61–62, 94
"informing the public," 38, 40, 89
Infowars, 50–51
In-Q-Tel, 32
in real life (IRL), 24–29, 90
Instagram, 61
Iraq, 4, 7, 79
Ireland, 131
IRL. *See* in real life
irrationalism, 17
Islam, 66–67
ivermectin, 82–83, 101

Jackson, Laura Lynne, 27
Jackson, Thomas, 129
JAMA (medical journal), 116
Jameson, Fredric, 32, 163n7
Janet, Pierre, 124–25
January 6th insurrection, 6–7, 54–55, 71,
    75, 163n3; disinhibition and, 65; irratio-
    nality and, 17; QAnon and, 26, 67, 73,
    77; Trump, D., pardons for, 81
Jones, Alex, 2, 50–51
jouissance, 79, 100, 166n40
Judt, Tont, 7
juridical authority, 129
juridical truth, 13, 38
justice, 34, 69
just wars, 7

Kafka, Franz, 141
Kakutani, Michiko, 158n4
Karen (slang term), 66
katallattein, 68
Kennedy, Robert F., Jr., 25–27, 83, 104
kinship, 93
KKK. *See* Ku Klux Klan
Klein, Ezra, 7
Klein, Melanie, 20, 33, 76, 98–99, 106
Klein, Naomi, 167n19
knowledge, fantasy and, 35
Ku Klux Klan (KKK), 24
Kyrgyzstan, 116

labor, 46
Lacan, Jacques, 20, 100–1, 122, 166n40
Lacanian psychoanalysis, 34–35
language, 121–22, 138
LARP (live action role play), 60–62, 78
LARPolitics, 59–69
law-preserving violence, 111, 141
leaking subject, 36
leaks, 41–42
"left behind," 8, 10, 55
lethal mothering, 133
liberalism, 88, 153n20. *See also*
    neoliberalism
libertarianism, 92
libido, 80
literary critical truth, 12
live action role play. *See* LARP

LMA. *See* "Reception of Asylum Seekers Act"
logos, 33
The Lord of the Rings (Tolkien), 32
lying, organized, 152n11

MAGA, 18
magic words, 126–35
MAHA (Make America Healthy Again) movement, 83
malingering, 137
Manning, Chelsea, 4, 36–38
Mannoni, Octave, 6
manufactured consent, 36
Marasco, Robyn, 57
Marcuse, Herbert, 40, 106
Marvel Comics, 110
Marxism, 16, 17
masculinity, 125
masochism, 100, 102
mass delusions, 58–59
mass hysteria, 132
mass panic, 132
mass psychogenic illness, 117
mass shootings, 26, 50
mastery, 21, 107
materialization, 123, 139
maternal superego, 99
May, Theresa, 111–12, 131
Mazzarella, William, 154n31, 174n1
McGowan, Todd, 169n36
McVeigh, Timothy, 5
medical dissent, 14
medical freedom, 25–26, 83, 89–91, 95–98, 102, 105–8, 145, 166n4
Melley, Timothy, 163n7
Memoirs of my Nervous Illness (Schreber), 20, 21–22, 57
Meta, 32
metadata, 42
mimicry, 60, 69, 137
minority populations, 9
Mirowski, Philip, 159n9
misinformation, 31
misogyny, 126
Mitchell, Juliet, 16, 123, 125
modernity, 13, 20, 34

Modi, Narendra, 10
Moms for America, 83, 104
Moms for Liberty, 85–86, 90–92, 104–5, 145
mood, exposure as, 48–53
mothers/motherhood, 93, 99, 133
Moyn, Samuel, 9–10
Musk, Elon, 147
Muslims, 66–67
"my body, my choice," 84
mystery illnesses, 109; AHIs, 114–18, 120, 124, 132, 139–44, 171n10; Havana Syndrome, 25, 113–19, 128, 142, 147, 170n5; RS, 25, 127–41

narcissism, 112
National Academies of Sciences, Engineering, and Medicine (NASEM), 117
National City Christian Church, 65
nationalism, 9, 72–73, 79
National Security Agency (NSA), 5
National Socialist Front, 129
natural rights, 88–89
Nazism, 39, 107; Neo-Nazi movement, 131–32; salute ("Sieg Heil"), 147
negative liberty, 92
neoliberalism, 2, 15, 47, 92, 101–2, 153n20, 162n35; authoritarianism and, 28; entrepreneurship and, 49; Foucault on, 46; freedom and, 85, 87; populism and, 10; post-truth politics and, 8; QAnon and, 11; roll-back phase of, 79
Neo-Nazi movement, 131–32
Nero, Dante, 26
the Netherlands, 131
Neumann, Franz, 70–71, 72
neurotic anxiety, 70–71, 140
news sources, fracturing of, 35–36
New World Order, 66
The New York Times, 36
9/11 terrorist attacks, 8
1984 (Orwell), 4
Nixon, Richard, 152n7
normative delusions, 59
Norway, 131

NSA. *See* National Security Agency
nudge economics, 52

Oath Keepers, 55, 77
Obama, Barack, 18–19, 114, 139
Obama, Michelle, 59
obscenities, 139
Occupy Movement, 80
Oklahoma City bombing (1995), 5
Onafur, Tina, 113–15
On the Government of the Living (Fou-
cault), 33–34
opinion: belief compared to, 7–8; delu-
sions and, 58–59; as value-neutral, 58
Orban, Viktor, 10
The Order of Things (Foucault), 154n30,
158n7
organized lying, 152n11
Orwell, George, 4, 5
O'Sullivan, Susanne, 130
Oxford English Dictionary, 47
Ozark (TV series), 49

Palantir, 32, 158n3
Paltrow, Gwyneth, 2, 27, 50–51
Panama Papers, 37
Pappenheim, Bertha, 122
paranoia, 19–23, 54–58; anxiety and,
70–75; Black, 24–25; collective, 62;
double realities and, 75–81; ethics of,
90, 92; etymology of, 2; LARPolitics
and, 59–69. *See also specific topics*
paranoid delusions, 58
paranoid ideation, 75
"Paranoid Reading and Reparative
Reading" (Sedgwick), 157n49
"paranoid-schizoid" position, 76, 79
paranoid style, 162n2
paranoid thinking, 56
parental rights, 85–86, 89–90, 92, 95–98,
102, 105–6, 108
parrhesia, 37, 169n45
Party of the Swedes. See *Svenskarnas Parti*
Parus, Tanya, 82–83
pastel QAnon, 25, 69
pedophilia, 98
Peltz, Rachel, 134

Pennsylvania, University of, 115–16
Pentagon, 115, 117
people of color, 26; African Americans,
24–25, 134; Asian Americans, 23
Perkins, Jo Rae, 69
personal choice, 96
personal liberty, 96
personal protected sphere, 95, 102, 107
phobias, 70
"plain sight," 31–33, 36
platform capitalism, 51–52
play instincts, 62
pleasure, 39–40
Poitras, Laura, 5
Poland, 116
political action, 90
political animal. See *zoon politikon*
political polarization, 1, 25, 28
political transparency, 32
politics of exemption, 92–97
Polymeropoulos, Marc, 118, 126
populism, 8, 9, 10
post-facts, 159n9
post-truth, 6–11, 33, 58, 78, 152n7
power, 33; biopower, 47; blind, 101; sovereign, 37; truth and, 13–15
precarity, 162n40
predictive policing, 158n3
preppers, 86
primary process thinking, 122
Princeton University, 105
private property, 95
projection, 3, 68, 71, 73–75
projective fantasy, 21
projective identification, 76
Project Veritas, 3, 4
propaganda, fascist, 65
The Protocols of the Elders of Zion, 59
Proud Boys, 26, 55, 56, 77
psychic distress, 120
psychoanalysis, 16–18, 22–23, 33, 97, 120–
21, 137, 146, 154n30; border politics and,
119; Foucault and, 158n7; hysteria and,
124; Lacanian, 34–35
psychopolitics, 15–19, 147–48
psychosocial analysis, 28
public health measures, 169n40

public sphere, 38
the Punisher (fictional character), 110

QAnon, 1, 3, 8, 10, 17–18, 53, 58, 121,
    163n3; anxiety and, 70–75; as big tent
    conspiracy, 55; COVID-19 pandemic
    and, 56; deep state and, 5; double reali-
    ties, 75–81; "Enjoy the Show" and, 55;
    games of truth and, 57; January 6th
    insurrection and, 26, 67, 73, 77; LAR-
    Politics and, 59–69; neoliberalism and,
    11; pastel, 25, 69; "the Storm," 59, 79,
    80–81
QAnon Shaman (Jacob Chansley), 25,
    54–55
Q clock, 73
Q Proofs, 73, 74
qualifying disqualification, 168n26
queer people, 98
"Question Authority" (dictum), 5

racial entitlement, 96
racism, 21–22, 46, 132; Eastern despotism
    and, 7; Foucault on, 48; of Trump, D.,
    39
radicalization, 18, 55
Rana, Aziz, 87
Rancière, Jacques, 153n15
rational truth, 7
Reagan, Ronald, 47, 85, 96, 111
realistic anxiety, 140
realities, double, 75–81
reason/reasoning, 13; cynical, 39;
    Enlightenment, 16
"Reception of Asylum Seekers Act"
    (LMA), 131
refugees, 49, 112
regimes of truth, 11–13
regressive fascism, 147
Remnick, David, 7
repression, 70
repressive desublimation, 40–41
Resignation Syndrome (RS), 25, 127–42,
    144, 147; See also Anomalous Heath
    Incidents
ressentiment, 70
revelation, exposure as, 33–41
Rhodesia, 46

rights: European Court of Human Rights,
    38; natural, 88–89; parental, 85–86,
    89–90, 92, 95–98, 102, 105–6, 108
role-playing, 60
Röpke, Wilhelm, 46
Rosenfeld, Sophia, 155n32
Rowling, J. K., 104
RS. See Resignation Syndrome
Russia, 31, 116, 117, 119, 171n10

sadism, 100
Sallin, Karl, 134, 173n39
Sanders, Bernie, 10
Sandy Hook shooting, 50
Santner, Eric, 20–23
Scandinavia, 111, 130
scapegoats, 70
schizophrenia, 21, 126
Schreber, Daniel Paul, 20–23, 57, 59, 80,
    121
scientific truth, 12, 13, 29
Scott, Joan, 154n30, 167n5
Second World War, 7, 66
secularism, 12
Sedgwick, Eve Kosofky, 22, 157n49
self-certainty, 8
self-cultivation, 72
self-enrichment, 51
self-formation. See Bildung
self-making, 61
self-mastery, 107
self-ownership, 88, 92
self-preserving vigilance, 129–30
self-reproach, 101–2
self-sovereignty, 92, 96
Septimus Severus (emperor), 33–34
"1776" (meme), 91
sex panics, 98
sexual assault, 39, 136
sexual harassment, 111
shootings, mass, 26, 50
Shorter, Edward, 134
Shrier, Abigail, 105
"Sieg Heil" (Nazi salute), 147
Silicon Valley, 19
Sleeping Beauties (O'Sullivan), 130
Slobodian, Quinn, 26, 46, 104
Sloterdijk, Peter, 39

Snowden, Edward, 4–5, 36–38
social critique, 16
social order, 7, 22, 32, 58, 95
social relations, 120
South Africa, 46
sovereign citizen movements, 86
sovereign power, 37
speech, parrhesiatic, 37
spontaneous action, 78
Srnicek, Nick, 51
State Department, US, 114–15
state protections, 167n119
status quo, 74, 94
Stigler, George, 159n9
stigmata, 124
Stimmung (mood), 50
"Stop the Steal" (activist movement), 6,
    18, 54, 71, 74
"the Storm" (QAnon), 59, 79, 80–81
Stovall, Tyler, 87
Strauss, Leo, 159n9
stress, 119
sublimation, 106
Sunstein, Cass, 52
superego, 98–100, 105, 106
superegoic sublimation, 90
"Support Our Troops" (slogan), 81
surveillance, 5, 115
surveillance capitalism, 19, 45, 46, 52
Svenskarnas Parti (Party of the Swedes),
    129
Sweden, 25, 109, 113, 126, 128–32
Switzerland, 131
symbolic investiture, 23
symbolization, 121–22
syphilis, 24

Taibbi, Matt, 104
Taiwan, 116
talking cure, 121–22, 133
Tamas, Gellert, 129
targeted ads, 31
Tarrio, Enrique, 26
Telegram, 4, 77, 90, 163n3
TERFs. *See* trans-exclusionary feminists
terrorism: 9/11 attacks, 8; Oklahoma City
    bombing (1995), 5
Thaler, Richard, 52

Thatcher, Margaret, 47
the "therefore," 15
TikTok, 65
Tolkien, J. R. R., 32
Toscano, Alberto, 87–88
tradwives culture, 167n19
trans-exclusionary feminists (TERFs),
    102, 104–5
trans people, 17, 84, 98, 104
Traverso, Enzo, 10
Trump, Donald/Trumpism, 31–32, 51,
    71–72, 77–78, 114–15, 119, 147, 158n1;
    AHIs and, 139; antisemitism and, 111;
    assassination attempt on, 27; disinhibi-
    tion and, 40; irrationalism, 17;
    Kennedy and, 27; people of color and,
    26; populism and, 10; QAnon and,
    55–56; racism of, 39; sexual assault by,
    39; trans people and, 104; Truth Social
    and, 3. *See also* January 6th
    insurrection
Trump, Melania, 78
truth, 3; autonomy of, 12; games of, 11–15,
    18, 32–33, 57, 153n15; juridical, 13, 38;
    post-truth, 6–11, 33, 58, 78, 152n7;
    regimes of, 11–13; scientific, 12, 13, 29
The Truth Fairy (Shrier), 105
truth-freedom, 82–92
"truthing," 3–4, 18
Truth Social, 3–4
Turner, Patricia, 24
Tuskegee Institute, 24
Twitter, 61

Uber, 45
the unconscious, 44, 146
unconscious processes, 3
undocumented people, 112
United Kingdom, 8, 10, 32, 46, 116
United States, 6, 8, 15, 25, 79, 110, 117;
    African Americans in, 24; AHIs in,
    142–43, 171n10; anti-lockdown protes-
    tors in, 26; anti-trans legislation in,
    104; Declaration of Independence, 91;
    Defense Department, 115; freedom in,
    84; games of truth in, 18; populism in,
    10; State Department, 114–15. *See also*
    Trump, Donald/Trumpism

"Unite the Right" rally (2017), Charlottesville, 17, 66
University of Pennsylvania, 115–16
uppgivenhetssyndrom. *See* Resignation
    Syndrome
utopias, 79
Uzbekistan, 116

vaccines, 1–3, 27, 83–84
Veritofobi (Truth Phobia) (Jackson, T.),
    129
Vietnam, 116
violence: law-preserving, 111, 141; sexual
    assault, 39, 136
vulnerability, 49, 52, 107

Wahnbildung (delusional formations),
    58
wandering wombs, 125
Warrior Mom, 93, 99, 107
wars: Cold War, 31, 66–67, 79, 103, 115;
    just, 7; on terror, 59, 66, 67, 110; World
    War I, 125; World War II, 7, 66
Watkins, Jim, 67
wealth, 68, 107
weapons of mass destruction, 7
Weeds (TV series), 49
welfare queen, 111
Wennman, Magnus, 127, 127
"We the People," 91–92

We the People Health & Wellness Center,
    82
"What is Critique?" (Foucault), 14
whistleblowing, 3–6, 36–41
white exceptionalism, 96
White Freedom (Stovall), 87
white nationalist movements, 26
whiteness, 107
Whitney Museum, 5
"Why Am I So Effing Tired?" (Goop
    product), 50
WikiLeaks, 36, 38, 41
Wilson, Elizabeth, 118, 172n27
Winnicott, D. W., 33, 62
Wolff, Naomi, 104
women's emancipation, 93
world catastrophe, 57
world-making, 61
World Press Photo competition (2018), 128
World War I, 125
World War II, 7, 66
Wylie, Christopher, 36, 161n24

YouTube, 44, 61, 84

zero-hour contracts, 46
Žižek, Slavoj, 36, 38
zoon politikon (political animal), 98
Zuboff, Shoshana, 19
Zupančič, Alenka, 145, 166n40

Zahid R. Chaudhary is Associate Professor of English at Princeton University. He is the author of *Afterimage of Empire: Photography in Nineteenth-Century India*.

www.ingramcontent.com/pod-product-compliance
Lightning Source LLC
Chambersburg PA
CBHW031151020426
42333CB00013B/613